SECRETS OF THE EXODUS

"This is far from all the hair-brained publications that have already appeared concerning supposed hidden messages in the Bible. This thesis certainly contains some rather abrupt shortcuts, and some errors. But it is not the work of charlatans. They launch a passionate path."

Rabbi Marc Alain Ouaknin, interview in Evénement de France Soir, *October 28, 2000*

Contents

☥

Translators' Introduction

Sigmund Freud speculated that Moses was not a Hebrew, but an Egyptian.[1] In Freud's time the idea upset some and outraged others. But, as the decades have rolled along, Freud's concept has sunk into the consciousness of Western thought, and at the beginning of the new millennium, it no longer seems outrageous.

Now, sixty years after Freud's thesis, two French-Jewish researchers have pushed the envelope further. After twenty years of research, they have discovered not only that Moses was not a Hebrew, but that the Patriarch Abraham wasn't either. Both, it turns out, were Egyptians. And not just any Egyptians; they were in fact pharaohs.

In retracing the history of monotheism, the researchers ran into tales of treachery, murder, fanaticism, duplicity, romance, and statesmanship in that great kingdom that endured over millennia in the Valley of the Nile. As they dug deeper into recent archeological and historical discoveries, they found that the Hebrews never were slaves in Egypt, and that the "Chosen People" were Egyptian inhabitants of the holy city of Akhet-Aten.

Messod and Roger Sabbah unearthed the origin of the Hebrew alphabet from Egyptian hieroglyphic sources. They demonstrate that the Book of Genesis reproduces Egyptian cosmology. They show how the "historic" characters of the Old Testament – Abraham, Moses, Aaron, Joseph, Sarah, and Laban – represent Egyptian names and titles. They present evidence that Abraham was the pharaoh Akhenaten and that Moses was Ramesses I. In their findings, Sarah and Nefertiti turn out to be one and the same person.

[1] Sigmund Freud, *Moses and Monotheism*, 1939.

These astounding discoveries were published in French under the title *Les Secrets de l'Exode*. It was thus restricted to those who read French. The translators have attempted to make the findings of the French researchers available to an English-reading audience. In doing so, we have not only translated the language, but also the spellings of Egyptian gods and persons. We have also made some modifications in the dating system of the French original. French Egyptologists speculate on the dates of the reigns of the pharaohs in a different manner from their English-speaking colleagues. The differences are a matter of very few years and the differences are infinitesimal when viewed over the span of more than four millennia. Nevertheless, for English readers, we have chosen to stick with dates generally agreed to by English writers on ancient Egypt. The French are accustomed to seeing Egyptian names spelled one way, English readers another. We have chosen spellings and terms familiar to the English-speaking world.

The organization of the book has also been modified by the translators. We have separated historical material from linguistic-cultural studies, which are presented in the final few chapters.

So, welcome to a whole new view of the Books of Genesis and Exodus. And to the intriguing story behind the story.

ART AND LOIS BANTA

Gods, People, and Places

Since Egyptian writing did not have vowels, there are alternative spellings for many of the names of pharaohs, gods, and places. The translators have attempted to use the spellings most often found in books in English on the subjects covered in this book. The following listing gives the name the translators have chosen, sometimes followed by alternative spellings.

Pharaohs of the Tenth Dynasty (Partial list)

Akhtoy (Achthoes, Khety) III	Reigned 2050–2015 BC
Merykare	Reigned 2015–2000 BC

Pharaohs of the Eighteenth Dynasty (Partial list)

Thutmose (Tuthmosis) III	Reigned 1479–1425 BC
Queen Hatshepsut	Reigned 1479–1458 BC
Amenhotep (Amenophis) II	Reigned 1426–1400 BC
Thutmose (Tuthmosis) IV	Reigned 1400–1390 BC
Amenhotep (Amenophis) III	Reigned 1390–1353 BC
Amenhotep (Amenophis) IV, who became Akhenaten	Reigned 1353–1336 BC
Smenkhkare	Reigned ?–1332 BC
Tutankhamun	Reigned 1332–1322 BC
Ay (The Divine Father)	Reigned 1322–1319 BC
Horemheb	Reigned 1319–1292 BC

Pharaohs of the Nineteenth Dynasty (Partial list)

Ramesses (Ramses) I	Reigned 1292–1290 BC
Sety (Sethos) I	Reigned 1290–1279 BC

Egyptian Gods (Partial list)

Amun (Amen, Amon) Amun-Re (Amon-Ra)	King of the Gods
Anubis	Dog god
Aten (Aton)	The One God; the Solar disk
Atum	The god who existed before creation, together with [or the same as] the primordial waters
Bes	Goddess of childbirth
Hathor	The cow that nourishes Egypt
Horus	Son of Isis and Osiris
Isis	Wife of Osiris and mother of Horus; a Madonna figure
Maat	Goddess of justice and truth
Mut	Amun's wife; the vulture
Nut	Sky goddess
Osiris	God of the dead
Ptah	Creator of the world; God of "the opening of the mouth"; patron of skilled artisans
Re (Ra)	Sun god
Seth (Set)	Evil god
Thoth (Toth, Dahuty)	God of knowledge

Others Mentioned in this Work

Akhensenamun	Wife first of Tutankhamun then of Ay
Champollion	Jean François (1790–1832); decipherer of Egyptian hieroglyphics from the Rosetta Stone, and founder of the science of Egyptology
Nefertiti	Queen of Egypt, Eighteenth Dynasty, wife of Akhenaten
Rashi	Born AD1040 in France. His *Commentaries* on Hebrew scriptures influenced later theologians. Actual name, Rabbi Shelomoh ben Yishaq.
Teye (Tiy)	Wife of Amenhotep III
Yuya	Father of Teye; father-in-law of Amenhotep III

Hebrews

Aaron	Moses' brother
Abraham (Abram)	Father Abraham, the first Patriarch
Esau	Firstborn son of Isaac
Hagar	Abraham's second wife, mother of Ishmael
Haran	Sarah's father
Isaac	Abraham's second son
Ishmael	Abraham's first son
Jacob (Israel)	Son of Isaac, Grandson of Abraham
Jethro	Moses' father-in-law
Joseph	Son of Jacob and Rachel, became Lord of Egypt
Joshua	General and, after Moses' death, leader of the Children of Israel into the Promised Land
Korah	Leader of a revolution against Moses
Laban	Rebecca's brother, Jacob's uncle
Leah	Jacob's first wife, Laban's daughter and Rachel's older sister, mother of six of the children of Israel (Reuben, Simeon, Levi, Judah, Issachar, Zebulun)
Moses	Leader of the Exodus
Rachel	Laban's daughter, Jacob's second wife, mother of two of the children of Israel (Joseph and Benjamin)
Rebecca	Isaac's wife
Sarah (Sarai)	Abraham's first wife, mother of Isaac
Terah	Abraham's father
Zilpah	Leah's maid, mother of two children of Israel (Gad and Asher)

Hebrew Deities

Adonay	Lord, often a substitute word for Yahwe so the Divine Tetragram does not get spoken in vain
Elohim	The Gods, or Sons of God, or Family of God (a plural)
Tetragram	The four Hebrew letters that spell Yahwe
Yahwe	The One God, the Divine Tetragram, the Name that must not be taken in vain

Locations

Akhet-Aten	Akhenaten's capital
Karnak	Temple on east bank of the Nile at Thebes
Malkata	Theban palace of Amenhotep III on west bank of the Nile
Nun	The primordial ocean where the gods are born
Tell el-Amarna	Current name of the location of Akhet-Aten
Thebes	Capital of Egypt during the Eighteenth and Nineteenth Dynasties (except during Akhet-Aten period)

Peoples

Apiru	Nomadic brigands in the province of Canaan
Hittites	A warlike people from the area of Anatolia

Prologue[1]

The second book of the Bible, the Book of Exodus, tells the story of how 600,000 male slaves, accompanied by "a great multitude," including their wives and children went from Egypt to Canaan. In all, some two million people – men, women, children, plus another "multitude" – are reported to have made the journey. That number would represent nearly as many people as the entire population of Egypt at that time.

The slaves purportedly had been in Egypt for 430 years (Exodus 12:40-41) before they made the great escape. As a prelude to their escape from slavery, ten dreadful plagues infested Egypt, including one that killed the firstborn sons of every Egyptian. The slaves and the "multitude" made their escape by walking right through the waters of the Red Sea.

As important as such an event would have been to Egypt, there is no record outside the Bible that an event like this ever occurred. Ancient Egypt left behind a great written record. Archeologists have brought additional insight to our knowledge of that cradle of civilization. Yet, try as they might, no researcher has been able to find any proof of such an exodus. There is not a single reference to any group of people called "Hebrews."

Is it possible that an enormous horde of people, resident slaves in the country for so many years, who brought down horrendous plagues on the land, and who escaped by a parting of the Red Sea, could have left no historical or archeological trace behind? This puzzle has bothered historians and archeologists ever since the nineteenth century when the French

[1] This prologue is not a translation from the original French text.

Egyptologist, Champollion, deciphered the hieroglyphic writing that recorded the history of Egypt. The question that has persisted for over a hundred years remains: Is the Hebrew Exodus history or legend?

On the other hand, Egyptian history and archeology do happen to report a significant exodus, which occurred around 1344 BC. The population of an entire city – the capital of Egypt at the time, Akhet-Aten – departed from Egypt and settled in the Egyptian province of Canaan. The people who made this astounding trip were monotheists, believers in the One God. They left the polytheistic land of Egypt in an exodus that is well recorded in Egyptian history, and is verified by modern archeology.

Could the historical exodus have provided the basis for the Book of Exodus? This is the question posed by this book. For over twenty years the authors have been studying the evidence that history and archeology present. That research is presented in the following pages.

CHAPTER 1

☥

The Tomb and its Secrets

In the Fall of 1923, Howard Carter was excavating a site in the Valley of the Kings. On November 4 of that year, one of his workers made a momentous discovery – a step leading into the tomb of the "boy pharaoh," King Tutankhamun, who had died in 1322 BC.

News of the discovery spread across the globe like a lit trail of gunpowder. The media, scientists, politicians, and men and women in the streets, were all enraptured by this magnificent archeological discovery. After months of studying and classification, all the contents were removed from the tomb except the red granite sarcophagus in which the king's mummy had lain. The treasures, objects at least 3250 years old, were all removed to the Cairo Museum and exposed to the view of admiring visitors.

The tomb itself was opened to tourists, who were often surprised by its small size compared to other buried tombs in the Valley of the Kings.

The tomb was studied from top to bottom, but it still withheld many of its secrets. On the east wall of the funerary chamber, above the figures of twelve priests bearing the mortuary catafalque, were eight painted columns of religious inscriptions. The figures, and the inscriptions did not excite great interest at the time. More recently, however, they have been further studied, and have shed new light on that time in human history when monotheism was invented.

On the north wall of the tomb is an enigmatic figure, wearing the crown of Egypt. Attached to the crown is the uraeus – a rearing cobra – the ancient symbol of royalty. The name of this mysterious person appears on two royal cartouches[1] placed above his face. He was called The Divine Father Ay – Pharaoh Ay. His name is written in double signed hieroglyphs.

Researchers noted that his name, Ay, is the name of God in the Aramaic Bible, Yod-Yod **יי**, which is our earliest source for the Old Testament.

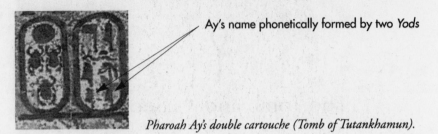

Ay's name phonetically formed by two *Yods*

Pharoah Ay's double cartouche (Tomb of Tutankhamun).

Researchers noticed that some of the objects found in the tomb bore close resemblance to articles mentioned in the Hebrew Bible. For instance, at the entry of the treasure room, seated on a pole-born chest, a statue of the Dog God, Anubis, guarded Tutankhamun's tomb. The dog and the chest were covered by a fringed linen shawl, "adorned with a double braid of blue lotuses, recalling the blue bands of the *tallith* with the *tsitsit*,"[2] the fringed prayer shawl of the Hebrews.[3]

The pole-born chest of sculpted wood, covered inside and out with gold leaf, recalled, in its form and in its religious conception, the Ark of the Covenant.

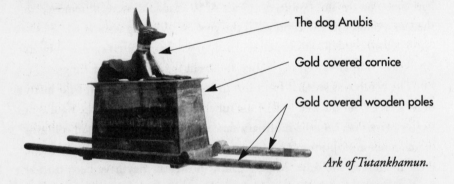

The dog Anubis

Gold covered cornice

Gold covered wooden poles

Ark of Tutankhamun.

The funerary chamber of Tutankhamun held four overlapping containers, one inside the other. The containers were covered by a large linen cloth, placed on a wooden frame, giving the whole thing the look of a tent, or tabernacle. This frame was compared at the time of its discovery with the tabernacle of the Old Testament, the Holy of Holies, constructed of gilded wood and holding the Ark of the Covenant.[4]

Canopic box of calcite-alabaster covered by a linen cloth (Tomb of Tutankhamun).

When Howard Carter opened the third container, he noticed on one of its lateral panels two angels with their wings spread high, evoking the angels placed on the Sacred Ark of the Biblical story. They were reproduced on the two sealed doors of the fourth and last container, as well as on the lid of the golden body mask.

These and other archeological finds caused researchers, both at the time of their discovery, and even more so recently, to consider that Egyptian archeology might shed a great deal of light on Hebrew scripture. In the tomb of King Tutankhamun there were indications that the Biblical story of the Exodus might have much closer ties to Egyptian religious beliefs than formerly believed.

The Book of Exodus tells of a people called the "Hebrews." Much is known of Egyptian history, yet nowhere at all is there a description of a people called the Hebrews. Nor, indeed, is there an account of any exodus from the country of any group of slaves. Historians and archeologists have searched in vain for any hint that the Exodus described in the Bible ever occurred.

In the Biblical story of the Exodus, the pharaoh of Egypt is never mentioned by name. He is described as "the one who never knew Joseph."[5]

Panel of the third box container of Tutankhamun. Sculpted wood plated with gold foil.

He believed that the Hebrew slaves were "more numerous and stronger" than the Egyptians: "Come, let us deal shrewdly with them, lest they multiply, and, if war breaks out, they will join our enemies and fight against us and leave the land" (Hebrew Bible, Exodus 1:10[6]).

The Bible indicates that there were two kinds of people in Egypt at the time: the Egyptians and the Hebrews (Children of Israel). Pharaoh had no fear of the Hebrews as long as their numbers remained reasonable. His fear was mainly that he might lose the workforce he so sorely needed.

Conscious of the demographic danger of the growing slave population, he decided on a radical measure. He decreed that all the firstborn of the Hebrews be killed. Fearing God more than they feared Pharaoh, the midwives refused.

Then, Pharaoh ordered the people to throw the firstborn Hebrews into the river. Here is where the Moses story begins.

Saved from the waters of the Nile by Pharaoh's daughter, "he became her son."[7] One day, Moses killed an Egyptian who was mistreating a Hebrew. Another day, he separated two Hebrews who were fighting. The fear of seeing himself denounced by one of them provoked his flight into the land of Midian. There, he married Zipporah, one of the seven daughters of Jethro, the high priest of Midian. After the miracles of the burning bush, the leprous hand, and the rod that turned into a serpent, Moses returned to Egypt and joined his brother Aaron.

Together they approached Pharaoh, who refused to let the Hebrews leave. A deluge of plagues followed. The tenth plague, bringing death to the firstborn of the Egyptians, overwhelmed Pharaoh. The defeated king of Egypt yielded and allowed the people to leave. However, he asked Moses and Aaron to bless him first.[8]

There then begins the story of the great exodus toward the Promised Land. The familiar story traces the crossing of the Red Sea, the wandering in the Sinai desert, the gift to Moses of the Tablets of the Law, the Ark of the Covenant, the Tabernacle, the episode of the Golden Calf, then the rebellion of the common people. After forty years of wandering in the desert, and after the deaths of Aaron and Moses, the conquest, so long awaited by the Hebrew people, finally began with the capture of Jericho. Thereafter all the Canaanite cities submitted to the mighty armies of Joshua.

That is the story that is so familiar to Jew, Christian, and Muslim. It is a story at the heart of the continuing conflict between Israel and Palestine in the year AD 2000. For a different version of the story, it is necessary to turn our attention to what history and archeology tell us about a city located in Egypt in 1350 BC. To understand this alternate version of the Exodus story, we need to spend some time learning about that amazing ancient city.

Notes

1. Cartouche: an oval frame in which the name of the pharaoh is written in hieroglyphics.
2. Howard Carter, *The Tomb of Tutankhamun.* Pygmalian, 1978. See also Nicolas Reeves, *The Discovery of Tutankhamun.* Thames and Hudson, 1990, p. 133.
3. The Israelites wore a prayer shawl called *tallith* or *tsitsit*. In the CD Rom of *Tutankhamun*, Christiane Desroche-Nobelcourt shows a fringed shawl that closely resembles the prayer shawls of the Hebrews.
4. See Exodus 26 for a description of the tabernacle. Cf. Richard Friedman, *Who Wrote the Bible?* Exerge, 1997, p. 191.
5. Exodus 1:8.
6. Translation from the Hebrew, and all subsequent Hebrew texts, by Art Banta.
7. Exodus 2:10.
8. Exodus 12:32.

☥

CHAPTER 2

The City of Gold and Light

In the Egypt of 1350 BC there existed a "city of gold and light." Akhet-Aten, the capital of the Egyptian Empire, was considered the most beautiful city in the world. It was the holy city of Pharaoh Akhenaten and his queen, Nefertiti, a city of palaces, temples, and obelisks covered with gold as far as the eye could see. It had luxurious gardens, and a long royal road extending over more than four kilometers. A royal bridge crossed that road. The art, the beauty, and the refinement of Akhet-Aten reflected the very height of Egyptian civilization. The most beautiful women of Egypt, as well as numerous Canaanite, Phoenician, Hittite, Midianite, Nubian and Babylonian princesses were invited to inhabit this terrestrial paradise.

There were entire neighborhoods of alleyways, where all classes of people rubbed shoulders: priests, businessmen, vintners, and bakers, who had come there from every corner of the known world. There was also a large group of artisans, artists, and intellectuals: sculptors, engravers, goldsmiths, painters, stone workers, masons, medical embalmers, architects, contractors, surveyors, scribes, and accountants. There were many people employed to care for the royal palaces and the temples of the god Aten. This entire population participated in the activities of the holy city, which teemed with life.

All these people had received from Pharaoh the immense privilege of coming with their families to live in this sacred city, the Holy City of God Aten. By order of Pharaoh, they had converted to the new religion, the new cult of the One God, to monotheism. Those who found favor in the eyes of Pharaoh Akhenaten or Queen Nefertiti could look forward to the immense honor of being buried in the necropolis situated on the periphery of the city, within the sacred territory of Akhet-Aten.

The city was delimited by border stelae, and for the second time in Egyptian history, Akhenaten had established a difference between a region designated as "sacred" and the rest of Egypt. His first attempt had been to build a sacred site in the center of the sanctuary of the god Amun at Karnak, with temples similar to those he later constructed at Akhet-Aten. The problem there was that the One God, Aten, would be in the company of the King of the Gods, Amun. At that early point in his reign, the pharaoh bore his first royal name, Amenhotep IV (meaning "Amun is in peace"), later known in Greek as Amenophis IV. In the fifth year of his reign, he changed his name to Akhenaten ("the grace, the light, which is used by Aten").

From the viewpoint of the old polytheism, Akhenaten was a heretic. He had forsaken the gods of his father Amenhotep III and embraced the concept of there being but One God, Aten. Aten was seen as the creator god of the universe, and was represented by the solar disk, which extended its beams over all terrestrial creatures.

Amenhotep III had constructed a city called Malkata, containing the royal palace and administration buildings. Imitating his father, Akhenaten decided to construct a new capital for Egypt, from which he would conduct the affairs of state. In the new order, the polytheistic clergy of Amun would be excluded from power. Akhenaten abandoned the sacred land of Karnak, the religious center of the ancient religion of Egypt, and established his new "Holy Land," Akhet-Aten. It was located on the west bank of the Nile, about halfway between Memphis to the north and Thebes to the south, on a site later called Tell el-Amarna.

The pharaoh proclaimed that he had been led to this new region by the god Aten himself, with the promise of life and prosperity for him and his descendants forever. When Akhenaten arrived at the site, he made, as did Abraham in the Bible, a sacrifice in honor of his God, on the very place where he later built the great temple of Aten.[1] Following these acts, which are confirmed by Egyptologists, Pharaoh addressed his assembled court. He declared that God had guided him to the holy land of Akhet-Aten in order for temples to be built for his worship. He promised that this land would be the capital of Egypt forever.

All the riches of the country flowed toward Akhet-Aten. Sacred food was offered to the god Aten before being consumed. Consecrated bread and wine were offered in abundance. Approved animals were consecrated in the Atenian temples and redistributed across the country, as happened centuries later in the Temple of Solomon.[2]

Akhenaten instituted morning and evening prayer, at sunrise and sunset, thus glorifying the appearance and disappearance of the solar disk Aten. The hymns to the glory of God, recited and chanted in the temples, are the origin of the later psalms and prayers. In his capital, as in all Egypt, Akhenaten was worshiped as Aten. He was proclaimed the "Son of Aten," but in the Egyptian mind, that phrase did not exclude his being Aten himself. Inside his royal cartouche, the name "Aten" appeared in translation as "He who is pleasing to Aten." His wife also changed her original name, and became Nefertiti, "perfect is the beauty of Aten." Installed in the capital, Akhenaten reigned as absolute master of the city and of all Egypt, distributing tasks and functions to his intimates.

Ardently desiring to institute one universal religion, Pharaoh had temples built to the glory of Aten throughout Egypt. The expressions "forever" and "eternally" occur regularly in the hymns. These proclamations and declarations were written by Akhenaten himself, and he taught them to his disciples and followers.

If events had developed as planned by the king and queen, the religion of Aten would have spread over all Egypt from the capital Akhet-Aten, the holy place of the new belief. The pharaoh was, above all, a teacher. He diffused his knowledge to the thousands of priests who dwelt in the capital. They had the task of propagating the new religion throughout Egypt, in the name of the new god Aten, and of his supreme representative, Akhenaten.

Akhenaten insisted quite particularly on his role of teacher in the sacred domain, which made him a spiritual teacher. Several texts indicate that Akhenaten conversed daily with his disciples to whom he attempted to make known the nature of Aten.[3]

Akhenaten also bore the title "He who sees the Great God." As High Priest of the new religion, he was the only intermediary between God and the

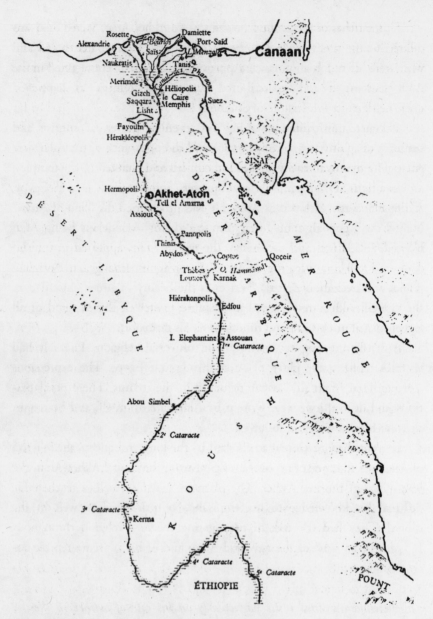

Map of Egypt at the time of Amenhotep IV – Akhenaten.

people, the only one with the power to present the great offering in the Temple of Aten. But, even as High Priest, he could not present the great offering alone. That ritual required the presence of both Pharaoh and his queen.

This earliest form of monotheism had a strong base of what today are called "family values." The research carried out at Tell el-Amarna (Akhet-Aten) tells us much about worship practices in the homes of the people. Each house in the city was provided with a stone altar, inscribed on two sides. Cyril Aldred describes it as follows: "All the houses of this kind had a similar trait. They had a sanctuary placed in one of the main rooms. It had the form of a false door with painted red posts and a niche to receive a stela portraying the royal family engaged in cult-based activity."

As a tie-in with the Biblical Exodus story, the red posts are a reminder of the blood the Hebrews were reported as painting on their doorposts. "Yahwe[4] will pass through to slay the Egyptians. And when he sees the blood on the lintel and on the two doorposts, Yahwe will pass over the door, and will not allow the destroyer to enter your houses and slay you" (Hebrew Bible Exodus 12:23).

In his devotion to the new religion of monotheism, Akhenaten had the names of Amun chiseled away in the temples and on the obelisks. Pushing his heresy further, he profaned the name of Amun inside the cartouche of his father Amenhotep III. To suppress the name of a god was considered a true sacrilege by the inhabitants of ancient Egypt. The Biblical monotheists echo this in the words of their One God: "I will utterly erase the name of Amalek from under heaven."[5]

In chiseling out the name of Amun, Akhenaten was suppressing the existence of that god. He went on to have the statues, the objects of the paternal cult, broken. Akhenaten had committed a sacrilege, something that had never before been done in ancient Egypt. In the Biblical tradition, Abraham also broke the idols of his father.

Akhenaten was a powerful and a mystical pharaoh. The entire nation prostrated itself before him. Kings of other lands came to pay tribute in his capital and to render him homage. He was the Glory of Aten, and promenaded the length of the royal road of Akhet-Aten, accompanied by Nefertiti on his gold and silver carriage, heading for the great temple of Aten.

The pharaoh loved to appear in the company of his wife at the view window of the palace. It was there that he appeared to the people. And, just as the Moses in the Bible did, he held up before the people the two stone tablets where the two cartouches of Aten's name were inscribed. The people prostrated themselves before the name of God. These tablets, inscribed on both sides, could be read from either side. The similarity to the Biblical tablets of Moses is noteworthy. Both were rounded on the perimeter with writing on both sides. "Moses turned and went down the mountain with the two tablets of the covenant in his hands, tablets that were written on both sides" (Hebrew Bible, Exodus 32:15).

Akhenaten and Nefertiti elevating the name of Aten on stone tablets engraved on both sides. Behind the royal couple the little princesses are shaking the sistra.

As previously mentioned, the new religion emphasized the family. Akhenaten was particularly fond of the company of his six daughters and his wife, giving the people an image of a happy couple. In many homes, the inhabitants kept an effigy of the royal family watched over by the Sun God Aten. The sacred union was made part of the cult of the new religion. It fused the people to the royal family, so that the birth of a social model based on the sharing of family values can be seen in this image.

This social model is even more visible in the homes in the outskirts of Akhet-Aten. Each house was constructed along the same plan – a prime example of social planning. There was a living room, where the Pharaoh's cult could be practiced, plus bedrooms, bathrooms and toilets.

Everything was pre-planned in that amazing capital, where one could contemplate God every day. What the inhabitants could not know was that simply by living in the Sacred City, they were playing out one of the greatest dramas of Egyptian history, a drama with consequences for all humanity for more than three thousand years.

Most pharaohs were represented in postures evoking power and strictness. Akhenaten is shown as the relaxed pharaoh. The royal sculptor represents him with elongated neck and meditative eyes, a new artistic vision for Egypt, probably one imposed by Akhenaten himself. There was never a pharaoh like him before or after.

♀ ♀ ♀

In the seventeenth year of his reign, Pharaoh Akhenaten died and was buried in the royal tomb in the valley (*wadi*) located in the extension of the axis of the Great Temple of Aten.

The tomb must have harbored even more riches than Tutankhamun's. It must have contained an ark (without the god Anubis represented on it), a funerary altar, some "sanctuaries" interlinked with each other, and the "tablets" with the name of Aten on two cartouches. The God of the Dead, Osiris, certainly would not have been represented, but the pharaoh would have had his arms crossed in the "Osiris position," holding the royal scepter in his right hand and the whip in the left. The goddess Hathor would not have appeared as herself, but as the effigy of Nefertiti.

Pharaoh Smenkhkare, Akhenaten's successor, reigned for barely two years, in a hazy historical period, before dying at the age of about twenty-five. The cause of his death is unknown. Murder is one option, particularly with the religious politics of the time. Since he was faithful to the religion of Aten, Smenkhkare may have been in the way of the counter-reformation that was brewing at that time.

At the death of Smenkhkare, his half-brother, Tutankhamun, was eight years old. Since he was too young to reign, it was the "Divine Father," High Priest Ay, who took over the reins of the kingdom. Ay's father, Yuya, bore the title "Divine Father" before his son. "Divine Father" also meant "Father of the God." Yuya had been thus honored by Pharaoh Amenhotep III, who had elevated him to Divine Father as well as Commandant of

Chariots (Grand Master of Cavalry). In other words, Yuya was the commander-in-chief of the armies. Yuya bequeathed part of his functions to his son Ay. Later, when Nefertiti, Ay's daughter, married the future Akhenaten, Ay became the father-in-law of the new king while he also bore the title of "Divine Father."

Ay was venerated by the population of Akhet-Aten. A carving of the period shows him standing in the garb of high priest. Before him, the inhabitants prostrate themselves in worship. Ay's status had already become nearly as high as pharaoh's.

Divine Father Ay is little known by Egyptologists. Some don't even mention him when they speak of the Amarnian period, or forget him when they cite the pharaohs of the Eighteenth Dynasty. Still others speak of him in a rather succinct manner, rapidly passing over the subject. Ay didn't leave many traces of himself when, ten years later, he had become the sacred pharaoh of Egypt. He reigned for only four years before passing power to General Horemheb. However, as it turns out, Divine Father Ay is a central figure in the history of Egypt and in the Biblical story of the Exodus.

Ay was the high priest who, well before becoming pharaoh of Egypt, made the most important decision of that period. He was to change the destiny of not only an empire but of the religious history of the Western world.

☥ ☥ ☥

At the death of Pharaoh Smenkhkare, Ay took over the government of Egypt, since Tutankhamun was still a youngster. He participated in the coronation, and decided early on to "transfer" the new pharaoh to either Thebes or Memphis – Egyptologists disagree as to which city.

Tutankhamun was crowned pharaoh and, under the influence of the Divine Father Ay, he changed his name from Tutankhaten to Tutankhamun. Thus, he erased the name of the One God Aten from his name and added that of the King of the Gods, Amun. This change indicated clearly the gravity of the politico-religious situation in Egypt at the time. It meant the return to Amun by a pharaoh too young to understand what had been imposed on him.

Tutankhamun was a child naturally obedient to his presumed grand uncle. Ay was the only man to have the wisdom, intelligence, and experience to lead a country that he knew inside and out. Smenkhkare's convenient death permitted Ay to act at last – to put into operation his plan of counter-reformation.

Ay didn't simply want to destroy the work of Akhenaten. He wanted to obliterate his memory and reduce his spiritual power to nothingness. The image of the God-Man, whom Ay perceived as detrimental to Egypt, had to disappear from the land. The temples would have to be destroyed or

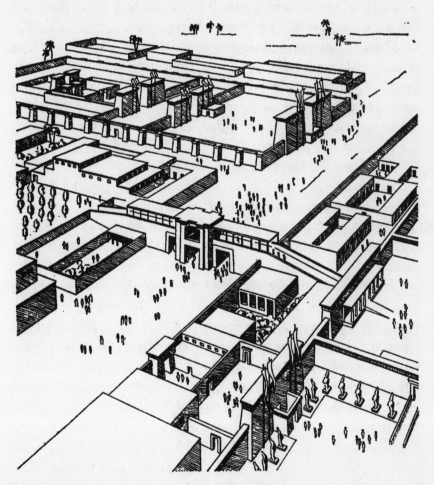

A reconstruction of the city of Akhet-Aten. Taken from Pierre Grandet, Hymnes de la religion d'Aton.[6]

torn down, thus suffering a fate more dramatic than that of the Amun temples in the time of Akhet-Aten's splendor.

In order for all the names of Aten engraved on the walls of Egypt to be obliterated, the names of the king and of Nefertiti had to be effaced as well. The god Aten, the One God, disappeared as rapidly as he had come, a period of but a single adventure.

The most important decision, though – the one to toll the knell on the Aten religion – was to abandon the city of Akhet-Aten, the city that had been the religious and political capital of the empire. Ay declared that city "cursed land," heretical and impure. It was pronounced forever uninhabitable and was to be erased from memory for evermore.

The abandonment of Akhet-Aten by its inhabitants did not take place naturally and without obstacles. The abandonment of the most beautiful city in the world, the terrestrial paradise, had to have been extremely traumatic. The archeologists and Egyptologists are in accord that the inhabitants actually took away all their riches. The city had not been conquered nor destroyed, but abandoned. It was deserted in obedience to the orders of the new power in Egypt, the Divine Father Ay.

Some inhabitants probably left for Thebes or Memphis, or elsewhere in Egypt. The others are the subject of the story of the Exodus.

Akhet-Aten became a veritable phantom city. It had to await the reigns of Horemheb, Ramesses I, Sety I, and Ramesses II to see its temples at first dismantled, then destroyed, transforming the city into a vast field of ruins.

Today, the sands have completed the work of destruction, entirely covering the plain of Amarna. It was three thousand years later, in November 1714, that a Jesuit priest, Claude Sicard, visited this desert region and stumbled upon an unusual stone. As he approached, he discovered that it had the appearance of a border stela of an abandoned ancient city. The stela represented a king, a queen, and a princess.

It was the stela of Akhet-Aten, the city that had been built to endure forever.

Notes

1. Cyril Aldred, *Akhenaten, King of Egypt*. Le Seuil, 1997, p. 49.
2. Christian Jacq, *Nefertiti et Akhénaton*. Perrin, 1996, p. 146.
3. *Ibid.*, p. 136.
4. Most translations of the Bible substitute the words "Lord" or "God" where the Hebrew uses the name "Yahwe." The translators have chosen to use the original Hebrew words to keep the meaning as close to the original as possible.
5. Exodus 17:14.
6. Pierre Grandet, *Hymnes de la religion d'Aton*. Le Seuil, 1995.

CHAPTER 3

☥

The Pharaoh of the Exodus

Is it possible that the exodus from Akhet-Aten and the Biblical Exodus are one and the same story? Sigmund Freud suspected that the origin of the Biblical Hebrews was related to the story of Akhet-Aten. More recent research indicates that Freud was correct in his speculation and that much that is written in the books of Genesis and Exodus is linked to the City of Gold and Light.

Archeologists and historians have spent two centuries looking for evidence of the Exodus described in the Bible. They have always come up empty-handed. Champollion, the great French Egyptologist who first deciphered Egyptian hieroglyphics, insisted that it was necessary to understand the Egyptian experience in order to bring the Exodus into the field of history. He was on the right track. He wrote:

> *The tribes [Hebrews] that had, by a ruse, escaped from a people much more advanced than they were themselves, could not, just by entering the desert, simultaneously rid themselves of concepts of order and civil habits. Nor could they forget the practice of the arts acquired during their prolonged stay on the banks of the Nile, within an agricultural nation. The Hebrew leader renewed the most ancient form of Egyptian government, the theocracy, which lent itself in a most efficient way to the accomplishment of his views. He left the Valley of Egypt, not to lead the tribes back to their primitive state, to the nomad and pastoral life of their fathers, but with the preconceived design of placing them in a limited territory, acquired by conquest, and to establish them, like the Egyptians, as a sedentary nation*

*composed of cities, cultivating the land, and devoting themselves to all
the industrial arts. To the extent that local circumstances allowed,
Moses applied the civil institutions of the Egyptians to the organization of Hebrew society. He proclaimed religious dogmas essentially
distinct from those of Egypt. But, in the exterior forms of worship,
and particularly in the material of the religious ceremonies, he had
to imitate, and actually did imitate Egyptian practices. Study
of Egyptian monuments, whether interior or exterior, in Moses'
time, will give more complete understanding of the original texts
of the Bible.[1]*

Sigmund Freud, in *Moses and Monotheism*, declared: "We must choose the
interregnum sometime after 1350 as the date of the Exodus. The later
periods, up to the definitive implantation in the land of Canaan, are
particularly impenetrable to investigation."

The era Freud mentions corresponds to the one immediately following
the death of Akhenaten. The era is that of Pharaoh Smenkhkare, who
became pharaoh after Akhenaten. Smenkhkare's brother, Tutankhamun
was "exiled" to Thebes for his coronation before the abandonment of the
city of Akhet-Aten. It is possible to deduce that the Exodus took place at
the beginning of the reign of King Tutankhamun, coinciding with the
desertion of the monotheistic capital. The Egyptologist Cyril Aldred also
places the abandonment of Akhet-Aten during the first year of
Tutankhamun's reign.[2]

When he was eight years old, Tutankhamun succeeded Smenkhkare.
He does not fit the description of the pharaoh of the Exodus. The eight-
year-old would hardly be the pharaoh who was so evil, obstinate, and piti-
less towards the Hebrews. Besides, the pharaoh of the Bible had a firstborn
son, according to the story. Tutankhamun was eighteen years old when he
died, without an heir.

If the Exodus took place at the beginning of King Tutankhamun's
reign, we are led to reconsider the troublesome period Freud discussed,
beginning with the ephemeral reign of Smenkhkare. In the Biblical tale
(Exodus 1:22) Pharaoh orders the death of all the first-born Hebrew sons.
Christiane Desroches-Noblecourt, in her book *Ramesses II, The True Story*,
says there was never any time in Egyptian history when a massacre of

infants would have been possible. No document or fresco attests to the historical reality of any such event, nor to the plagues described in the Book of Exodus.

There is, however, a clue in the Book of Exodus that relates to a situation in Akhet-Aten. It is the mention of the increase in the birthrate that apparently so bothered the pharaoh of the Bible. In the ruins of Akhet-Aten, the most recent research reveals the presence of delivery rooms, which indicates a cult of midwives.

The great increase in the birthrate in Akhet-Aten was the result of the increase in the number of women. Beautiful foreign women kept arriving in the city, princesses who were offered to Pharaoh.

At the beginning of Exodus, the midwives are described as courageous, disobeying Pharaoh's orders by allowing male new-borns to live.

> So the Elohim[3] were kind to the midwives. And because the midwives feared the Elohim they gave them families. Then Pharaoh commanded all his people, "Every boy that is born to the Hebrews you shall cast into the Nile, but you shall let every girl live." (Hebrew Bible, Exodus 1:20-22)

Pharaoh was well aware of Egyptian wisdom teachings and was conscious of the sacred character not only of human life but of animal life as well. He would not have been able to commit such an abomination. Pharaoh could not have been Smenkhkare. One of the very rare representations of him shows him to be an affable man in the company of his wife, Merit-Aten, one of Akhenaten's surviving daughters. Smenkhkare was a monotheist who practiced the religion of his father Akhenaten. He was an adept of the philosophy of ancient Egypt. That philosophy taught respect for human life, love of beauty and of nature, as revealed in the Hymns to Aten and Amun. In those hymns it is stated that the king must consider foreigners as human beings created by God.

As Akhenaten's co-regent after Nefertiti's death, Smenkhkare was indoctrinated with these teachings from his earliest years. He never wished to return to the polytheistic religion of Amun deliberately, nor did he modify his name. In Egyptian tradition, just as in the Bible, to change one's name implied a change of religion or of destiny. His persistent monotheism is further demonstrated by the double cartouche of Smenkhkare, bearing the name of the "One God," Aten. Faithful to the religion of his father, Smenkhkare had to endure enormous pressure from the High Priest Ay to return to the old religion. His refusal to abandon his One God, Aten, probably cost him his life.

Ay wanted to deport all of the priests of Akhet-Aten from Egypt. Smenkhkare was clearly opposed to that exodus. As a monotheistic pharaoh, he does not fit the description of the pharaoh of the Book of Exodus. Yet, Smenkhkare was the firstborn son of Akhenaten. The Bible recalls that the Pharaoh was a firstborn son who asked Moses and Aaron for divine benediction. While Smenkhkare was chronologically the pharaoh at the time of the Exodus, his actual behavior does not fit the description of that pharaoh's actions. So, who held the power to cause the actual exodus?

The ephemeral reign of Smenkhkare and the youth of Tutankhamun make it obvious that power was held entirely by the one man influential enough to make all the religious, political and military decisions. That man was the Divine Father Ay, High Priest of Akhet-Aten, and regent vizier.

The Divine Father Ay worshipped by the priests and population of Akhet-Aten after having been honored by Akhenaten with a gift of gold necklaces.

Ay's decisions would transform the reign of Tutankhamun into the time of the return of Amunian orthodoxy and the exile of the monotheistic priests. It was the Divine Father Ay who succeeded Tutankhamun as pharaoh, and pursued the policy of restoring the old religion.

During Akhenaten's reign, Ay had an important governmental role. Akhenaten was thoroughly preoccupied by the cult of Aten that he had instigated. He was adored by his courtesans and was continually receiving foreign emissaries offering slaves, women, and material gifts. He was busy distributing gifts and largess to the people from his view window. With all these concerns, he did not have time to bother himself with the affairs of Egypt. The affairs of state he left entirely in the hands of his grand vizier, the Divine Father Ay. It was Ay who traversed all the country's provinces to attend to the task of governing. Ay was diplomatic and intelligent, and had a perfect knowledge of Egypt's political situation. As Akhenaten's reign was approaching its end, Ay found the country in a state of decay, and its people in distress.

Akhet-Aten – the holy city among all cities, the terrestrial paradise – had as its corollary the great misery of the rest of Egypt. At Akhenaten's death the unhappy condition of the land outside the holy city impelled Ay to make his irrevocable decision. The monotheistic religion, the worship of Aten alone, had proved catastrophic for the country. Ay concluded that the hardships endured by the country were caused by the abandonment of the old gods. The monotheistic priests seemed to be to blame for the wrath of the gods. Like the pharaoh of the Bible, Ay had a large number of people that he had to dispose of in some manner.

The Bible places the number of Moses' people in the thousands: "The Children of Israel journeyed from Ramesses to Succoth, about six hundred thousand men on foot, besides women and children. A great multitude also went up with them, as well as very many cattle, both flocks and herds" (Hebrew Bible, Exodus 12:37-38).

Most of the numbers mentioned in Exodus are contested. Chaim Potock estimates the numbers to be clearly exaggerated, since it brings the total number of people to around two million.[4] Such a displacement of population was impossible for the period, since the number represents nearly the whole population of Egypt. Besides, six hundred thousand men on foot, that is to say, armed, could have held back the Egyptian force without any difficulty, even if that force was quite powerful. Finally, these two million people could never have been able to live in one single region of Egypt – the region of Goshen mentioned in the Bible – without leaving any trace. The exaggerated numbers are attributed to scribes who, according to Redford[5] and Friedman,[6] wrote the Exodus story about seven hundred years after the event.

According to all the evidence, if the Hebrew people had represented such power in Egypt, they would have left an imprint on Egyptian writing, art or literature. We do know that Amenhotep III organized a census of the population because of the growth of foreign residents in Egypt.[7] The Book of Numbers tells of a census of the tribes of people who left Egypt. The verse mentions a "great multitude"[8] which accompanied the people of the Exodus. This multitude appears to be a mixture of converts that followed the monotheists. The Bible does not tell us anything about those hordes that accompanied the Hebrews, but a mixed multitude of people had dwelt in Akhet-Aten. John Pendlebury, an Egyptologist at the beginning of last century, wrote that the city of Akhet-Aten was quite cosmopolitan. "It was," he said, "during its short existence, the greatest imperial city in the world. All matters of the kingdom were dealt with there. In its streets all nations of the known world rubbed elbows, the Minoans, the Mycenaeans, the Cypriots, the Babylonians, the Jews,[9] and many other races."[10]

When Ay became pharaoh, the Egyptians became, again, worshipers of Amun and the other gods. They were relentless in effacing all traces of Pharaoh Akhenaten.[11] However, this has not impeded archeologists from reconstructing a large part of that king's history. Sculptures, names, psalms, prayers, family scenes, vestiges and objects of all kinds, including bricks were retrieved from inside the foundation of the pylons of the Temple of Karnak.

With all this excavation and research, much has been learned about Akhenaten. But in all that archeological treasure trove there does not exist the least trace of Hebrews in Egypt.

One theory proposed by historians is that the Hebrews were the Apiru. The Apiru were a semi-nomadic people who possessed none of the culture, traditions or language of the Egyptians, and were dispersed all over Egypt and Canaan. The temptation to confuse the Hebrews with the Apiru is quite strong. But the more archeologists have learned about the Apiru, the more they admit the absence of any connection with the Hebrews of the Bible.

The population of Akhet-Aten consisted essentially of priests, their families and slaves, and a multitude of workers and peasants. On leaving the city, the population appeared like nomads, but their vocation was never nomadic, since they profoundly aspired to establish themselves in the Promised Land. To agree to leave a city as beautiful as Akhet-Aten, there would have to have been a promise of "a marvelous land flowing with milk and honey."

Egypt had suffered for the glory of Akhet-Aten. The bulk of the wealth produced by the country made its way to the capital. The city had not only become the sacred center of Egypt, but its economic one as well. Christian Jacq notes, "Everything that the land of Egypt produced had to come to the temple [of Akhet-Aten] to be consecrated and then redistributed to the population."[12] Just as at the time of Solomon, this redistribution couldn't be made until after an appropriate percentage was skimmed off for the new capital.

Akhenaten had already levied a sacred tax on the country and had set up numerous forced labor projects for the construction of the Theban temples as well as other temples to Aten in the rest of the country. Then he decided that a large part of the revenues of the old capital of Thebes would be directed to Akhet-Aten. He doubtless did the same to the other cities of Egypt,[13] strangling, bit-by-bit, the whole country to the profit of the City of Light. All Egypt worked for the grandeur of its god-king Akhenaten.

The writers of the Bible describe such a situation. "Yahwe said to Moses, 'I have heard the wailing of my people who are in Egypt. I have heard their cry because of their taskmasters. I know their sufferings'" (Hebrew Bible, Exodus 6:5). The Biblical scribes have to be describing the afflictions of the Egyptian people, since the Hebrews have no historical reality in ancient Egypt.

Brickmaking plays an important part in the Biblical tale of the Exodus. Archeology and history teach us that brickmaking was an essential part of ancient Egyptian life. The Hebrew Bible tells us the same in Exodus 5:12: "So the people were scattered throughout all Egypt, to gather stubble for straw [to make adobe bricks]."

Akhenaten had the idea, still in use today, of replacing the enormous, heavy cut stones with bricks of smaller size, which could be carried by a single man. These bricks, called *"talatates"* allowed the buildings and temples of Aten in Karnak to be built rapidly. To build Akhet-Aten, however, it was necessary to redouble the speed of construction, so Pharaoh also used bricks made of straw and clay, building the capital in record time. Memories of the forced labor, as well as of the bricks of straw and clay, remained engraved in the memory of the Biblical scribes: "The same day, Pharaoh ordered the taskmasters of the people and their foremen, 'You shall no longer supply the people with straw to make bricks, as you did before'" (Hebrew Bible, Exodus 5:6-7).

These verses must indeed deal with the suffering of the Egyptian people who constructed Akhet-Aten, the magnificent city.

All over Egypt they made bricks (Karnak talatates).

☥ ☥ ☥

Akhenaten had an interesting strategy to entice the clergy of the polytheistic Amun religion to the holy city of gold and light. According to the Amarna Letters[14], he had the most beautiful women of Egypt brought there, as well as numerous Canaanite, Phoenician, and Mitanite princesses, along with their retinues and their dowries, offered by subject kings. The priests of Amun were invited to change their residence and their religion and move into the grandiose city teeming with beautiful women, leaving behind the cities and temples of their ancestors.

Akhenaten used both sex and material enticements to attract priests and worshipers to his new monotheistic religion. Princesses, foreign women and slaves were waiting for the new adherents. Akhenaten also distributed jewels and material riches. This extract from one of the El Amarna letters is an example of the approach Pharaoh took toward his vassals:

> *To Milkilul, a man of Gazru: Thus speaks the king [Akhenaten]: I send you this tablet saying, "With this he sends Hanya, a guard of the archery cavalry, along with all he needs for the purpose of acquiring very beautiful serving-wenches: money, gold, linen clothing, carnelian, all kinds of stones [precious], an ebony chair; all of them equally beautiful things: Total value: 160 dibans.*[15] *A total of 40 serving wenches, 40 sicles of silver being the price of one serving wench." (EA 369)*

Princesses and women of lesser rank, chosen for their beauty, were installed at Akhet-Aten to marry royal princes or priests. The train of servants that accompanied them augmented the female population of the city even more. The new capital of the Egyptian Empire became, for several years, a veritable paradise, a Garden of Eden, peopled by the most beautiful women in the world.

In this way, Pharaoh attracted and converted the priests of Amun into priests of Aten, enticing them into a true "golden trap" – Akhet-Aten.

During this time, the rest of Egypt was ignored and abandoned. The populace was condemned to forced labor and great suffering. The centralization desired by Pharaoh was also the cause of that subversion which spread through the cities that formerly were sacred, like Thebes, Heliopolis, Memphis, and Hermopolis.

This double Egypt, one composed of the beautiful city with the beautiful people, one composed of the struggling masses, was seen by the pharaohs following Akhenaten and Smenkhkare as unacceptable. Their successors returned to the old polytheistic religion of Amun, abandoning the religion of Aten. If the inhabitants of Akhet-Aten had freely consented to return to the old religion, they never would have had to abandon the capital. All that would have been needed was to transform the temples of Aten into temples of Amun, remove Aten's names, and build new temples (as Akhenaten had done for his reformation).

Egyptian life would then have returned to its normal course. But, the new religion had taken firm root in the hearts of its converts who lived the good life in the golden city.

Some partially damaged stone inscriptions provide important clarifications about the new religion. According to Pierre Grandet's commentary:

> *The king affirmed that the gods, so far as they were known, were only statues created by human hands, in a form which immemorial tradition had seemed to lend a sacred character. But the gold and gems with which they were ornamented did not manage to hide that they were merely useless objects.*[16]

During his reign, Akhenaten, as teacher to his disciples, preached the new doctrine, which carried a revolutionary notion concerning the concept of the divine. This teaching, glorifying One God, later became the basis of the ideology of an abstract god, invisible, transcendent, omnipresent, and omniscient. This One God, Aten, incited in his followers the will to eliminate the ancient cult of images and idols. The concepts of the ancient polytheistic religion were anathema to the people of Akhet-Aten. The uniqueness and exclusivity of Aten were paramount – concepts repeated over and over in the psalms and hymns of Akhenaten.

The Little Hymn to Aten, which is found in five tombs of Akhet-Aten, is distinguished by the notion of a venerable, unique god, who

> *... was fashioned by himself alone. Who created the earth and all that is found thereon: all people, herds, and wild beasts, all trees which thrust themselves from the ground. They live when Thou appearest for them. Thou art the father and the mother of all that Thou hast created. Thou art the Living Aten, whose symbol endureth. Thou hast created the far heavens, there to shine forth, to observe what Thou hast created. Thou art the One in whom is found a million lives.*[17]

The verses of this hymn contain the foundation of the Biblical religion: the worship of the One God, the creator of the universe.

The Great Hymn to Aten repeats the same ideas:

One God without equal, Thou didst create the universe according to the consciousness of Thy heart, so that Thou art One alone. Thou extractest eternally thousands of forms originating from Thyself. Thou dwellest in Thy Unity. No being engendered by Thee exists for any reason other than to contemplate Thyself Alone.

The religion of Aten revealed a truly new form of divinity. The ancient wisdom of Egypt had already advocated the virtues of the One God before the writers of the Bible had transcribed it. The Stela of Lyon is an Egyptian monotheistic poem:

Thou art One.
Thou art the being whose manifestation existed before manifestation.
Thou art the creator of the heavens and the earth,
Who offerest ceaselessly the plenitude of all being.[18]

♀ ♀ ♀

The scribes who wrote the Books of Genesis and Exodus tell of how the One God was revealed to the patriarchs. The story is followed by describing the gift of the Tables or Tablets of the Law on Mount Sinai. The Biblical story was recounted out of memories engraved in the consciousness of the Jewish people. The oral tradition, handed down from generation to generation after leaving Egypt, had to be integrated into a politico-religious context in order to conform to the beliefs of kings and emperors who dominated the Middle East in their own lifetime.

The hypothesis that the Bible was written in part in Babylonia has been put forward by numerous historians.[19] At the time of the Jewish exile to Babylon, in the time of Nebuchadnezzar, king of Babylon, the Judahite survivors found themselves in a new land, and they submitted to their new masters. The story of Esther indicates that this adaptation succeeded and was brought to completion when some of the exiles returned home under the reign of Cyrus the Great. At that time, it was the priest and scribe Esdras who, having returned to his homeland, reassembled with the bless-ing[20] of King Artaxerxes I (486 BC) the Five Books of the Bible.[21] The lands of Canaan, Judah, and Israel were no longer vassals of Egypt. Babylonia had conquered them, and Pharaoh was a distant memory. By then Egypt had become the hereditary enemy of the Hebrews. A hundred years before, at the beginning of the Babylonian Exile in Nebuchadnezzar's time, the prophet Ezekiel had composed the Oracles of Condemnation and of Chastisement against the "seven nations: Ammon, Moab, Edom, the Philistines, Sidon, and particularly against Tyre and Egypt." He held them responsible for the fall and deportation of the people from Judah and the destruction of Jerusalem and the Temple.

It was during the Babylonian Exile, a period of total submission to the Persian kings (Cyrus was called the Messiah) that the Bible was modified, and that the story of the Exodus was recast to the detriment of the Kingdom of Egypt, which, by then, had also submitted to the Persians.

The scribes in Babylon could remake the Exodus story only by conserving the authentic framework of a minute part of the truth. It is impossible to determine how long this practice lasted. Rashi[22] confirms in his Commentary on Exodus 12:41, "This is one of the passages of the Torah that was modified for King Ptolemy."

How many passages of the Bible were modified to suit the kings and emperors who ruled over the Hebrews after the exodus from Egypt, masking the historical reality?

Notes

1. *Grammaire égyptienne, principes généraux de l'écriture sacrée égyptienne appliquée à representation de la langue parlée.* Champollion le Jeune. Reissued as *Grammaire egyptienne de Champollion* by Christian Jacq, Solin, 1997.
2. Cyril Aldred, *Akhenaten, King of Egypt.* Le Seuil, 1997, p. 192.
3. The Hebrew word *Elohim* is usually translated as God or Lord. However, it is definitely a plural, and refers to Gods, Sons of God, or the Family of God. The translators have left the original words, "the *Elohim*," wherever they appear in quoted Bible verses.
4. Chaïm Potock, *Une histoire des Juifs.* Ramsay, 1996.
5. D. Redford, An Egyptological Perspective on the Exodus Narrative, *Egypt, Israel Jnl.* 1987. pp. 137–69.
6. Richard Friedman, *Who Wrote the Bible?* Exerge, 1997.
7. Philipp Vandenberg, *Nefertiti.* Pierre Belfond, 1987, pp. 117–18.
8. Exodus 12:38.
9. Pendlebury assumes the Biblical evidence of a Jewish people.
10. Christian Jacq, *Nefertiti et Akhénaton.* Perrin, 1996.
11. Cyril Aldred, *Akhenaten.*
12. Christian Jacq, *Nefertiti et Akhénaton*, p. 146.

13. Claude Vanderseyen, *Egypt and the Valley of the Nile*, Vol. 2. Nouvelle Clio, 1995, p. 435.

14. The El Amarna Letters are clay tables written in cuneiform, discovered in 1887 in the ruins of the administrative buildings of the capital Akhet-Aten, dating from1350 BC.

15. The El Amarna Letters, 10 sicles = 1 diban = 91 grams of gold.

16. Pierre Grandet, *Hymnes de la religion d'Aton.* Le Seuil, 1995, p. 17.

17. Christian Jacq, *Nefertiti et Akhénaton.*

18. Christian Jacq, *La sagesse vivante de l'Egypte ancienne.* Robert Laffont, 1998, p. 35.

19. Richard Friedman, *Who Wrote the Bible?* See also D. Redford, *An Egyptological Perspective on the Exodus Narrative*, pp. 137–69.

20. *Dictionnaire Encyclopédique du judaïsme.* Le Cerf, 1993, p. 326.

21. Richard Friedman, *Who Wrote the Bible?* D. Redford, *An Egyptological Perspective on the Exodus Narrative*, pp. 137–69.

22. Rashi (Rabbi Shelomoh ben Yishaq), AD 1040–1105. French-Jewish scholar and commentator on the oral tradition concerning the Pentateuch. His teaching is one of the most important in the Jewish tradition. It is based on written and oral traditions and he used the Aramaic Bible as his reference source.

CHAPTER 4

☥

Pharaoh Ay

The Bible and Egyptian history conceal information about the dispersion of the priests and notables of Akhet-Aten, yet reveal a great deal about the hidden pharaoh, the Divine Father Ay.

When the old, polytheistic religion was restored, an official stela was set up, announcing the re-established order. Archeological evidence of the Biblical and historical Exodus is engraved on this Stela of Restoration, also known as the Stela of Tutankhamun. The Stela is in the form of a half table of the law, engraved by order of the Divine Father Ay. It informed the ancient world (and us, now) about the tragic and miserable situation that prevailed in Egypt at the time. It reveals the fact that the Egyptian leaders had made the decision to abandon the monotheistic religion of Akhenaten and the reasons for the restoration of the previous, established religion.

> *The temples of the gods and goddesses, from Elephantine to the marshes of the Delta, have begun to collapse. Their sanctuaries are falling, little by little, into ruins in front of piles of rubble covered by weeds. Their homes have been destroyed. Roads run through their fences. The country has a sick feeling and the gods have turned their backs on our land.*[1]

Other translations of the Stela tell of the catastrophic state of the rest of the country.

> *The temples of the gods have fallen into detestable times. Their courts have become roads where everyone can pass through. The country has*

*been exhausted by curses and the gods have been neglected. His
Majesty [the new king, Tutankhamun, guided by Ay] seeks a solution
pleasing to Amun. The gods have turned their backs on the country.
The gods do not respond any more when their counsel is sought.*[2]

John Adams Wilson, in *Egypt, Life and Death of a Civilization*, analyzes the
inscriptions of the Stela, attested to by Bennet's translations. He takes note
of the vivid reaction of the child-king Tutankhamun. The Stela asks the
question, "What did the repentant pharaoh do?" The engraving on the
Stela gives the answer: "He drove out deceit from one end of the two lands
to the other. And Maat [goddess of justice and truth] was re-established.
The lie [monotheistic religion] became an abomination within the land."

*The Stela of the Return (1330 BC),
or the Stela of the Restoration of the
cult of Amun. It can equally be
called the Stela of the Exodus
(Cairo Museum).*

The expression, "He drove out deceit from one end of the two lands to the
other," is an historical reality, reaffirmed by the Bible – "They were driven
out of Egypt and could not tarry." (Exodus 12:39).

Only one man could have caused those words to be engraved on the
stela – the Divine Father Ay, a fervent servant of Maat, goddess of truth
and justice. Knowing the suffering of the Egyptian people, he had the
ability, will, and power to decide upon the radical action that had to be

taken. The texts that have come down to us testify to the urgency he felt to re-establish the ancient gods in order to recover the equilibrium of the country.

The High Priest Ay was the only person assured of the power in Egypt after Smenkhkare's death. Egyptologists describe him as a great diplomat and an outstanding strategist, who maintained a certain cohesion in the country during the second part of Akhenaten's reign, while the pharaoh was cloistered in his capital.

Nicolas Grimal writes, "The return of Amunian orthodoxy probably occurred under the influence of the Divine Father Ay, who guided the steps of the young Tutankhamun. Tutankhamun sent out an edict for the restoration of the previous cults, and described the miserable state into which the errors of Amenhotep IV [Akhenaten] had reduced the country."[3]

Ay was the "Father of the God," as well as the perceived father of the commoners of Egypt. These commoners, the inhabitants of the rest of the country, did not have the right to travel to the new capital. Men and women suffered from having lost the religious and spiritual values of their ancestors. Their gods were struck down and their priests displaced to Akhet-Aten. They were left alone, without resources, and with the further constraint of conscription into work crews to carry out the tasks of the new religion.

Ay well understood the foundations of Aten's religion. He had contributed to its ascension, and had sincerely believed in it. Now, he saw the misery and suffering of the Egyptian people as a consequence of that religious reformation.

The new monotheistic religion had brought tragedy to Ay personally. During Akhenaten's reign, he saw his loved ones suffer and die. His parents (Yuya and Tuya), his brother Anen, and several of his granddaughters died. His sister, Queen Teye, died soon after her husband Amenhotep III. His adopted daughter, Nefertiti, died soon, as did two of his great-granddaughters.

The death of Akhenaten must have dealt the ultimate blow to Ay's dream of the cult of the One God, the Protector. Akhenaten was his son-in-law, a person he had admired during the glory days of Akhet-Aten. Ay was deeply disappointed in the One God Aten. This One God had provided no protection to him at all. He had lost practically his entire family while Aten's cult grew. And Egypt had sunk into a lamentable state. The Stela of Tutankhamun demonstrates that the misfortunes that befell the Divine Father Ay were interpreted by him as punishment from Amun.

Akhenaten had abandoned and desecrated the statues of Amun. He had forsaken the people of Egypt as well as their ancestral gods. Ay felt that it was urgently necessary to repair the fault and calm the wrath of Amun. A mere return to polytheism would not suffice unless it was accompanied by a grandiose action to regain Amun's confidence. Amun had allowed Aten the privilege of living, and of expanding until he, Aten, had grown the more powerful of the two. And Aten, far from expressing his gratitude, tried to destroy Amun. So the law of Talion, a law well known to the Egyptians,[4] would have to be invoked. Genesis 9:6 presents the law in Biblical terms: "Whoever sheddeth the blood of another person, by that person shall his blood be shed." It is the ancient law of vengeance.

Ay found himself confronted with the most difficult decision of his life. He would have to blame the population of Akhet-Aten for the woes of the country. The cosmopolitan life created by Akhenaten became a pretext for the accusation of corruption, adultery, and exhibitionism against the city. Akhet-Aten had to be destroyed, and its monotheistic priests had to be exiled or killed. They had, after all, been guilty of corruption and of fraternization with foreign women.

Killing priests was certainly not an Egyptian custom. Such an act was considered the crime of crimes. Besides, Ay himself had been venerated and deified by the monotheistic priests.

Smenkhkare had opposed exiling the monotheistic priests, which probably cost him his life. After his death, the Divine Father Ay became the sole initiator of the restoration of the old religion. He could act freely, since the young pharaoh Tutankhamun was under his tutelage.

To save Egypt from the misery and scourges described on the Stela, the Divine Father took his stand against the population of Akhet-Aten. Akhet-Aten's populace, however, attached to their privileges and to their One God, refused to abandon their beliefs and their wealth.

The condition of the Egyptian people, exhausted by the scourges of the One God religion, caused Ay to negotiate a compromise with the monotheistic population of Akhet-Aten. Ay promised them the Egyptian province of Canaan (the Promised Land), along with all the wealth of Akhet-Aten.

The venerated Divine Father Ay shooting at a target held by two prisoners. The population of Akhet-Aten greets the high priest by kneeling. In the center are two royal cartouches of the pharaoh, who is not wearing the royal uraeus, which leads one to suppose that these cartouches were added to the engraving later (Gold foil engraving).

The Bible describes the wealth taken from Akhet-Aten in the Book of Exodus: "The Children of Israel did as Moses told them, and asked the Egyptians for gold and silver jewelry, and for clothing. Now Yahwe had caused the Egyptians to be favorably disposed toward them, and the Egyptians gave them what they asked for. So, they plundered the Egyptians" (Hebrew Bible, Exodus 12:35-36).

The monotheistic priests, the Yahuds, took with them the wealth of Akhet-Aten. The city wasn't abandoned in a disorganized manner; the departure was well planned.[5] Cyril Aldred discovered that the excavations at the city of Thebes were far more rewarding than the meager loot gleaned from Amarna. Very little was left behind when Akhet-Aten was deserted, providing slim pickings for the archeologists millennia later. The latest research indicates that the capital was dismantled at the beginning of Tutankhamun's reign. And, it was dismantled by order of the Divine Father Ay.

With the capital of Egypt deserted and abandoned, where would its inhabitants have gone? Having left the terrestrial paradise, what happened to the priests of Aten and to the prominent citizens? They were deported to the Egyptian province of Canaan. Not only were the priests and nobles deported, but the Egyptian artists and artisans, who were an integral part of the Yahud class (the Tribe of Judah), went along with them.

The traditional view of what happened to the monotheistic priests is that they returned to their old cities and resumed the priesthood of the old monotheistic gods. However, there is strong evidence against this view.

The Stela of the Restoration gives an archeological indication about the disappearance of the priests of Akhet-Aten. According to Claude Vandersleyen, the Stela specifies that Egypt, lacking enough priests for the restoration of the cult of Amun, organized a massive recruitment drive. "The only written indication of social reorganization of the priests states that from then on, the priesthood would consist of children of the functionaries of their city."[6]

The new priests had to be recruited, not from priestly families, but from families of the bureaucratic class – a very strange course since the priesthood in Egypt had, from time immemorial, been a truly exclusive caste unto itself.[7] In the same way that Ay succeeded his father Yuya, the ancients transmitted their traditions, secrets, and teachings to their descendants. The tradition is promulgated in the Bible. "And the priest who is anointed and consecrated as priest to succeed his father shall make atonement, wearing the holy linen garments" (Hebrew Bible, Leviticus 16:32).

If the numerous priests of Akhet-Aten abandoned their God to return to the old religion of Amun, how could there be a lack of priests? Why did those who had returned to power feel obligated to recruit priests elsewhere, among the uninitiated, in disregard of the ancestral traditions?

The answer is that the priests of Aten, the One God, never returned to the worship of Amun. The leading citizens of Akhet-Aten never returned to anonymity. The people of Akhet-Aten – priests, nobles, artists, and common people – disappeared from Egypt to go to the desert of Moab, and later to the province of Canaan.

☥ ☥ ☥

By a religious alliance with the monotheistic priests, Ay settled a crucial political problem at the same time, dealing with the region's equilibrium. He repopulated the province of Canaan, which had been abandoned by Akhenaten and invaded by bands of Apirus. Many of the Amarna Letters affirm that Akhenaten had received many real cries of distress and appeals for his help. For instance: "Rib-Hadda says to his lord: 'I fall to my lord's feet seven times seven times. Why dost thou remain thus seated motionlessly, doing nothing, so that the Apiru dog takes thy cities? When that dog took Sumur, I wrote thee, why hast thou done nothing …?'" (EA 91)

By moving his own Egyptian subjects, who venerated him like a god, to the land of Canaan, Ay had reached a solution that allowed him to put an end to the anarchy reigning over the land. By this means, he held back the advance of the Hittites from the North. The Hittites now became, equally, the enemy of the new arrivals. The Divine Father created a "buffer zone" protectorate for Lower Egypt by sending his armies along with the new settlers. The Aramaic Bible frequently speaks of Ay's armies accompanying the Exodus: "On exactly that day, all the armies of Ay left the land of Egypt"(Aramaic Bible, Exodus 12:41).

♀ ♀ ♀

On Tutankhamun's death, the Divine Father Ay assumed the crown of the Egyptian empire. The succession took place without conflict, and in accordance with the Egyptian tradition of the immortality of the pharaohs, the cult of Tutankhamun was replaced by that of the Divine Father Ay (Adon-Ay). Then, after the death of Ay after a four-year reign, the new pharaoh, Horemheb, faithfully followed the directives of his predecessor, restoring the worship of Amun throughout Upper and Lower Egypt. He made a final, decisive rupture with the religion of Aten, the only truly exclusive monotheism that had ever existed in ancient Egypt. He established judges in the land, putting an end to the disorder and corruption that had grown endemic. Enthused by his religious passion, he went so far as to represent himself as the direct successor of Amenhotep III.

Always following the example of the Divine Father Ay, Horemheb was accustomed to saying that "he traveled the country far and wide," the better to know it and provide for its needs.

Horemheb usurped numerous statues and effigies of the monotheistic pharaohs, effacing their names and their memory by engraving on them his own. He made no exception of Ay. His rancor towards his monotheistic predecessors had adequate reason. Under monotheism, Egypt had suffered the loss of the fundamental symbol of its existence – its clergy. The priests had been the bearers of Egypt's mysteries, knowledge, and traditions.

Unlike Horemheb, Pharaoh Ay is scarcely represented in sculptural form. The rare works discovered which do show his image are paintings and bas-relief murals, or engravings on gold leaf. Ay seems to have accorded slight importance to images representing himself. For him the emphasis was on Egypt's need to return to the worship of the polytheistic god Amun. Although he reigned only four years, Ay had been "pharaoh without a crown" for more than twenty.

During Akhenaten's last ten years, while the pharaoh was cloistered and worshiped within the capital, and during the reigns of Smenkhkare and Tutankhamun, Ay was lord of the land, the Divine Father, respected and venerated throughout Egypt.

It was Ay who presided over the burial of Tutankhamun. And it was Ay who chose the secret location for Tutankhamun's tomb in the Valley of the Kings, filling it with treasures found three thousand years later.

Ay is the forgotten pharaoh. The discrete sovereign of Egypt, he is above the pharaohs. He is the one "whose face is never seen." Ay was the artisan and sculptor of the Great Exodus. He would impose his seal upon the face of all consequent Western civilization.

Notes

1. Translation of Claude Vandersleyen, *Egypt and the Valley of the Nile*, Vol. 2. Nouvelle Clio, 1995.
2. Translation of Christian Jacq, *Nefertiti et Akhénaton*. Perrin, 1996, p. 219.
3. Nicolas Grimal, *Histoire de l'Ancienne Egypte*. Fayard, 1988, p. 294.
4. Elisabeth Laffont, *Les livres de sagesse des pharaons*. Folio Histoire, Gallimard, 1979, p. 22.
5. Cyril Aldred, *Akhenaten, King of Egypt*. Le Seuil, 1995, p. 73.
6. Claude Vandersleyen, *Egypt and the Valley of the Nile*, p. 476.
7. Lionel Casson, *Ancient Egypt, The Great Ages of Man*. Time, 1969, p. 79.

CHAPTER 5

☥

Amun

To better understand the relationship between the Bible and ancient Egypt, let us go back 200 years before the Exodus to the reign of Ahmose, the founder of the Eighteenth Dynasty, a turning point in the history of ancient Egypt. It was the Pharaoh Ahmose who drove out the Hyksos, who had conquered the country and ruled it from about 1630 to 1523 BC.[1] These invaders founded Avaris, a garrison town, as their capital. Manethon, an Egyptian priest of the third century BC, described Egypt's capture: "Without warning, people of an unknown race, coming from the East, had the audacity to invade our country [Egypt] and, without difficulty or combat seized it by live force."

In addition to their culture and their philosophy, the Hyksos introduced the use of the horse, the war chariot, and bronze work, thus definitely making their imprint on Egypt. In turn the Hyksos adopted the Egyptian gods, their sacred hieroglyphic writing, and Egyptian traditions. A hundred and fifty years after their conquest of the country, they became, in their own minds, true Egyptians. The expulsion of the Hyksos undertaken by Ahmose foreshadowed the events of the Exodus that occurred two centuries later. The reconquest was bolstered by the retaking of Avaris, around 1520 BC, and by driving the invaders back towards Asia. The Hyksos became the "sacred enemy," an appellation that left its mark on future dynasties century after century.

The Egyptians left us a great deal of information about the Hyksos and their invasion. Does it not, then, seem strange that they left us not even a footnote about the Hebrews? Here are "Chosen People," who refused to accept the established gods and beliefs of Egypt, who, as slaves of Pharaoh, remained in the country for 430 years, yet who are never mentioned in any way in the writings that were penned on papyrus, chiseled into temple and tomb walls, or engraved on gold leaf.

How could the Egyptians ignore the God of the Hebrews who had caused them so much suffering with ten successive plagues and ruined the kingdom? Egyptian scribes would, without doubt, have recorded some information, at least a few traces of such devastation.

The Book of Exodus, chapter five, mentions that Pharaoh himself appeared to be unaware of the One God of the Children of Israel after 430 years of their presence, 210 of those years in slavery.[2] "Afterward, Moses and Aaron went to Pharaoh and said, 'Thus saith Yahwe, "Let my people go, that they may hold a festival to me in the desert."' But Pharaoh said, 'Who is Yahwe that I should obey him and let Israel go? I do not know Yahwe, and will not let Israel go'" (Hebrew Bible, Exodus 5:1-2).

There does not exist any kind of Egyptian statement about the Hebrews, whereas, for the expulsion of the Hyksos,[3] the Egyptian scribes show them belittled, made petty, and driven out of the country.

After their victory over the Hyksos, the Eighteenth Dynasty was founded and Egypt pursued territorial advances to the South as well as to the North, as far as the Euphrates. Thanks to Thutmose's conquests, Pharaoh added to his name and to his title the supposed qualities that had accrued through these conquests: greatness, power, force (the weaponed arm of pharaoh), and beauty. These were the qualities that were customarily used either in Pharaoh's throne name or in his royal cartouche. Pharaoh's attributes are identical to those claimed for the God of the Bible.

Amenhotep III had the good fortune to possess a veritable empire bequeathed to him by his forebears. Thutmose III had conquered the Near East as far as the Euphrates. In the south of Egypt, he annexed Nubia, the Land of Kush, and extended his kingdom to the third cataract of the Nile (today's Sudan).

At the age of fourteen, Thutmose III's great grandson, Amenhotep III, married Teye, the daughter of Yuya, who came from a tiny village called Akhmin in Upper Egypt. After the marriage of his daughter to Amenhotep, Prince Yuya was promoted to the supreme rank of "Father of the God," or father-in-law of the God-King. He later passed this title on to his son, Ay.

At that time an ancient god, Aten, resurfaced in Egypt. Aten's origin, in all likelihood, goes back to Atum,[4] a primordial Egyptian god of around 2200 BC. This resurgence of Aten was favored by Amenhotep III's in-laws, and most particularly by Teye, Yuya's daughter, the future high queen of Egypt, and Akhenaten's mother. The education she gave her son was influenced by Yuya.[5] And so both Teye and Yuya played a role in the first stage of the process that led to the rise in power of the religion of Aten after the coronation of Akhenaten.

Amenhotep III was instructed, as were all the pharaohs, in sacred writing, in arithmetic, and in science. But, above all, he was initiated into the cults of the main Egyptian divinities. Among these, the principal god was Amun, whose temple – the great Temple of Karnak – was located in the capital, Thebes. The origin of this god is obscure. He may have issued from the metamorphosis of a "primordial serpent"[6] that transformed itself into a divine being. During the Old Kingdom (2625–2130 BC), Amun was a god without cachet. His name is mentioned in the Pyramid Texts, but is not emphasized. Toward the time of the Ninth Dynasty his name became associated with the god Re, representing the sun (Amun-Re). By the Eighteenth Dynasty, Amun definitively took the first place in the Egyptian pantheon. Amun means "the hidden one." As in the Bible, no one could see the face of God.

Amenhotep III was not a conquering king. He had already inherited an empire, and now he had to consolidate it with alliances with his powerful neighbors, mainly Mianni (Mesopotamia), with which he made a pact by marrying Gilheba, the daughter of King Sutarna. At the death of Sutarna, Amenhotep III sealed a new pact with his Midianite successor Tushratta (or Dushratta), who gave him his daughter Taduheba in marriage.

The peace thus established predisposed Amenhotep III to concentrate his energy on constructing numerous buildings throughout Egypt to encourage the different cults in the land. Among the most important was the magnificent Temple of Karnak (Thebes), and its replica in Soleb, in Upper Egypt.

Amenhotep III also had a sumptuous palace built near Thebes, which is now called Malkata. At that time, ancient Egypt had attained a very high degree of refinement in its arts and sciences.

The power of Amun's clergy accrued considerably. This supremacy generalized into the acquisition of real estate, with an increase of bare land, cultivated land, and vineyards awarded to the priests of Amun, making Thebes the religious and political capital of the country. Amun was consecrated there as King of the Gods, next to whom the other divinities seemed to play only a secondary role. The surface area of the Temple of Karnak was augmented by the addition of imposing columns, and its façade was enlarged. The pharaohs of the Eighteenth Dynasty began to inscribe the names of the gods Amun and Thoth inside their cartouches.

The Eighteenth Dynasty, which included the pharaohs involved in the Exodus, was extinguished with the death of Pharaoh Horemheb in 1292 BC. The pharaohships of the Ramesseans established the Nineteenth Dynasty. By then, the events of the Exodus were old history.

☥ ☥ ☥

Abraham's sacrifice of the ram is the symbol of a rupture with the god Amun. At the beginning of the Book of Exodus, the "Hebrews" were asked by Pharaoh to "sacrifice the abomination of the Egyptians." "Moses said [to Pharaoh], 'It would not be right to do so, for we shall sacrifice offerings abominable to the Egyptians to our God Ay'" (Aramaic Bible, Exodus 8:22; Hebrew Bible, Exodus 8:26). One of Rashi's most important commentaries follows:

> *The abomination of the Egyptians. The idol worshiped by the Egyptians cf: and for Milkom, the abomination of the sons of Amun (II Kings 23:13). With regard to Israel, the test calls it an abomination. It can still be explained in another sense: the abomination of the Egyptians would be something detested by the Egyptians that is the sacrifice we are going to offer, since it is their idol that we sacrifice.*

The text associated with the commentary confirms that it dealt with a religious conflict between a monotheistic Atenian people, "sacrificing" the Amunian gods that existed then. This explanation makes it possible to establish a bridge between the Bible and history, since in all the history of ancient Egypt, the only period when there was a conflict similar to that in the Bible (the One God Adonay against Amun's idol) is found, as Freud suspected, just after Akhenaten's death.

Notes

1. The dates are always approximate, cf. Claude Vandersleyen, *Egypt and the Valley of the Nile*, Vol. 2. Nouvelle Clio, 1995, p. 663. The translators have chosen dates commonly agreed on in the English-speaking world.

2. Exodus 12:40. For a stay in Egypt of 210 years, see Rashi, *Pentateuch According to Rashi, Exodus*. Samuel and Odette Lévy, 1990, p. 89.

3. John Adams Wilson, *Egypt. Life and Death of a Civilization*. Arthaud, 1961.

4. Sigmund Freud, *Moses and Monotheism*. Gallimard, 1986.

5. Cyril Aldred, *Akhenaten, King of Egypt*. Le Seuil, 1997, pp. 214–15.

6. *Ibid.*, p. 86.

☥

CHAPTER 6

The Bible of Ay

A study of the Aramaic translation of the Bible reveals that the Hebrews were the Yahud priests, the Judahites, the followers of Pharaoh Ay. Following their exile from Akhet-Aten, the "Judahites" (the Yehudim or Yahuds) settled in Judah and the "Hebrews" (the Children of Israel, the "multitude") were relegated to the northern territories.

The Aramaic Bible, called the Targum, is a prime reference source because of its precedence in time. It is a translation of a Hebrew Bible into the Aramaic language. All extant copies of the Books of Genesis and Exodus in Hebrew were written after the Aramaic Bible. Aramaic is an ancient Semitic language very close to Hebrew and Arabic; it was the spoken and written language of Jesus of Nazareth. By Jesus' time, Hebrew had been a dead language for centuries. The Aramaic Bible is the one that Jesus would have read.

The Aramaic Bible states the name of God as "Ay." When the Divine Father Ay granted the Land of Canaan (the Promised Land) to the monotheistic priests, they deified his name, and used it as one of the names of the One God. The Aramaic Bible also reveals Ay as a "warrior" or "a man of war." "Ay is a warrior. Ay is his name" (Aramaic Bible, Exodus 15:3). "Yahwe is a warrior" (Hebrew Bible, Exodus 15:3). This verse illustrates the anthropomorphism of the God of the Bible. The concept of an abstract god was a later development.

Ay was the god of the Yahuds. It was probably after Akhenaten's and Smenkhkare's death that Ay's name became Adon-ay – Lord Ay. With this continuing tradition, much later during the Babylonian exile, God was referred to as "Adonay," even though the name was written on the page as

"Yahwe"; in this way the holy name was avoided, the name "which was never to be spoken."

The Aramaic Bible reveals the history of the Yahuds, worshipers of Pharaoh Ay and, by deduction, the other Egyptian pharaohs. The Yahuds were deported by Ay, but they revered him. Back in Egypt, the Amunian scribes and population saw the Divine Father Ay as a god of the Egyptian pantheon. As such, he was worshiped in the subject province of Canaan. A comparison of the Hebrew and Aramaic Bibles demonstrates that relationship: "And Abram answered, 'Adonay-Yahwe'" (Adonay is Yahwe) (Hebrew Bible, Genesis 15:2); "And Abram answered, 'Ay Elohim'" (Ay is "the gods") (Aramaic Bible, Genesis 15:2).

Egypt returned to the polytheistic religion of Amun during and after the time when Ay was Pharaoh. The Amunian artisans engraved Ay's name on temple walls within many cities in the Kingdom of Judah, which testifies to the persistent vitality of the worship of Pharaoh Ay, as well as of the Egyptian symbol "Yod-Yod," one of the more important symbols of "the Creative God" in the ancient Pyramid Texts. For the Yahud people, Ay's divinity integrated all the gods (Elohim), including Jehovah (Yahwe). Monotheism still lived within that concept.

A reading of both versions of the Bible reveals that there were two classes of people who were involved in the Exodus. There were the Yahuds, the priestly class, and there were the Children of Israel, the commoners, the "multitudes." Taking into account these texts as well as a study of the African monotheists, we can deduct that there was another class, the *Meses-Ay,* the police of Akhet-Aten, who went south and whose descendants live today in Kenya and Tanzania. These last group of Massai monotheists took the route south and will be discussed at a later point in this book (see Chapter 19).

The Aramaic Bible makes a clear distinction between the Hebrews (Children of Israel) and the Yahuds. The Hebrew Bible does not make such a distinction. The Aramaic version related that it was the Yahuds who went out of Egypt under the aegis of their god Ay. The Hebrews were assimilated into the Children of Israel, the Egyptian commoners, the "multitude."[1] "Then they [Moses and Aaron] said, 'The God of the Hebrews has met with us'" (Hebrew Bible, Exodus 5:3); "Then they [Moses and Aaron] said, 'The God of the Yahuds has met with us'" (Aramaic Bible, Exodus 5:3).

The Moses of the Bible was a Yahud, a son of Levi. The two Bibles deal with this fact differently. "At that time, Moses had grown up. He went out among his people and saw them toiling at hard labor. He saw an Egyptian beating a Hebrew, one of his own people" (Hebrew Bible, Exodus 2:11); "At that time, Moses had grown up. He went out among his people and saw them toiling at hard labor. He saw an Egyptian beating a Yahud, one of his people" (Aramaic Bible, Exodus 2:11).

In the latter case, Moses the Yahud did not defend a Hebrew, but one of his own Yahud class. It was a Yahud who was being mistreated by an Egyptian. So, Moses could strike an Egyptian for having humiliated a dignitary of his own rank and caste. In the episode that follows this, Moses encounters two of his fellow Yahuds (Aramaic Bible) and not two Hebrews (Hebrew Bible). In the Aramaic version, Moses intervenes as a judge. It is these passages translated from the Hebrew Bible that have thrown historians into confusion, as they desperately seek any trace of Hebrews or Children of Israel in ancient Egypt. If they had researched the Yahuds, the results would have been strikingly different. This reasoning is indispensable vis-à-vis the Jewish, Christian, and Muslim communities' other sense of the Hebrew word "slave": servant of pharaoh.

The Aramaic Bible reveals that the Yahuds were the priests of Egypt, of a different caste from the Hebrews, the "multitude," in ancient Egypt. "Yahud" (or "Yahut") is a hieroglyph meaning official or civil servant, an hereditary position of one charged with serving pharaoh. Hebrews as a distinct and separate people simply are not to be found in the ancient land. They were an invention of scribes who wrote centuries later, in a far-off, foreign land.

Rashi first raises the question of "slaves subjugated by Pharaoh." The commentator affirms that the people who came out of Egypt were "servants of Pharaoh." As a matter of fact, since they themselves had slaves, and consequently wealth, they could not be considered slaves.

From a house of bondage. From the house of Pharaoh where you were his slaves. Does this rather mean: from the house of bondage where you were slaves of other slaves? Scripture makes it more specific: "And he delivered you from the house of bondage from the hand of Pharaoh, King of Egypt (Deut. 7:4). Thus you can conclude they were slaves of a king [servants] and not slaves subject to other slaves." (Rashi, Exodus 20.2)

According to this explanation, the social status of the Hebrews was located between the highest rank in the empire, the Egyptian nobility, and the "Egyptian slaves." The slaves were, more correctly, "servants." Slavery, as we would define it today, did not exist in Ancient Egypt. From the vizier to the simplest shepherd, every person was Pharaoh's servant: as Christiane Desroches Noblecourt puts it, "Everyone in Egypt made bricks." In return, Pharaoh, the symbol of abundance,[2] assured the redistribution of wealth and food to the people.

Rashi gives a solution to this puzzle by specifying the other sense of the word "Avodah" – slave – as "servant of the cult," in the sense of "he who sacrifices in the temple."

He who sacrifices to the gods. In order to tell you: Just as the sacrifice is a service practiced toward God within the temple. I would like to add here the offering of incense or libations that are acts of worship practiced within the temple.

Only the nobles and priests had the privilege of entering within Egyptian temples and worshiping there. The Hagada (the traditional story of the leaving of Egypt) gives an explanation commented upon later in the Treatise of the Fathers. It teaches that "Pharaoh had excluded the tribe of Levi from Egyptian slavery." The tribe, composed of priests, nobles and their families, thus would have escaped the servitude imposed by the King of Egypt: "It [the Tribe of Levi, the Yahuds] owed its fortune to the maintenance of noble and extensive ancestral practices, like circumcision and study of the Law."[3]

Rashi's commentary on Genesis 18 is also quite specific: "The Midrash states further that the Tribe of Levi, to which Moses belonged, had never been Pharaoh's slave."[4] These explanations from the oral tradition mention the presence of Levite priests among the populations of the Biblical Exodus, that could only be representatives of the Egyptian nobility and clergy of Akhenaten's time. It is simply impossible to admit a cohabitation between two religions in ancient Egypt – two clergies and two nobilities coming from different origins. The division between Amun and Aten was settled by a massive exodus precisely because the priests of Aten, who were Egyptians, were accused of being "dissidents" by Ay, and subsequent pharaohs. In the words of Sety I, the son of Ramesses I, "I drove out for him [i.e., for my father the Pharaoh] the dissidents [the monotheistic Yahuds of Akhet-Aten] into the desert lands."[5]

☥ ☥ ☥

In Chapters 8 and 9 of the Book of Jeremiah, the prophet, several times, puts the people on guard against the "lying Bible" of the scribes: "How can you say, 'We're the wise ones who have the Law of Yahwe with us?' Behold, the lying pen of the scribes hath transformed the law into a falsehood" (Hebrew Bible, Jeremiah 8:8).

Jeremiah had escaped to Egypt with part of the Judahite population after the conquest of Jerusalem by Nebuchadnezzer. The flight toward the land of the fathers reveals that the prophet refused to submit to the new masters and did not consider Egypt an abomination. Paradoxically, in order to save the people, Jeremiah extolled the subjugation of Judah and Israel to Babylon (Jeremiah 27:7).

The people who could not escape to Egypt were forced into submission to the new conquerors. The result of that submission was that in Babylon the Biblical story, which had been fundamentally Egyptian, was transformed into a Mesopotamian story. Jeremiah was railing against the lies that were being promulgated by the false prophets at that time.

> So do not listen to the words of the prophets who say, "Do not submit yourselves at all to the king of Babylon." For they are prophesying lies to you. "I have not sent them," saith Yahwe. "They prophesy lies in my name. Therefore I will banish you and those false prophets." Then, I said to the priests and people, "Thus saith Yahwe, 'Do not listen to the words of the prophets who say, "The vessels of the House of Yahwe will soon be brought back from Babylon," for they prophesy a lie to you.' Do not heed them. Serve the king of Babylon and live." (Hebrew Bible, Jeremiah 27:14-17)

The Yahuds managed to save their own lives, but adopted the Babylonian superstitions and gods, Murdoch and Ishtar, which are introduced in the Book of Esther. Mordecai (Mordoch-Ay) is the image of the god Murdoch. Esther represents the goddess Ishtar. The god to be hated henceforth,

Amun, is personified by Haman and his partisans. The battle between Aten and Amun was perpetuated in Babylonia. And the Biblical version of the history of the Judahites suffered the twists and turns necessary to satisfy the new Babylonian rulers.

Notes

1. According to Erman and Ranke, a strong movement of immigration from Canaan toward Egypt took place in the time of the kings of the Eighteenth Dynasty. Adolphe Erman and Hermann Ranke, *La civilisation égyptienne.* Payot and Rivages, 1994, p. 208. Although the "multitude" may have left Egypt at the same time as the Yahuds, it is not representative of the "Chosen People" of Moses, but will serve as a scapegoat after the rebellions in the desert.

2. Pharaoh was identified with the Nile, as is shown by an effigy of Ay as God of the Nile, the dispenser of the wealth of Egypt.

3. David Berdah, *La Hagada de Pâque.* Editions Alpha Magium, 1986.

4. Rashi, *The Pentateuch According to Rashi: Genesis.* Samuel and Odette Lévy, 1990.

5. Dominique Valbelle, *Histoire de l'etat pharaonique.* Edition PUF, 1998, p.288.

☥

CHAPTER 7

Genesis

When the people of the Exodus reached Canaan, the Yahuds established themselves as the Kingdom of Judah and the multitude formed the Kingdom of Israel. Over the following centuries, power in the Near East shifted from Egypt to Chaldea (Babylonia). In 597 BC, Nebuchadnezzar, ruler of Chaldea, attacked and conquered Judah and razed its capital, Jerusalem. The Yahud classes that ruled Judah were taken away into exile in Babylon. That exile lasted 58 years.

During the Exile, the Yahud scribes began to compile accounts of Judahite history and traditions. In doing so, they modified the stories to make them acceptable to their Babylonian captors. The Book of Genesis is one of the results of the scribes' retelling of Yahud legends. The first of these legends is the story of Creation.

The Yahud retelling of the creation story harks back to the Egypt of 4700 years ago. Memphis was the capital of the kingdom at that time. The god of that city, who protected the first known great pharaohs, was called Ptah. The theology surrounding the creation of the universe by Ptah is called Memphite theology.

Memphite doctrine affirms that at the beginning of creation, there existed a cosmic void, a kind of chaos plunged in darkness, identical to the Biblical "*tohu-bohu*": "The earth was formless and void (*tohu-bohu*), and darkness was over the surface of the deep; and the Spirit [wind/breath] of the Elohim hovered over the waters" (Hebrew Bible, Genesis 1:2).

In the Egyptian version, there was a primordial ocean formed of celestial waters called "Nun." The void was filled by the Nun, the celestial waters, echoing the Biblical creation. Genesis 1:2 speaks of the Spirit (wind/breath) that hovered over the surface of the waters. The Nun, which existed before the creation of the world, gave birth to rivers and streams, and most particularly to the Nile. Genesis relates, in the same way, the creation of the primal rivers from the primordial waters.

The waters eventually lowered, allowing the firm land gradually to appear. This emergence gave birth to the sacred Nile. The primordial mound, the image of the pyramid that contains Pharaoh's Ark (Kheops and his Ark), is found in the Biblical story of Noah's Ark[1]: "On that day, all the springs of the great deep burst forth, and the windows of the heavens opened up." Then, later on: "The springs of the great deep and the windows of the heavens were closed, the rain stopped ... and the ark came to rest on Mount Ararat."[2]

The first Divine word in the Bible was addressed to the elements: "'Let there be light.' And there was light" (Genesis 1:3). This echoes the Memphite theology, which stipulates that the creation of the world was directed by the sacred word of the god Ptah. This also foreshadows the Christian doctrine of the Word, found in John 1:1, "In the beginning was the Word, and the Word was with God, and the Word was God."

Ptah, "the god who opens,"[3] had the power to create by pronouncing the sacred words: "He created all things and caused the gods to be born ... So Ptah was satisfied after he had created all things so they were in divine order."[4]

In the Hebrew Bible, it is stated repeatedly that, "God saw that it was good [*Tov*]".[5]

♀ ♀ ♀

Two thousand years before the appearance of the Bible, the concept of a divine force prior to creation existed already in Memphis, providing a basis of belief for the entire Egyptian society.

This religious concept permitted local populations to integrate in an environment propitious for religious beliefs and contributed to the rein-forcement of the national expression of the country. This common identity led to the invention of the 365-day Egyptian calendar. This calendar developed around the annual flooding of the Nile and is the origin of New Year's cerebrations in all countries and religions of the western world, thus rendering homage to the most ancient of all the Egyptian traditions: the flood.

Work in the fields depended on the floods of the Nile. When the harvest season finished, the ancient Egyptians devoted themselves to non-agricultural tasks: artistic and scientific endeavors and construction work, which necessitated efficient organization. The alternation of agricultural and collective activities gave the people the feeling of participating in the life of the nation, in its material and spiritual domains. This community of labor among the Egyptians produced strength and optimism, a fervor that we find later among the Yahuds.

From the Fourth through Sixth Dynasties (roughly 2600 to 2100 BC, a period of some 500 years), the Egyptians undertook the task of controlling the annual inundation. The drainage and irrigation work contributed to the creation of new wealth. The people were minions of the pharaohs, who exercised a centralizing power. The emergence of a new national cohesion, concentrated on the "god-king," permitted the construction of the cities, temples, and great pyramids – symbols of the primordial landing of the Ark, akin to the tale of Noah.

Egypt soon saw itself as a holy land. Well before Akhet-Aten and the writing of the Bible, the notion of a holy land was associated with ancient Egypt, a land naturally protected by mountains and deserts, and blessed by the Nile. This advantageous geographic situation, perceived as a gift of the gods, was also the origin of the concept of a "chosen people."

The people of ancient Egypt were chosen by the gods, and thus were living in the "holy land." John Adam Wilson writes:

Egypt believed itself chosen among all nations and that its setbacks could only be temporary. Everyone sensed that life could be enjoyed in familiar simplicity. This fundamental optimism towards life here below extended to the life beyond. The blessings of immortality were promised to every good Egyptian.[6]

The blessings of immortality are the same promises made to those faithful to Biblical monotheism. Election and sanctity remained always fixed in the hearts of the people who "came up out of Egypt." Egyptian mythology and memories of life in Egypt remained with the Yahuds in their new promised land of Judah. The memories persisted through the exile to Babylon. Among the prized memories were those of the man who had given them the gift of monotheism – Akhenaten – and of the wonderful paradise he had constructed – Akhet-Aten.

Notes

1. Genesis 7:12.
2. Genesis 8:4.
3. John Adams Wilson, *Egypt. Life and Death of a Civilisation*. Arthaud, 1961, p. 60.
4. K. Seth, *Dramatische Texte zur Altägyptischen Mysterienspielen,* p. 59. Cited in John Adams Wilson, *Egypt. Life and Death of a Civilisation.*
5. Genesis 1:12, 1:18, 1:21, 1:25, 1:31.
6. John Adams Wilson, *Life and Death of a Civilisation*, p. 66.

☥

CHAPTER 8

Akhenaten and Adam

Akhenaten was regularly represented on temple walls under the god Aten, who was symbolized by the divine sun. Aten is shown sending down his rays, materialized as lines directed toward Pharaoh's face. Most of the rays fall on Akhenaten's hands. Some beams carry the "Ankh," the symbol of life. Others carry the symbol of royalty (the Scepter of God).

To be precise, the Ankh appears before Pharaoh's nostrils. This represents the breath of life, the same breath that God (the Elohim, Adonay) breathes into Adam's nostrils in the Genesis story. Only those of royal rank could receive this symbol of life. No ordinary Egyptian had the right to that "divine breath," which was the prerogative of Pharaoh and his family.

Akhenaten and Nefertiti offer incense to Aten in the temple. Aten sends the breath of life into their nostrils by means of the Ankh sign (Cairo Museum). Genesis 2:7: Yahwe and the Elohim fashioned man from the dust of the earth and breathed the breath of life into his nostrils, and man became a living being.

Akhenaten required his people to worship him as the sacred image of the god, Aten. The god-king of the Eighteenth Dynasty proclaimed himself son of Aten, then son of Re (another aspect of the sun god). Pharaoh had become the representative on earth of the One God. He called himself the "first prophet of Aten." This quality conferred on him the primacy of the new cult. The people could worship Aten only through Pharaoh. In his capital of Akhet-Aten, as in all of Egypt, he had magnificent temples built and consecrated to the cult of Aten, his own cult, since he was the only representative. To worship Aten was to worship Akhenaten. At the entrance of the temples, before the two monumental pylons separated by the great central door, colossal statues majestically imposed the authority of the great pharaoh.

♀ ♀ ♀

Many of the statues and other representations of Akhenaten show him as both male and female. Early in the Bible, we have this male–female blend. Genesis 1:27 says: "So the Elohim created humans in their own image, in the image of the Elohim they created them. They created humans male and female."

Is the image of the Elohim (the gods, the sons of God) the image of man? Does the verse relate to the anthropomorphism we encounter in Egyptian imagery? Most of the Egyptian gods are represented by people or animals, or by people with heads of animals. The expression "male and female" attaches masculine and feminine characteristics to Adam's person. Representations of Akhenaton show both masculine and feminine characteristics.

What are the reasons behind Akhenaten's desire to have himself represented as both male and female? Frölichs' syndrome, an hereditary deformity of the body, has been advanced as one explanation, making him deformed and incapable of procreation. However, Akhenaten had six daughters, without counting the many other children he had by his royal wives or concubines.

It could be that this double representation, male and female, was envisioned as some peculiarity of Amarnian art characterizing the art of the epochs of Akhenaten and his father Amenhotep III. Another explanation posits Akhenaten and Nefertiti as the primordial couple of creation.[1]

Colossus showing an asexual Akhenaten, male and female (Cairo Museum). The colossus is red, which is "Adom" in Hebrew = Adam = Atum "The Elohim created man in their image. It is in the image of the Elohim that he was created" (Genesis 1:27). "He will be united with his wife and they will become one flesh" (Genesis 2:24).

This last explanation finds its parallel in the Adam and Eve story.

In one of the giant statues of Akhenaten (above) he is shown standing in the Osiris position (arms crossed). He is asexual, without loincloth – the image, like Adam, of the first human created on earth. Unlike Adam, though, Akhenaten is shown as both male and female. He had proclaimed himself "the father and mother of humanity," a notion which applies allegorically to Adam,[2] and to Abraham[3] (Father of Nations).

Aten had fashioned Akhenaten in his own image. Akhenaten and Adam were both fashioned by the One God in his own image.

In Genesis 2:4, a new and different version is presented of the creation of man.[4] It begins: "This is the description of the creation of the heavens and the earth. When Yahwe and the Elohim created the earth and the heavens …"

This second version of Creation contradicts the first. In this new tale the earth was created before the heavens. Then came man, the plants, the animals, and woman. Even though the order is different, God breathes the indispensable breath of life into Adam's nostrils. "Then Yahwe and the Elohim, from the dirt of the earth, formed man into a living creature by breathing the breath of life into his nostrils" (Hebrew Bible, Genesis 2:7).

In the second creation myth it was no longer a question of man being made in the image of God, but of creation from dirt. Death was symbolized by a return to the dirt of the earth. Egyptians covered their bodies with dirt during the mourning ceremonies, to mark their affliction and as a sign of humility. It was also done by the many mourners who lamented while following the funeral procession.

Scene of mourning for Princess Maketaten. Akhenaten and Nefertiti spread dust in a sign of mourning. The princess is mummified, standing inside the kiosk.

In addition to the application of dirt to the body, Egyptian male mourners abstained from shaving. Pharaoh let his beard grow for 70 days when one of his daughters died. John Pendlebury[5] writes that a sketch of Akhenaten shows him with several days' beard growth and a child's toy in his hand, possibly to express his mourning for his daughter Maketaten. A painting of Ramesses II, wearing several days' growth of beard in mourning for his father Sety I, reminds us that this tradition, continued by the Yahuds, had an Egyptian origin.

*Ramesses II in mourning for his
father, wearing several days'
beard growth.*

Crying, wailing mourners, cinders and dust, prayers for the dead and
purification with holy water, incense ritual, beard ritual, blessings over
food, funeral meals in the temples, inscriptions engraved on stone with the
name of the departed, the passage of the soul of the corpse to the Great
Beyond, celestial tribunal, resurrection, fast, and a period of mourning –
all these traditions and beliefs which came out of ancient Egypt were
preserved in the Bible, under the aegis of the priests of Akhet-Aten. These,
in turn, have influenced all the subsequent monotheistic religions.

In the Egyptian notion of creation, there is a reference to Atum, a god
who created himself and who fashioned man by dismembering himself.
According to Freud,[6] Atum was a distant ancestor of Aten. Atum, god of
Heliopolis (a city which the Bible calls On) personifies the celestial deep.

Atum was the first god and Adam was the first man of the creation
stories. Eve, the first woman (Isha) is reminiscent of Isis.

Adam, then, came out of remembrance of the Egyptian god Atum, the
god who existed prior to creation, a personification of the celestial deep.
And *Isha* (Woman, Eve) came out of remembrance of Isis, with whom
Nefertiti was identified.

The roots of Genesis seem to have grown in Egyptian soil.

Notes

1. Pierre Grandet, *Hymnes de la religion d'Aton*. Le Seuil, 1995, p. 30.
2. Genesis 1:27.
3. Genesis 17:4-5.
4. Richard Friedman, *Who Wrote the Bible?* Exergue, 1997, p. 53.
5. H. Francfort and J.D.S. Pendlebury, *The City of Akhenaten*, II. Egypt Exploration Society, XL, 1933, pl. XXXI.
6. Sigmund Freud, *Moses and Monotheism*. Gallimard, 1986.

✇

CHAPTER 9

Forbidden Fruit

In the first version of the creation story, God made a gift of all creation to man. In Genesis 2:8-11 (Hebrew Bible), we learn about the Garden of Eden and the tree that bore forbidden fruit:

> *And now Yahwe and the Elohim planted a garden in Eden, in the East. And they put the man they had formed in it. Then Yahwe and the Elohim planted all kinds of trees in the ground, trees that are pleasant to see and good to eat. In the middle of the Garden, they planted the Tree of the Knowledge of Good and Evil. A river that watered the garden flowed out of Eden. It divided into four streams. The first was named Pishon. It is the one that flows through Havilah, where there is gold. The gold of that land is good.*

Rashi claims that the Garden of Eden was located in Egypt. The word Pishon means the Nile, the primordial river of Creation, which watered the Garden: "That is the Nile, the Egyptian river called Pishon, because its waters, by the blessing of God, overflowed and watered the ground."[1]

The Pyramid Texts report that Pharaoh was responsible for the flooding of the Nile. Rashi has an interesting commentary on the relationship of the Pharaoh and the Nile. Genesis 47:7-10 states: "Then Joseph brought in Jacob his father and presented him to Pharaoh ... and then Jacob blessed Pharaoh." Rashi comments: "What blessing did he give him? That the waters of the Nile would rise to his feet, because Egypt does not receive rain water. It is the Nile that waters by its floodings. But since he had received Jacob's blessing, Pharaoh could approach the banks of the Nile, and the waters of the Nile would rise and water the land."

The Nile waters the land of Havilah, linked to the gold deposits in the south of Egypt. Gold was considered the flesh of the gods – the flesh of Pharaoh.

The second river cited by the Bible is called the Gihon, in the land of Kush, which is in the south of Egypt. Consequently, it is a branch of the Nile. The other rivers, the Tigris and Euphrates, are in what was then Assyria. So the limits of the Garden of Eden correspond to the borders of the Egyptian Empire from the reign of Thutmose to that of Ramesses I, i.e., the time of the Eighteenth Dynasty. Strangely, the Bible locates a "Garden of Adonay" in Egypt:

> *Lot raised his eyes and observed that the entire plain of Jordan was well-watered, like the garden of Yahwe, like the land of Egypt, toward Zoar. This was before Yahwe destroyed Sodom and Gomorrah. (Genesis 13:10)*

In Genesis 2:16-17 the next reference to the Tree occurs: "And Yahwe said to the man, 'You may eat the fruit of any tree in the Garden.' But the Elohim commanded, 'You must not eat from the Tree of the Knowledge of Good and Evil. For when you eat that fruit, you shall die'" (Hebrew Bible, Genesis 2:16-17).

Then, God created woman from one of Adam's ribs. Along came the crafty serpent, coaxing Eve to transgress the divine order. She tasted the fruit of the tree and gave it to Adam, who also ate it. Because of her transgression, the Bible states that the woman will bear children in pain and be dominated by the man, who must toil "by the sweat of his brow."[2] Following the eating of the fruit, the first couple was condemned to return to dirt, after having been driven from the Garden of Eden.

♀ ♀ ♀

There is historical and archeological data that place the Garden of Eden in Egypt. Among the numerous temples erected by Akhenaten there is the Great Temple of Aten, or the "*Gem-Pa-Yten*" or "*Gempa-Aten.*" It covers an area 200 meters wide by 800 meters long. Like the other temples of Akhenaten, it was first constructed at Karnak, where its original foundations were found. Its exact replica, built afterwards in the capital of Akhet-Aten, was surrounded by an immense estate, which consisted of basins of purified water, vineyards, orchards, and green spaces protected by an enclosing wall.

Within the Garden stood the sacred tree, called "*Ished.*" Its fruit was destined only for Pharaoh. A priest or priestess had to write or engrave on each fruit, within an oval or cartouche, the name of the king. The fruit thus marked became sacred in the eyes of the people, and constituted divine food. Christiane Desroches Noblecourt states that the fruit of the tree of Pharaoh Amenhotep III at the Temple of Karnak conferred immortality, like the Biblical tree.

The Hebrew Bible alleges that the Garden of Eden (*Gan-Ba-Eden*),[3] like that of the temple of Akhenaten, faced East, and was also irrigated by the waters of the Nile.

There is another of Akhenaten's temples, the "*Gem-Aten,*" which also could be identified as the Garden of Eden, with the Ished Tree. The Hebrew term "*Gan-Eden*"[4] gets confused with the Egyptian "*Gem-Aten.*" This temple, like *Gem-Pa-Aten,* existed both at Karnak and at Akhet-Aten. It was composed of the same elements: gardens, temples with columns, a sacred tree, vineyards, and a basin of sweet water fed by the Nile.

Fruit of the divine tree gave power, knowledge, beauty, majesty, intelligence, and longevity to Pharaoh and his divine wife Nefertiti. The monotheistic priests tasted the forbidden fruit, and each one who did so then considered himself as godlike, identifying himself with Pharaoh.

☥ ☥ ☥

The story or legend of Original Sin is at the base of the Biblical laws governing the relationship between man and woman. The concept submitted women to religious constraints. Such constraints are still in force today in many countries. The legend has allowed men to prevail physically and intellectually over women.

The legend that gave rise to the concept of original sin harkens back to the earliest days of ancient Egypt. The pharaohs of that period probably associated their names with primordial Egyptian gods like Atum, who gave birth to Shu and Tefnut, the divine couple who gave birth to Geb (the earth) and Nut (the heavens). Geb and Nut engendered four divinities, thus forming the Great Ennead[5] of Heliopolis.

Atum = Adam   Isis = Isha = Eve   Thot = Daat = Knowledge

Pharaoh = Re is in peace = Atov = Hotep

The tree "Ished" of Pharaoh, each fruit of which is marked with his name by the priest and priestess, bears identical symbols to the tree of Creation in the Book of Genesis. The Tree of Knowledge (Daat) of Good (Tov) and Evil (Ra) (Genesis 2:9).

In Egyptian mythology Osiris was king of Egypt. Isis was his queen. The name Isis is a Greek translation of the Egyptian root "*Isa*" or "*Isha*," which is the Hebrew root word for woman. Osiris,[6] the god of darkness, symbolized the strength and abundance conferred at Pharaoh's death. Seth, Osiris' brother, jealous of him, assassinated him. Then Horus, the son of Isis and Osiris, challenged Seth in order to avenge the death of his father. This intrigue is classic in Egyptian thought. It places the seizure of power at the deepest base of its culture. There follows the permanent battle between Horus and Seth – between good and evil.

Horus was aided in his battle against Seth by his mother, Isis. The celestial tribunal finally agreed with Horus and Seth was condemned to submission. Seth appears in the Bible as Cain, Adam's son who murdered his brother Abel.

Another Seth legend tells how he was called by the sun god Re to be one of the occupants of the royal boat, to protect it against the incessant attacks of the serpent, Apophis. In that battle, Isis joined Seth and used her

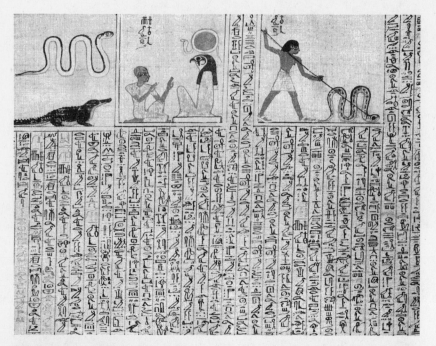

The battle between Seth and Apophis.

Apophis the serpent finally submits to the god Seth, who is shown transformed into a fabulous animal.

magic charms to bewitch the serpent, depriving it of its senses, thus facilitating its annihilation.[7] This was the victory of Isis and Seth over Apophis, who incarnated evil, the demon brought to earth. This legend, much earlier than the Biblical tale, shows the serpent under the sacred tree, where the fruit, always coveted by the priests and priestesses, bloomed.

It is the Biblical interpretation of the story of Apophis that results in the concept of Original Sin. In ancient Egypt, women were somewhat liberated. Although they did not have the right to perform administrative functions, some women, like Hatshepsut and Nefertiti, acceded to divine status. Women could obtain the same basic rights as men. They could dispose of some parts of their inheritance, they could go to court, etc. Work for women of the lower classes was difficult, but they were represented among the ranks of artists, artisans and goldsmiths. What the Bible considered defeat of man and woman in the face of urges and desires was seen by the Egyptians to be not defeat, but victory. The battle of the god Seth and the goddess Isis against the serpent was won because man and the woman were united heroically against Apophis.

In the Biblical story, Original Sin came into the picture when Adam and Eve had both eaten the forbidden fruit. They became aware of their nudity. Nudity was considered natural to them before they ate the fruit. After eating the fruit, they perceived it as a sin before God. The shame concerning their sexuality on the day after Creation seems to contradict the stages in which God (or the Gods?) was "satisfied"[8] with His work. The shame the couple felt is intentionally linked to evil.

In the Biblical telling, evil is tied to sexual urges. From the moment of the awakening of that desire, the "evil tendency" of sex required strict laws to govern sexual relations between men and women. These laws broke down later, the Bible teaches, leading Solomon, Judah, and Israel into transgressions.

The Egyptian case was quite different. The art of Amarna shows Nefertiti and Akhenaten naked or lightly dressed. A mural shows them in the flesh, embracing without showing any shame. The carnal act, amorous and consecrated, did not symbolize decadence, but, on the contrary, an image of the divine couple at its best, naked before their god. They were in the state described in Genesis 2:25, before the primordial couple ate the fruit. "The man and his wife were naked, but were not ashamed."

The royal princesses are often shown naked in their parents' presence (for example, on Huy's tomb) and sparsely dressed when taking part in some of the ceremonies of the cult. Cyril Aldred, a specialist on the Amarnian period, describes this situation thus:

> *The cult of nudity attained its apogee under Akhenaten's reign. This cult was represented not in the formal attitudes of worship repeated so insistently in every section of the temple, or even as triumphal conquerors striking the foreign enemy, but rather in intimate circumstances, full of life, as human beings engaged in everyday activities: 'while embracing their children, prancing about in their bare skins ... banqueting in the intimacy of their palace.'*[9]

Christian Jacq comments on this:

> *Akhenaten and Nefertiti demonstrated their love by kissing each other, even in front of the populace ... In several instances, the royal couple is represented naked as they banquet, as shown in Huy's tomb, and in decorations in Ay's as well ... That the royal family lived naked in their apartments was quite the way things were done.*[10]

As in the Bible before the doctrine Original Sin, notions of good and evil in Pharaoh Akhenaten's capital had nothing at all to do with the sight of one's own nudity or that of another person. The vision expressed then, by the beauty of the human body, was divine creation influencing all artistic inspiration, including sacred art.

Here, a teaching is revealed concerning the meaning of good and evil for the ancient Egyptians. As in the Bible before Original Sin, good and evil were neither related nor opposites. Good was deified as *Maat*, goddess of justice and truth, qualities that were sacred and religious. These qualities were linked to the God who created the universe, having nothing to do with knowledge of evil.

Maat has the same root as the Hebrew *Emet*, meaning truth and justice. In this state of innocence, good was never the opposite of evil, as it is in the Bible. Evil was a well-known idea, under the name of *Isefet*. With the Egyptians, *Isefet* was a destructive force.

Isefet, or "evil," was demonstrated by the perversity of the priests of Akhet-Aten when they transgressed one of the sacred laws of Egypt. They tasted the fruit of the Divine Tree. By doing so, not only did they identify themselves with Pharaoh, but worse yet they demystified the ancient legend of the Tree of Life in the eyes of the Divine Father Ay, as the God of the Aramaic Bible states, "Here that man has become like one of us, in that he knows good [*Tov*] and evil [*Re*]" (Aramaic Bible, Genesis 3:22).

The serpent, that personification of women's perversity, is dealt with in Genesis 3:14, where God inflicts a heavy chastisement on the creature: "Yahwe and the Elohim said to the serpent, 'because you have done this, you are cursed above all the domestic and wild animals. You shall crawl on your belly and eat dirt all the days of your life.'"

Rashi[11] explains that the serpent was originally provided with legs, and that these were removed, obliging it to crawl on the ground. However, while the serpent is the animal cursed at Creation, ancient Egypt considered it a living god: the eye of Horus, protector of Pharaoh, ready to dispatch anyone looking at his face. Rashi's commentary gives us the state of the oral tradition about the "legged serpent," whose origin is purely Egyptian. One legend relates[12] "that Seth launched serpents against his enemy Osiris who was asleep beneath the Tree of Life. Awakened by the cries of an owl, he gave the order for them to creep on the earth."

The serpent with legs from the tomb of Amenhotep II.

The Tree of Life is encountered in the Great Hymn to the god Amun. It describes God as the creator of humanity, the animals, and the plants that nourish the cattle. In agreement with the Bible, the Tree of Life has the function of conferring longevity on Pharaoh or on whoever eats its fruit. In

Genesis 3:22, after chastising the primordial couple, Yahwe and the Elohim say, "Now he must not be allowed to take fruit from the Tree of Life, and eat, and live forever."

The Adam and Eve story is a remembrance of the expulsion from Akhet-Aten. This memory remained engraved in the consciousness of the people who were "driven out of Egypt," in order that they might worship their One God in another land "flowing with milk and honey." They received a promise in exchange for the paradise lost.

Genesis 3:23-24 of the Hebrew Bible says, "So Yahwe and the Elohim drove him [Adam] out of the Garden of Eden, to work the ground [dirt] from which he had been created. They drove the man out, and on the east of the Garden of Eden, they placed cherubim and a flaming sword, which flashed back and forth, to guard the way to the Tree of Life." The picture of the flaming sword, forever guarding access to the lost paradise recalls that, during and long after the banishment of its inhabitants, Akhet-Aten was guarded by the army of the Divine Father Ay.

"And He said to Adam, 'Because you listened to your wife, and ate from the tree I commanded you to avoid, the very dirt under your feet is cursed. You shall eat of it all the days of your life'" (Hebrew Bible, Genesis 3:17).

In the story of Sodom and Gomorrah, there is a similarity to the story of the expulsion from Eden. The Aramaic Bible describes it in this way:

> *Ay said, "Because the outcry against Sodom and Gomorrah has increased, and the perversity is very grave, I will go down and I will see for myself. If they are behaving as the outcries indicate, I will exterminate them. If not, I will warn them." The men turned from there and went towards Sodom. And Abraham remained standing before Adon-Ay. (Aramaic Bible, Genesis 18:20-22)*

According to these verses, Adon-ay decided to destroy the two cities because of the perversion reigning there. Although they were located in Canaan, in desert regions close to the Dead Sea, there exists not a single archeological trace of Sodom and Gomorrah. Paradoxically, the Bible compares the cities to a "Garden of Yahwe" in Egypt. "And Lot looked up and saw that the plain of the Jordan was well watered, like the garden of

Yahwe, like the land of Egypt toward Zoar" (Hebrew Bible, Genesis 13:10).

The corruption of Sodom and Gomorrah is similar to Ay's perception of Akhet-Aten. Ay doubtless wished to destroy the city at first, but finally compromised in favor of deporting the population to Canaan and dismantling the buildings.

In the Aramaic Bible, Ay sent messengers to warn Lot and his family: "Lot went out and said to his sons-in-law, engaged to his daughters, 'Look! Abandon this place. For Adon-Ay is going to destroy this city.' But he appeared to the eyes of his sons-in-law to be joking" (Aramaic Bible, Genesis 19:14).

"The sun had risen over the earth when Lot arrived at Zoar. Adon-Ay caused brimstone and fire to fall from the skies, to rain on Sodom and on Gomorrah. He destroyed those cities and the whole plain – all the inhabitants of those cities. And even the vegetation on the ground" (Aramaic Bible, Genesis 19:23-25).

The name Gomorrah, in Hebrew, is *Amora*, which means "people of Re" or "people of Pharaoh." The verse can be translated as, "Ay caused it to rain on Sodom and on *his* people of Re, the Great God."

Rashi comments as follows on these verses: "The rain fell over Sodom. He [Lot] arose in the night, as it is written: when dawn broke (Verse 15), the moon was still in the heavens, at the moment when the sun had just risen. For he was one who worshiped the sun, and others worshiped the moon."

As at Akhet-Aten, the inhabitants of Sodom had the sun cult. The moon was considered by them to be Re's second eye. The perverted picture of Sodom is encountered in Akhet-Aten's cult of nudity. Sodom, considered in the Bible as "a garden of Adonay in Egypt" could well be the metaphor for Akhet-Aten.

God saved the family of Lot, Abraham's nephew, just as Ay saved the young pharaoh Tutankhamun and his family before deporting the population. Zoar, the name of the refuge city, is close to the Hebrew, *Shaar*, meaning door. Thebes was called "the city of a hundred doors." The city of the light of Aten, the sun god, the Garden of Eden, abandoned and destroyed by Ay, is revealed in the written and oral tradition of the legend of Sodom and Gomorrah.

♀ ♀ ♀

The Biblical legend of Original Sin, under the cover of the ancient Egyptian legend, symbolizes, above all, the drama of Akhet-Aten.

The serpent personifies the perversity of the women of Akhet-Aten, who, succumbing to the desire to taste the fruit of the Tree, gave it to the priests so they could accede to the throne of Egypt and thus to the eternal life of the pharaohs. In that way, they destroyed the secular myth of the sacred tree, provoking the wrath of the Divine Father Ay.

The goddess Nut under the Tree of Life. "The woman saw that the tree was good for food and that it was attractive to the eyes and could make one wise; she plucked its fruit and ate. She also gave it to her husband and he ate it" (Genesis 3:6).

Ay made them feel guilty, and cursed the population of the capital for their corrupt morals and their unbridled sexual lives. He accused the monotheistic priests of having succumbed to temptation by obeying their wives. This pretext allowed him to curse forever the sacred land of Akhet-Aten, and to excommunicate the men and women who had inhabited it. And to drive them out of Egypt.

Notes

1. Rashi, *Pentateuch According to Rashi, Genesis* 2:11. Samuel and Odette Lévy, 1993.
2. Genesis 3:14-20.
3. Genesis 2:8.
4. Genesis 2:15.
5. The Heliopolitan creation story has Atum evolving into a group of nine gods, called the "Ennead": himself (Atum), Shu, Tefnut, Geb, Nut, Osiris, Isis, Seth, and Nephthys. Sometimes a tenth god, Horus, the son of Isis and Osiris, is added to the group. Sometimes even Re joins the Ennead.
6. Robert Jacques Thibaud, *Dictionnaire de mythologie et symbolique égyptienne.* Dervy, 1996, p. 243.
7. Aude Gros de Beler, *La mythologie égyptienne.* Molière, 1998.
8. Genesis 1:14.
9. Cyril Aldred, *Akhenaten, King of Egypt.* Le Seuil, 1997, p. 137.
10. Christian Jacq, *Nefertiti et Akhénaten*, Perrin, 1996, p. 154.
11. Rashi, *Pentateuch According to Rashi, Genesis* 14:3.
12. Robert Jacques Thibaud, *Dictionnaire de mythologie et symbolique égyptienne*, p. 322.

☥

CHAPTER 10

The Elohim

The scribes of both the Aramaic and Hebrew Bibles often use the first person plural to describe God, as in Genesis 1:26: "Let us make man in our own image, in our own likeness." Rashi explains this plural form for God by saying that God speaks in the name of his "family," the celestial beings (the Elohim). "Man, being in the image of the celestial beings, could make the Elohim jealous. God took care to consult them. And when God judges the kings of the earth, He, in the same way, takes counsel with his 'family.'"

According to Rashi, the "upper" world is made up of a celestial host, the angels, sitting on the right and left hand of God, who is seated on His throne. The divine family is a mirror image of Pharaoh and his assembly. The expression "on the right (or the left) hand of the king" was included in the titles of the nobility of ancient Egypt. Ay held the title of "fan bearer seated at the right hand of the king, responsible for all his majesty's horses, true scribe of the king, father of God."[1] For important decisions, Pharaoh had to seek the counsel of the nobles seated around him. He also had to consult the gods, those celestial beings with whom he communicated. The upper world was multiple, in the image of ancient Egypt.

In the expression "as one among us," the Bible reveals Ay's (Adonay's) membership in the Elohim, the pharaohs of Egypt.

Once Adam and Eve were driven from the Garden of Eden, earth's population began to increase. By the time of Noah, there were many attractive human women. "When mankind began to increase in population on earth and daughters were born to them, the sons of the Elohim saw that the women were beautiful. And they married those of them that they wanted" (Hebrew Bible, Genesis 6:1-2).

Rashi offers this explanation about the beings that appear in these verses:

> *The sons of the Elohim: children of princes and judges. Another expla-*
> *nation of the* Midrash *[Hebrew commentary on the Bible]. They were*
> *heavenly beings, accomplishing a divine mission. They were also*
> *mixing with the women. In any case, the word Elohim always carries*
> *with it the sense of supremacy. It is thus that God said to Moses:*
> *"Thou shalt be for Aaron one of the Elohim" (Exodus 4:16). Or again,*
> *"Behold, I shall cause you to be one of the Elohim for Pharaoh"*
> *(Exodus 7:1).*

The commentary gives us a better glimpse of the priests of ancient Egypt. The pharaohs succeeded one another in the course of the different dynasties, and each one had numerous wives and children. They assured the futures of the princes by assigning them functions in the government, the army, and, above all, the priesthood. The priests of Akhet-Aten and the prominent citizens and functionaries formed the people of the Elohim[2] (sons of the gods). These were the children of all the pharaohs of the past, who were seen as the gods of Egypt. They belonged to the secular pharaonic royalty (the heavenly beings). Describing the Egyptian nobility in general, and of Akhet-Aten in particular, Cyril Aldred states:

> *In Egypt, the aristocrats often had direct ties with the sovereign. They*
> *were the "children of the court," descendants and relatives more or less*
> *close to the pharaohs, through the pharaohs' secondary wives. And they*
> *played an important role in the government, as for example, Yuya, the*
> *commandant of chariots under Thutmose IV, or Ay, chief of cavalry*
> *under Akhenaten.[3]*

The true meaning, then, of the word Elohim is the pharaohs of Egypt. It is thus that the first verse of the Bible meets the Pyramid Texts, proclaiming loud and clear that the king of Egypt is a cosmic being, called upon to mount the celestial ladder or stairs, to sit on a shining throne, nourished by heavenly fruit and reigning over a celestial world.

"The Nephilim were on the earth in those days and afterward too, when the sons of the Elohim mixed with the daughters of men. And those daughters bore children to them. They were the ancient heroes and men of renown" (Hebrew Bible, Genesis 6:4).

Although the Hellenists translated *nephilim* as "giants," the sense of the verse was contested by Fabre d'Olivet:

> *The simplest things are always those the scholars see least. They go searching into the beyond, with infinite pains, neglecting the truth right under their noses. The savants had the Latin word* nobilis, *under their eyes, which carries the same root as the Hebrew* Nephilim *… and which has to be seen in the* Nephilians *of Moses, not as giants or men of colossal height, but the grandees, distinguished, illustrious men. In short, the nobles.*[4]

This explanation, based on semantics, permits us to reinforce the sense of "sons of the Elohim" as those belonging to the pharaonic nobility, ambitious and proud of its past. The new nobility, mentioned by those Egyptologists who are specialists in the Amarnian reform, represented the majority of the population of Akhet-Aten, both in the government and the clergy. The power, thus constituted, rapidly disquieted the old Theban nobility, which had to find an ally in the person of the Divine Father Ay.

In monotheism, God has several names. This resembles the ancient Egyptian tradition of regrouping the names of all the pharaohs, representative of the supreme god. In brief, "Pharaoh is God"[5] = "Pharaoh is *the gods.*" "In the beginning the gods [the Elohim, all the pharaohs of Egypt] created the heavens and the earth" (Genesis 1:1). Since Pharaoh never dies, he is a plural being, representing all the gods. He is also a singular being, personifying the oneness of god. This is the origin of monotheism: unity comes from plurality, *e pluribus unum.*

Cyril Aldred[6] notes that Akhenaten had forbidden the use in sacred writing of the plural for the word "God," in order to highlight its oneness unambiguously. Rashi adds information on this subject: "God (the Elohim) was/were revealed to him (Genesis 35:7). Since the word Elohim is plural, the verb used here is plural. It often happens that the word God and Lord are in the plural."

The Bible uses the singular and the plural to designate God in accord with the theological concepts of the Eighteenth Dynasty.

For Yahwe is the great God of Gods, Lord of the Elohim [Eloheh Aelohim, Adone Adonim], *mighty and awesome. He is impartial and does not take bribes. He defends the fatherless and the widow, and loves the foreigner, giving him food and clothing. (Hebrew Bible, Deuteronomy 10:17-18; the words of Moses to the people of Israel)*

The plural Elohim, written in the first verse of the Bible, reveals the origin of monotheism. The Elohim are the many pharaohs, the fathers of Egypt.

Notes

1. Claude Vandersleyen, *Egypt and the Valley of the Nile*, Vol. 2. Nouvelle Clio, 1995, p. 479.
2. Deuteronomy 14:1 "You are the sons of Yahwe, your God (Elohekhem)."
3. Cyril Aldred, *Akhenaten, King of Egypt.* Le Seuil, 1997, p. 136.
4. Fabre d'Olivet, *La langue hébraïque* restituée. L'Age d'Homme-Delphica, 1991, p. 180.
5. Christian Jacq, *La tradition primordiale de l'Egypte ancienne selon les texts des pyramides.* Grasset & Fasquelle. 1998. p. 101.
6. Cyril Aldred, *Akhenaten*, p. 271.

CHAPTER 11

☥

The Flood

The story of Noah's Ark reflects the separation between the monotheistic people living within Akhet-Aten and the rest of polytheistic Egypt. "The earth was corrupt in the eyes of Adon-Ay, and full of violence. Adon-Ay saw how corrupt the world had become, because all the people had perverted their ways" (Aramaic Bible, Genesis 6:11).

The Noah legend cannot be understood literally. The Ark symbolizes Akhet-Aten, the holy land of the exclusive monotheist inhabitants. The Hebrew word "*tebah*" was translated as "ark" by the Hellenists many centuries ago. That ancient translation was refuted by Fabre d'Olivet. "The Hebrew word never meant vessel in the sense of a ship, as later understood … It is rather the symbolic name given by the Egyptians to their sacred city of Thebes, considered the asylum, the refuge, the home of the gods."[1]

The monotheistic ark (sacred city), Akhet-Aten, became a problem for the Divine Father. So, he began to make plans to get rid of it in order to save the rest of Egypt. He decided to evacuate the dwellers of the holy land and then destroy the city.

The Aramaic Bible expresses Ay's thought, as he considered the corruption that had become prevalent in the capital city. He was angry, and yet felt compassion for the population. The population, which he wished to save, is represented by Noah. Let us observe the state of mind of Ay (Adon-Ay), as revealed in the Aramaic version of the story:

Adon-Ay saw that the wicked thoughts of man had increased, and that all the thoughts of his heart were evil. And Adon-Ay was sorry that he had created man on the earth, and his heart was grieved. And Adon-Ay said, "I will wipe out from the face of the earth, mankind, whom I have created – men and beasts, crawling animals, and the birds of the air, for I am sorry I ever created them." But Noah found favor in the eyes of Adon-Ay. (Aramaic Bible, Genesis 6:5-8)

There were many things happening in Akhet-Aten (the "Ark") that Ay found subversive. Among them was the language of the inhabitants. A new language was developing among the people.

The city was cosmopolitan, composed of people not only from all over Egypt, but from throughout the known world. There was an urgent problem of communication. In order to converse with one another, a new language was adopted by the population.[2]

The new language of Akhet-Aten was created from the foreign dialects. This new language incensed the Divine Father Ay. He could not tolerate this insult, this heresy to the holy language of ancient Egypt. Ay could not speak or understand the new language. He needed an interpreter in order to be understood in the capital of his own country; Ay needed an interpreter to communicate with Pharaoh and the people of Akhet-Aten. This new language was the beginning of Hebrew.

Pharaoh had to hold audience with the many foreign residents in the capital, and made use of translators or interpreters to teach or to converse. Such is the origin of the prophets, guardians of the law, intermediaries between men and the gods, whose language they understand. In an Amarnian fresco kept at Cambridge, Akhenaten is depicted accompanied by a dignitary bearing the name of "prophet."[3]

Ay had to negotiate with Pharaoh Smenkhkare who spoke Hebrew, the new popular language of Akhet-Aten. The pharaoh also, of course, spoke Egyptian. However, an interpreter was indispensable in dealing with the court, since many of the courtiers spoke only their own foreign language and the new language, Hebrew. Thus we find Egyptian words in the Hebrew language. These words come from the Delta to Lower Egypt. Additionally there are words derived from Canaanite, Phoenician, Aramaic, Babylonian, and from many roots of the Arabic language. At the beginning of the last century, the learned linguist Frédéric Portal mentions, in his work on the symbols of the Egyptians:

It cannot be denied that intimate relations exist between the Ethiopian and Hebrew languages. Wansleben showed the parallels between five hundred roots that are the same in Ethiopian and Hebrew, independently of the other Semitic languages. This work is printed in the Dictionnaire Ethiopian de Ludolf *(p.475 et seq.) ... Hebrew and Ethiopian flow from a common source, proved by philology.*[4]

This analysis is confirmed by Rashi (Genesis 11:13): "They spoke to each other. One people to another, Egyptian to Ethiopian, Ethiopian to Put, and Put to Canaanite."

Consequently, the pronunciation of some Arabic-Hebrew words in the Bible similar to hieroglyphic Egyptian words (the sacred language) must prevail on conventional pronunciation. The *Dictionary of Jewish Civilisation* defines Hebrew as follows:

A semitic language. In 1887, a group of four hundred clay tablets was found at Tel El-Amarna in Egypt ... written by scribes who had poorly mastered this language, they present the "Canaanisms" and marginal glosses which allow a partial reconstruction of the vocabulary and grammar of a language, Canaanite, so close to Biblical Hebrew that it can be considered pre-Biblical Hebrew.

The birth of the Hebrew language, then, was another reason for Ay's wrath. That corrupt city, with its corrupt language, had to be destroyed. Ay even considered destroying all those who lived within it, but relented. The parallel with the Noah story is notable.

It is not as though actual arks were not part of Egyptian life. And the flood in the Noah story certainly has a strong Egyptian basis. Among the models of boats found in Tutankhamun's tomb, an alabaster one is the most beautiful and imposing. It is Pharaoh's Ark, with the stern and bow sculpted with gazelle heads.

☥ ☥ ☥

The annual summer inundation of the Nile began in mid-June and lasted until mid-October. During the 120 days of the flood (150 days in the

Bible), Pharaoh enjoyed "visiting" his country with his family and his favorite animals. Does the Biblical story of the flood carry a remembrance of that inundation?

The torrential rainy season in the west of the African continent resulted in the "bursting of the cataracts." For the ancient Egyptians, the bursting of the cataracts and the rising waters were seen as the birth of the celestial Nile.[5] When the consequent flooding occurred, part of the population lived on boats with their favorite animals. As the Biblical story suggests, a prolonged flooding, up to 120 days, could be a catastrophe for a large part of the country's population; a condemnation of the gods.

Ark of Huya, surmounted by a home and a shelter, where a couple of horses are visible (Tomb of Huya's).

The image of Noah's Ark, with all its animals, remains fixed indelibly in the popular mind. Could there have been such a vessel on the flooded Nile? Could the image have a basis in some past reality?

Cyril Aldred, in his book *Akhenaten, King of Egypt*, mentions the presence of a strange zoo at Akhet-Aten. Gifts to Pharaoh were sent to Akhet-Aten from the far reaches of the Empire and beyond. Among them could have been domestic animals (cattle, sheep, horses, etc.) or wild ones (giraffes, panthers, cheetahs, etc.). The animals would have been sent to Pharaoh in a boat, having the same characteristics as Noah's Ark – a boat with a house on the main deck. The roofs of Egyptian arks were either concave or slanted to allow the rainwater to roll off. For the same reasons, the encasements enclosing Tutankhamun's sarcophagus, as well as much of the furniture of his tomb, had their lids in inclined planes. "The Ark's roof came to a point, diminishing as it rose, until it was only a cubit in width. That was so the waters would fall to one side and the other" (Rashi's Commentary on Genesis 6:16).

Noah's Ark was a vessel that served as a metaphor for Akhet-Aten. But the image which the scribes used to represent this city may have been based on actual arks, sailing the Nile, loaded with exotic animals.

Notes

1. Fabre d'Olivet, *La langue hébraïque restituée*. L'Age d'Homme-Delphica, 1991, p. 191.
2. A kind of early Egyptian Esperanto seems to have been introduced [Translator].
3. Christian Jacq, *Nefertiti et Akhénaton*. Perrin, 1996, p. 138.
4. Frédéric Portal, *Archéoloie égyptienne*, vol. III. Les symbols égyptiens. La Maisnie, 1985.
5. Robert Jacques Thibaud, *Dictionnaire de mythologie et symbolique égyptienne*. Dervy, 1996, p. 220.

☥

CHAPTER 12

The Tower of Babel

Following the story of Noah's Ark, the Bible narrates a description of the building of the Tower of Babel. In the Temple of Abu Simbel there are engraved the following words: "The master builder constructed a temple whose summit is as high as the heavens. The sun rises for love of it." A prototypical tower "reaching up to the heavens" certainly existed in ancient Egypt. But the legend of the Tower of Babel goes beyond that simple fact.

Chapter 10 of Genesis lists the generations following Noah, stating that each one claimed land in accordance with his language, tribe, and people.[1] The statement that there were several languages comes up again in Genesis 10:20: "These are Ham's [Noah's son's] descendants, by their families, languages, territories, and people." Noah's families, with their multiplicity of languages, were dispersed by the God of the Bible, over the earth's surface after the Flood.

The chapter of the Bible following the Noah's Ark story, relating the story of the Tower of Babel begins: "The whole world had one language and one dialect." We have just been told in the previous chapter that there was a multiplicity of languages. This Biblical contradiction reminds us of the history of Akhet-Aten, where the mixture of people spoke different languages and finally forged a common language understandable to all.

The Bible tells of the construction of a tower hiding a city built, like Akhet-Aten, of rough bricks instead of heavy stones, within a valley,[2] by people speaking the same single language.

They said to each other, "Come, let us make bricks and cure them with fire." Instead of stones, they used bricks and instead of mortar they used tar. Then they said, "Come, let us build a city and a tower that reaches up into the heavens." Adon-Ay came down to see the city and the tower which the sons of man were building. And he said, "Behold, they are now a single people and they are speaking the same language. This is just the beginning of what they can do. From now on, nothing will be impossible for them to accomplish. Come, let us go down there and confuse their language so they cannot understand each other." Adon-Ay scattered them all over the earth, and they stopped building. That is why it was called Babel, because Adon-Ay confused the language of the whole world and scattered the people all over the land. (Aramaic Bible, Genesis 11:3-9)

Rashi cites the different languages spoken in Babel (Genesis 11:3), "To each other: one people against the other people, Egyptian to Ethiopian. The Ethiopian to Pout, and Pout to Canaanite" – all languages spoken in Akhet-Aten before the appearance of the common language, the holy language. "A same language: this was the holy language ... they had the advantage of being a single people and of having a single language, and it was thus that they began to commit evil." This language, discovered by the archeologists in the Amarna Letters, was called "Pre-Biblical Hebrew."

Ay was disturbed to see the inhabitants of Akhet-Aten speaking the same language. He saw it as a threat to Egyptian sovereignty. The city, like the city of Babel described in the Bible, was constructed of rough bricks and situated in a valley. Ay made the decision to disperse the inhabitants to other regions of the land and the abandoned city was never rebuilt.

The process of the building of the Tower of Babel is similar to what happened at Akhet-Aten. The workers, artisans, builders and priests came from all over Egypt, having been brought together previously, during the construction of the temples to Aten in Karnak. Their languages differed, but that did not keep the construction from continuing. During the building of Akhet-Aten, necessity caused the men to "create a new language, that they might understand one another," which leads to the Bible's statement, "They are speaking the same language."

After Akhenaten's death, the Divine Father Ay observed that the population continued to multiply and became more and more powerful. The population of Akhet-Aten could spread the cult of the One God over the rest of the country, exploiting all of Egypt as Aten suppressed the other gods. In Ay's view, the new religion had already done too much damage to the country. So, as the Bible story says, Ay "scattered" the inhabitants over all the land.

The story of Babel demonstrates the concerns of the Divine Father Ay in the face of the population of priests who identified themselves with the One God. Each priest presided over his own sphere of influence. This multiplicity of little One Gods, each one seen by his adherents as the very image of Pharaoh, engendered in Ay the fear of seeing himself dispossessed of his power by the "sons of the Elohim," the Yahuds of Akhet-Aten.

At the beginning of the Book of Exodus, the Biblical scribes describe Pharaoh's profound feeling of anguish and disquiet: "A new king who did not know Joseph came to the throne. He said to his people, 'Behold, the Children of Israel are more numerous and powerful than us. Come, we must deal ruthlessly with them or they will become more numerous still. If war breaks out, they could join the enemy and fight against us and leave the country'"(Hebrew Bible, Exodus 1:8-10).

After Akhenaten's death, a kind of anarchy ruled in his city. The priests, ambitious and avid for power, pressed by their wives, tasted the fruit of the sacred mystical tree, which was reserved only for the God-King. The priests, having defied the original prohibition, could now identify themselves with God and with Pharaoh, destroying the secular myth of ancient Egypt. This attack on the thousand-year tradition demystified and discredited Pharaoh both in the eyes of the priests and of the people. Ay judged the monotheistic priests internally corrupt in their beliefs, and externally corrupt in their comportment, their language, and their sexual relationships. Considering the situation irreversible, the Divine Father decreed that it was urgent to engage in a radical action to save an Egypt already "exhausted" by the centralization and by the loss of its gods and traditions. Only a return to the ancient cults could give the country an ultimate chance to survive. A return to Amun – a return to the ancestral protectors of the pharaohs and the recovery of the equilibrium and prosperity Egypt had previously enjoyed.

This trouble was brewing when Smenkhkare had become pharaoh of Egypt. Smenkhkare was still loyal to the new god Aten. Ay was planning to eliminate the adherents of the new religion. Civil unrest was imminent.

Smenkhkare knew from experience that in a period of internal trouble, it was necessary to assemble the people and the army by focusing them on the great construction projects of Egypt. All the people had to be involved, which explains Smenkhkare's return to Thebes to work out a compromise with the forces seeking a return to the god Amun. Pharaoh ordered the masters of the workforce to proceed with great work projects in the cities of Pitom and Ramesses. By this means, he hoped to reconcile Atenian and Amunian Egypt.

However, Smenkhkare did not know the strategies of the Divine Father. Ay would have no part in reconciling the two conflicting religious views. Nothing would stand in his way to save Egypt against the devastation the new religion had wrought on the holy land. The Divine Father also feared a religious conflict, which could end in his eviction from power.

First, Smenkhkare had to be taken care of. Then, the Yahud priests and their adherents had to be sent far away.

Ay, then, accomplished what Yahwe and the Elohim had done in the Genesis story. He dispersed the inhabitants of Akhet-Aten/Babel; the Yahuds were exiled to a new "Promised Land," the Egyptian province of Canaan.

Notes

1. Genesis 10:5.
2. Rashi, *The Pentateuch According to Rashi: Genesis*. Samuel and Odette Lévy, 1993. "Lack of stones, since Babel was in the valley."

☥

CHAPTER 13

Abraham the Egyptian

After the legend of Noah's Ark, the story of Abraham begins. In the Biblical telling, the patriarch Abraham was the first person to have had the revelation of the One God (Adonay). This God led him to the holy land of Canaan.

In archeological research no such person as Abraham has ever been found. Neither in Egypt nor in Mesopotamia does there exist any testimony in the writing of the period, nor are there any pictorial or sculptural representations referring to this famous individual.

Historians and archeologists have sought Abraham throughout the Near East, in vain. In their research through the Biblical texts themselves, they have pursued him, still without result. Is it possible that a man believed to have introduced monotheism to the Middle East (Mesopotamia, Canaan, Egypt) could have left behind no trace whatsoever?

According to the scriptures, Abraham would have lived around four centuries before the exodus from Egypt (sometime around 1700 BC). In the Bible, he is said to have testified to the existence of the One God at that time. Why isn't there any historical evidence of monotheistic teaching at that time in the lands traversed by Abraham? Did there exist in Mesopotamia, in Canaan, or in Egypt a person answering to Abraham's description?

☥ ☥ ☥

Evidence points to the fact that the historical Judahites were the Yehudim who made the exodus from Akhet-Aten to Judah. A look at the history of Judah has relevence to our story.

The Judahites (the *Yehudim* in Hebrew or *Yahudaes* in Aramaic) settled in Judah, and the Hebrews (the Children of Israel, the "multitude") in the Northern territories. Three centuries later the kingdom of Israel seceded from the kingdom of Judah. The two separated kingdoms then engaged in a lethal war. The Bible states that there were 500,000 killed in Israel:

> *The Children of Israel fled before Judah, and the Elohim delivered them into the hands of the Judahites. Abijah and his men [the Judahites] inflicted great losses on them. Five hundred thousand elite troops were killed in Israel. The Children of Israel were humiliated while the men of Judah were victorious because they were supported by Adon-Ay. (II Chronicles 13:16-18)*

The wars of Judah against Israel were a prolongation of a very ancient separation. The separation was that of the people of Akhet-Aten who had left Egypt, composed of the Yahud priests (Judahites), worshipers of Aten and of Ay (later Adon-Ay), and the multitude (Exodus 12:37-38), composed of the common people (Israel), who, after the Exodus, had suffered and had staged revolts regularly.

In 585 BC, the Egyptian Empire, considerably weakened, was unable to support the Yahud priests in Judah. Judah was conquered by Nebuchadnezzar's Chaldean army, and the people of Judah were exiled to Babylonia. The Yahud scribes carried the memory of their lost paradise with them, along with the memory of Pharaoh Akhenaten, the true father of monotheism. During the long exile in Babylon, they transformed their history into legend – the legend of Abraham.

Egypt was, by then, the sworn enemy of Babylonia. Yet Egypt was the country of origin of the exiled Judahite priests. In order to preserve the cult of the One God, they had to transpose Akhenaten in time and space. It was not possible to represent their hero as an Egyptian. That would make him an abomination to their new Babylonian masters. Instead, they had to depict him as an individual who had lived in a distant Mesopotamian period so that they could justify a new, Babylonian, origin of monotheism.

This maneuver allowed the scribes to survive in exile in their enemy's territory, while still keeping the base of their beliefs. The problem was vital – to make the monotheistic religion acceptable to the Babylonians, they had to delete every Egyptian trace. The Babylonians would never have tolerated an enemy religion in their own country.

During the troubled period of the Babylonian Exile, the Yahud priests abandoned their Egyptian god Ay in favor of the god Yahwe. The legend of the patriarchs had to be woven into the popular traditions and beliefs of the deported Yahudim. This ploy allowed the scribes and priests to save the most important parts of their ancestral traditions.

To protect their own lives, the Yahud priests disguised their history by claiming that Egypt, their land of origin, was the detestable nation responsible for all their troubles. Egypt became, in the new telling, an abomination – the cursed land. Breaking with the roots of their previous beliefs, the Judahite scribes created a new religion. However, they did remain faithful to their past and subtly hid the imprint of ancient Egypt in their Biblical writings.

☥ ☥ ☥

Camels often appear in the Bible stories. Early on in the Abraham story, Pharaoh offers camels to Abraham. Later, they are mentioned again: "Abraham's servant took ten camels from among those of his master and departed. And he had many other fine things that belonged to his master. He arose and went to Aram Naharaim [northwest Mesopotamia], close to the city of Nahor. He caused the camels to kneel outside the city" (Genesis 24:10).

Camels are there with Isaac (e.g., Genesis 24:61, 64) and Jacob, Abraham's grandson (e.g., Genesis 30:43; 32:16), as well as in Exodus where the camel is made part of Pharaoh's wealth.

The Bible places Abraham in time around 1700 BC. At that time, the camel was unknown in Egypt. It was not until around 1200 BC that the camel was domesticated in Mesopotamia. It does not appear in the Egyptian murals of the temples, nor in the tombs or pyramids, nor in the writings. In fact, the camel was not introduced into Egypt until much later, by the Romans in the second century BC.[1]

In the time of Ramesses II (thirteenth century BC), the Egyptians had neither domesticated the camel, nor did they use war chariots pulled by horses. It would take several centuries for the Egyptians, surprised by Asiatic invaders fighting from horseback, to become conscious of the equine revolution.

Ramesses II's Battle of Kadesh, where a soldier mounted on a horse is seen.

Biblical researchers believed that the presence of camels in the story of the patriarchs was an error of the scribes. However, the scribes went into great detail, as if they wanted to pass on a message. "He caused the camels to kneel …" (Genesis 24:11). "Rebecca looked up and alighted from the camel …" (Genesis 24:64). Presenting Biblical characters alighting from camels' backs is an anachronism that the scribes apparently wished to present.

By the sixth century BC, the camel, a symbol of wealth and power, had already been domesticated in Babylonia. At the time of the exile, the Yahud priests, led away into slavery, reconstituted the history of Akhenaten to agree with the values and usages of the times, in order to make themselves acceptable to their new masters. Had they forgotten that camels did not exist in ancient Egypt? Couldn't they have presented and described Abraham's power and wealth without camels? The camels give a Mesopotamian twist to the story, which would have been pleasing to their captors.

♀ ♀ ♀

The Yahud priests shifted Abraham's origin to a place far distant from Egypt, to Ur of the Chaldees, a city located at the eastern boundary of Mesopotamia. This premeditated maneuver removed him physically and geographically from Egypt. In that way, they could justify to their new masters their newly devised roots in the Mesopotamia, or rather Sumeria, of the distant past. In order to establish a convincing genealogy for Abraham, they introduced into the story the names of cities close by in the west of Mesopotamia,[2] Serug (Genesis 11:22), Nahor (Genesis 11:24, Haran (Genesis 11:27) and the figure of Terah (Abraham's father), thus legitimatizing a Chaldean origin for the patriarch. This procedure allowed the community of the Yahuds progressively to piece together their story, while mentioning cities within the Babylonian Empire.

Although the city of Ur existed in Sumeria, the name "Chaldea" (Chaldees) does not appear until sometime around the sixth century BC. Chaldea has never yielded any archeological proof of the existence of the great patriarch, Abraham.

In order to survive and for their traditions to survive as well, the Yahuds introduced anachronisms into the history of the Patriarchs. They made the story compatible with sixth-century Babylon. They recast a large part of their history at that time, probably under considerable restrictions. The new text of the story had no historical reality at all. The Biblical characters were conceived and projected into the very interior of the newly devised story. Nevertheless, through the invention of Abraham (as well as through other Biblical characters) the monotheistic Yahud scribes retained the image of the man who had profoundly influenced them for eight centuries. In the Bible written by the exiled scribes, Abraham represented the God-King, the monotheistic pharaoh of the greatest empire the world had known, Akhenaten.

☥ ☥ ☥

According to Cyril Aldred, the god Aten guided Amenhotep IV – Akhenaten – to the holy land of Akhet-Aten, the present site of Tell el-Amarna: "As a matter of fact, this was the place towards which King Akhenaten, visionary and religious reformer, was directed by divine inspiration in the fifth year of his reign; the site where his One God, Re Horakhty … had manifested himself at the time of the creation of the world."[3]

Now, let us look at a Biblical text that relates to this matter. "Yahwe said to Abram, 'Leave, for your own sake, out of your country, away from your native land, and from your paternal home. Go to the land I will show you. I will make you into a great nation, I will bless you. I will make your name great, and you will be a blessing'" (Genesis 12:1-2).

"'It is to your posterity that I will give this country.' He [Abram] built in this place an altar to Yahwe who had appeared to him. He left from there towards the mountain with Bethel to the west and Ay to the east. He set up his tent there and called on the name of Yahwe. Then, he headed toward the Negev" (Genesis 12:7).

Further on, the Biblical text resumes: "For Abram was very rich in live-stock, in silver, and in gold. He journeyed from the Negev up to Bethel and Ay [Beth-El = the house of God, analogous to the Pharaoh's great house; City of Ay located in Judah], to the place where he had pitched his tent in the beginning. To the place where he had first built the altar. There, Abram called on the name of Yahwe" (Genesis 13: 2-4).

The place to which Akhenaten was led, Akhet-Aten, was called "a site to the glory of Aten,"[4] home of God on earth for eternity. Akhenaten built an altar on the spot that his God indicated to him, and declared the land holy for himself and his posterity.

The parallel between Abraham and Akhenaten becomes clearer.

According to Cyril Aldred, it was always from inside his tent that Akhenaten supervised the great works of his capital. "The king was, at that moment, resting in a tent at Akhet-Aten, and it was from there that he left to set the main limits of the city."

Christian Jacq comments: "The documentation informs us that the king, during his first stay at el-Amarna (Akhet-Aten), resided under a great tent. It was there that he himself doubtless oversaw the great works and the activity of the builders."[5]

It was at the exact spot where he had pitched his tent that Akhenaten constructed the Great Temple of Aten. As in the Bible, the tent is a prefig-uration of the Holy of Holies, the sacred room of the temple.

Rashi's commentary reveals essential details about the relationship between Abraham and Akhenaten, nine centuries before the Egyptologists did:

> *Shaveh Valley. The name means the united valley. The Targum [Aramaic] translates as follows: The open plain, that is to say, free of any trees or other obstacles. The Valley of the King. The Targum says that it was the racetrack of the king. There was a track thirty units long, reserved for the king's amusement. Another Midrash. It is the valley where all nations, united in common accord, chose Abraham as king, as leader and guide. (Rashi, Genesis 14:17)*

So Abraham was the monotheistic king of a city located in a valley, which boasted a racetrack, and was acclaimed by many "united nations". The representatives of these nations could only have acclaimed a powerful king, the one who they had welcomed in the city. The oral tradition guarded the memory of Akhenaten parading on the Royal Road before his monotheistic people, who were made up of different nations, united by the same language, in the valley of Akhet-Aten.

According to Cyril Aldred's description, there was a processional "Royal Road" 40 meters wide, on which Akhenaten's royal chariot, followed by Nefertiti's, sped, followed by the chariots of the police and the elite guard. Aldred insinuates that it was a royal road adapted to racing: "A road so wide, stretched out like a bowline, suggests more a kind of track planned for chariots than for, say, the wanderings of pack animals."

Akhenaten and Nefertiti parade between the royal palace and the Great Temple of Akhet-Aten, on the "Royal Road", followed by the nobility and guards (Tomb of Ay; from Aldred, Akhenaten, King of Egypt, *p.80–1).*

Thus the "racecourse" Rashi discusses was a royal road, probably delimited by the north and south bridges, with the buildings limiting the cavalcade. King Abraham and King Akhenaten doubtlessly paraded down the same road.

♀ ♀ ♀

The Bible identifies "Abraham the Hebrew" as the chief shepherd leading his flocks across the plains and deserts of Mesopotamia, Canaan and

Egypt. The picture of a semi-nomadic shepherd coming into Egypt to the Pharaoh to receive wives and riches is in major contradiction to the customs of ancient Egypt.

The expression "shepherd of flocks" comes up frequently in the Bible. In Hebrew it is pronounced "*Roeh-Tseh-On.*" "Eve then bore his brother Abel. Abel became a shepherd of flocks (*Roeh-Tseh-On)*, and Cain cultivated the earth" (Genesis 4:2). "Moses became a shepherd of the flocks of Jethro, his father-in-law, priest of Midian" (Exodus 3:1).

Fabre d'Olivet compared the Hebrew expression "*Roeh-Tseh-On*" with Chaldean (ancient Aramaic), Samaritan, and Arab equivalents. As a result of his linguistic explorations, he finds that the expression "*Roeh-Tseh-On*" conceals a king with his army under the symbol of a shepherd and his flock. When the code is cracked, Abraham is revealed as a royal personage.

The scribes list Abraham's (Akhenaten's) royal lineage in the Hebrew term "*Roeh-Tseh-On,*" which permitted them to keep a humble attitude before the Babylonian kings. In the same vein, Joseph asked his brothers to present themselves before Pharaoh as descendants of generations of shepherds.

> *Joseph said to his brothers and to his father's family, "I will go and speak to Pharaoh, and I will tell him, 'My brothers and all my father's family who live in the land of Canaan have come to see me. These men are shepherds of flocks* (Roeh-Tseh-On), *for they have livestock. And they have brought their flocks and their herds and everything they own.' Now, when Pharaoh asks you, 'What is your occupation?' answer, 'Thy servants have been tenders of livestock from their youth even unto now, both us and our ancestors.' So you can live in the Land of Goshen. Because all shepherds are an abomination to the Egyptians." (Genesis 46:31-34)*

To save their lives, Joseph's brothers humiliated themselves before Pharaoh. The contradictory verses placing shepherds and kings together hide the alternative message, however. In order to survive in exile, the Yahuds humiliated themselves before Nebuchadnezzer, their new god-king, passing themselves off as shepherds who had come from Egypt, traveling easily from one country to another. To please the king, they placed their ancestor

Abraham in Mesopotamia, because the Egyptians were an abomination in the eyes of the Chaldeans.

The tradition of pleasing ruling kings was perpetuated from the time of Nebuchadnezzer to the reign of Ptolemy. The commentary of Rashi, discussing Exodus 12:40, shows that this practice was known in the oral tradition. He wrote, "This is one of the passages of the Torah which was modified to please King Ptolemy."

These frequent modifications, which were inflicted on the sacred texts to please Egyptian or Babylonian masters, disrupt the original document and are the reason for the many contradictions between the Bible and historical fact.

Nebuchadnezzer granted clemency to this population of shepherds, who traditionally were submissive. The Yahud priests used this recourse to obtain royal favor. They passed themselves off as a group of Hebrew shepherds, and thus saved their own skins.

⚥ ⚥ ⚥

Both in the story of Abraham and in the history of Akhenaten, we have a case of a dramatic break with the past. In the Jewish oral tradition, it is mentioned that Abraham broke the idols of his father. We know of a similar situation in Egypt.

In the fourth and twelfth years of his reign, Akhenaten demolished the statues of the Amunian gods.[6] A feeling of desolation swept over all of Egypt.[7] During the time of that iconoclastic reaction, he broke the idols of his father Amenhotep III, that is, of his ancestors, the Egyptian pharaohs (the Elohim). Akhenaten thus broke the old commandment of respect for "the fathers," creating a rupture in the very core of the traditional ancestral monarchy. Later, Horemheb and the Ramessides purposely omitted engraving Akhenaten's name and those of his sons Smenkhkare and Tutankhamun, and even that of the Divine Father Ay, on the wall of the Temple of Abydos. The names of the other ancestral pharaonic fathers appear on that wall.[8] Horemheb declared himself "the direct son of Amenhotep III," definitively wiping out the names of the heretic Amarnian kings from the list of the "Elohim."

Akhenaten glorified and proclaimed his name as well as that of Aten at Akhet-Aten. Here is an extract of Akhenaten's proclamation on one of the border stelae of the future capital.

The King of Upper and Lower Egypt, Living Example of Truth, Lord
of the Double Country, Beautiful as the Forms of Re, the Son of Re,
who is also the Living Example of Truth, Lord of the Two Crowns,
Akhenaten [the glorified spirit of Aten], Great during his Duration,
living forever and ever.

The Perfect God, the Only One of Re, from whom Aten created
Beauty, truly excellent for his creator, who satisfies him with whatso-
ever his soul desires, his servant whom he hath engendered, and
administrator of the country for which he has placed him on the
throne, supplying his home with very numerous possessions, sustaining
Aten and magnifying his name, causing them to belong to Him who
created it.⁹ Behold, proclaimeth Akhenaten. It is Aten who wanted this
city so that it would be created to commemorate his name. It is Aten,
my father, who governs the city.¹⁰

The king's words raise the following question. By excluding Amun, did
Akhenaten completely reject his father, Amenhotep III, or, quite to the
contrary, did he identify his father as Aten? The terms "son of Aten," "father
who governs the city," "Aten, the father," which appear in Akhenaten's
proclamations indicate a compromise between father and son. In the Temple
of Soleb, Amenhotep IV is shown worshiping his father Amenhotep III, who
was known as "Radiant Aten."¹¹ The cult of Aten would be crowned by an
"alliance" proclaiming Aten the father and Akhenaten the son.

The suggestion of a schism between Amenhotep III and his son does
seem plausible. At the time of Akhenaton's breaking of his father's idols,
Amenhotep III was still alive. A co-regency between the two monarchs
must have existed. A compromise between father and son allowed the new
monotheistic religion to live and thrive within the borders of the new holy
city. Peace was thus assured for Egypt at least until the death of
Amenhotep III.

♀ ♀ ♀

If, for purposes of Near Eastern politics, Akhenaten was transformed into
the legendary personage of Father Abraham, might we not surmise that his
wife, Sarah, was also an historical character in the drama of the holy city of
Akhet-Aten?

Abraham's wealth, his wives (princesses), his servants and slaves, and the submission to him of foreign nations and kings, all confer on him the stature of a monarch.

"Abram learned that his brother had been taken captive. Then, he had his well-trained men pass in review, 318 slaves, born in his house, and he set out in pursuit of the kings as far as Dan" (Hebrew Bible, Genesis 14:14). This verse shows that Abraham owned a mansion with 318 slaves (or servants), not counting the women. That shows that he had charge of enough personnel for a palace.

The number is also remarkably close to the 317 servants and ladies in waiting who accompanied Amenhotep III at his marriage with Princess Giluheba.[12] In these subtle ways, the Yahud priests and scribes hid in their texts the appearance of the immense Egyptian civilization.

The Bible insists on Sarah's great beauty. That beauty led to difficulties with Pharaoh and with others. Abraham's first wife was Sarai, whose name was subsequently changed to Sarah. Genesis 12:11 tells of her beauty: "When he [Abraham][13] was about to arrive in Egypt, he said to Sarah, his wife, 'Look, I know thou art a woman fair of face.'" Taking his beautiful wife into a foreign country seemed to Abraham to be fraught with danger. He feared for his own life at the hands of the Egyptians whom, he was sure, would kill him so that Sarah would be an available widow. For this reason, he asked Sarah to pretend to be his sister and not his wife.

When they arrived in Egypt Sarah was, indeed, noticed by the men of the country:

The Egyptians noticed that the woman [Sarah] was very beautiful. When the palace officials saw her they praised her to Pharaoh. And the woman was taken to Pharaoh's palace [Pharaoh married Sarah]. Pharaoh dealt well with Abraham, giving him sheep, oxen, asses, slaves, and camels in return for his [Pharaoh's] new wife. But Yahwe inflicted grievous diseases on Pharaoh because of Abraham's wife. When Pharaoh discovered that Sarah was Abraham's wife, not his sister, he confronted Abraham. "Why did you say 'She is my sister,' so that I took her to wife? Now, then, here is your wife. Take her and go!" And Pharaoh ordered his men to send him on his way. (Genesis 12:14-19)

For Sarah's sake, Pharaoh treated Abraham well, bringing him wealth. The scribes, in telling the Biblical story, were able to show Abraham as a rich and powerful person.

When we compare Abraham's wife, Sarah, with Akhenaten's wife, Nefertiti, we note some parallels. Nefertiti also was admired by the Egyptians for her perfection. Abraham referred to Sarah as his sister. Joyce Tyldesley notes that the expression "my sister" was customary among the princes and princesses of Egypt. "During a whole dynastic period, the expression 'sister' was employed in its widest sense. Consequently it could also equally designate a sister, a sister-in-law or a foster sister."

Erman and Ranke report a similar conviction.

> *In ancient Egypt, the word "sister" served to designate loved-one, exactly as in Egypt today the term "cousin" is used. In Egyptian lyric poetry, lovers always say "my brother" and "my sister," and there is no doubt that, in most cases, "his sister" cannot mean anything other than "his mistress," his concubine.*[14]

Sarah was the wife of both Pharaoh and Abraham concurrently. Nefertiti was married to Akhenaten's father, Amenhotep III. Thus, Nefertiti was married to two pharaohs. This marriage triangle parallels the marriage triangle in the Bible.

Nefertiti, Akhenaten's half-sister,[15] didn't have children by Amenhotep III, to whom she was married for a short time. The same was true for Sarah, temporary wife of the king of Egypt. The oral tradition claims that God plagued Pharaoh with impotence so that he would give Sarah back to Abraham. Amenhotep III, senile and sick at the end of his life, had more than seven hundred female statues made, each with the head of a lioness (Sekhmet),[16] in order to heal his impotence and the other illnesses that afflicted him.

The Bible claims that Sarah was the wife of a pharaoh, who historically would have been Amenhotep III, Akhenaten's father. Nefertiti was also Amenhotep III's wife. The Biblical scribes retained in their memory the picture of Nefertiti to describe Sarah.

Later in the Biblical story, new parallels are brought into the Sarah–Nefertiti question. Years after Abraham's sojourn in Egypt, Sarah had remained childless. The question of an heir was at stake.

In Genesis 16:3, when Abraham had been in the land of Canaan for ten years, Sarah, not having born a male child, offered her servant Hagar to Abraham. He lay with Hagar and she conceived. When Hagar was aware that she had conceived, her mistress became an object of disdain to her. Sarah said to Abraham, "Send that slave woman [Hagar] and her son away" (Genesis 21:10).

Rashi clarifies the subject of Hagar the Egyptian (Rashi, Genesis 16:1): "It was Pharaoh's daughter. When he saw the miracles of which Sarai was the object, he said, 'It would be better for my daughter to be the servant [of Abraham] in such a house than his mistress in another house'."

If Hagar is Pharaoh's daughter, she could only have been given, for the same reasons as Sarah, to a prince or co-regent belonging to the royal family, and must have dwelt in Egypt. Egyptian princesses were not allowed to leave their country. If Abraham had done so, he would have accomplished the impossible – leaving the country in the company of Sarah and Hagar, queen and princess of Egypt.

Nefertiti was the mother of six daughters. She did not produce a male child to assure the royal lineage. Akhenaten had a first-born son, Smenkhkare, with another wife, probably Queen Kiya, one of Amenhotep III's many daughters. Historical data indicate that Nefertiti sent away Queen Kiya.[17]

Like Nefertiti, Sarah was buried in a cave at the end of a field, recalling the valley and tombs hollowed out in the cliffs of Akhet-Aten. "So Abraham acquired the field of Ephron in Machpelah which was across from Mamre. The field and the cave which is there, and all the trees that are on the field, throughout the whole area were turned over to him in the presence of the sons of Heth, who had come to the city gates" (Genesis 23:17-18).

"Heth's children answered Abraham saying 'Hear us, Lord [Adoni]! Thou art a dignitary of God among us [Elohim]' … Abraham arose and prostrated himself before the people of the land [Am Aarets], before the children of Heth."

Abraham is designated by Heth's children as Adon, "a dignitary of the Elohim among us," belonging to their family. Consequently, Heth's sons, before whom Abraham prostrates himself, are dignitaries adoring the

Elohim, the One God. Hence the Biblical city of Heth is monotheistic, "worthy" to allot to Abraham a tomb located at its gate.[18]

In the last verse of Chapter 27 of Genesis there is a problem concerning "Heth," the city where Abraham and Sarah were buried. Heth is mysteriously transformed into "Canaan" in the following verse (28:1).

> *Rebecca said to Isaac, "I am weary of my life because of the daughters of Heth. If Jacob marries one of the daughters of Heth, such as these are, from among the women of this land [Aretz], what will my life be worth to me?"*
>
> *Isaac called Jacob and blessed him, and charged him "Do not marry one of the daughters of Canaan." (Genesis 27:46-28:1)*

Heth is the phonetic name of Akhet, the holy city of Akhenaten. This name is written in two hieroglyphs HT, as in Hebrew. Heth-Adon is similar to the sound Akhet-Aten, which would be read as Khet-Aton, and Akhet-Aten is where Akhenaten and Nefertiti were buried. Thus this curious transformation could be symbolic of the transformation by the scribes of Heth, the city of Akhenaten into Heth, the city of Abraham and Canaan, the Holy Land of Abraham.

♀ ♀ ♀

The Biblical account of Rebecca's betrothal to Isaac confirms her status as an Egyptian princess, crowned queen of Egypt. Genesis 24: 45-48 relates how Eleazar, Abraham's servant, brings Rebecca to Abraham and tells her story:

> *Before I had begun speaking to myself, behold, Rebecca came out, her water jar on her shoulder. She went down to the spring, and drew. And I said to her: "Please give me to drink." Quickly she let down her jar from her shoulder, and said, "Drink. And I will give your camels drink also." I asked her, saying "Whose daughter are you?" She said, "The daughter of Bethuel, Nahor's son, whom Milcah bore to him." Then I put a ring on her nose and the bracelets on her arms.*

According to Rashi (Genesis 15:2) the Midrash says that Eleazar had followed the kings to Damascus. So Abraham's servant must have had the power of a general who spread his master's teaching. The story is followed with the distribution of royal gifts.

Verse 47 describes the customs of Akhet-Aten, shown in the Amarna Letters, involved in reclaiming the princesses for Egypt's vassals. The ring passed through Rebecca's nose is the image of enthronement – a sign of royalty. It forms the sign of life, "Ankh," offered to her nose by Aten, and attributed to the kings and queens of the Amarnan period.

Rebecca's two bracelets share the same meaning as the ring. "And two bracelets. An allusion to the two double Tablets" (Rashi, Genesis 24:22). Rashi's explanation compares the bracelets to the Tablets of the Law. Going back to the oral tradition, he establishes the convergence of the word *tsemidym* (bracelets) and the stone Tablets (*mitsomedot*), similar to the two cartouches of Aten – the same golden cartouches in the form of bracelets that Akhenaten and Nefertiti are depicted as wearing.

☥ ☥ ☥

Jacob, Abraham's grandson, Isaac's son, is legendary for his dream in which a celestial ladder was erected between heaven and earth. "He reached a spot and spent the night there, since the sun had set. He took one of the stones from the place, put it under his head, and lay down in that place" (Genesis 28:11). Rashi relates that in the oral tradition, this passage is explaining that the stone was a headrest.

Several stone headrests were found in Tutankhamun's tomb. The alabaster funerary headrest on which the "boy pharaoh" reposed, like many objects in the tomb, had belonged to Akhenaten. Erman and Ranke[19] mention that several headrests were found in the homes of Amarna, adapted with cushions for comfort. This fact shows that the Hebrew oral tradition had kept a precise memory of objects in use from the Egyptian origin of the people.

Once Jacob settled down to sleep, with his head propped on the stone headrest, he dreamed: "Jacob had the following dream. A ladder was placed on the earth and its summit reached up into Heaven. And the messengers of the Elohim were ascending and descending the length of the ladder" (Hebrew Bible, Genesis 28:12).

The Pyramid Texts[20] speak clearly about a ladder, and a ladder with wings, recalling Jacob's ladder with its angels climbing towards the light.

Tutankhamun's alabaster headrest (Cairo Museum).

Each step of the ladder represented a trial for Pharaoh to undertake.

On the walls of the pyramid of the Sixth Dynasty Pharaoh Pepy I (2300 BC) are some of the first hieroglyphics relating to the life of that king. A ladder with six steps, probably representing the six trials of Pharaoh, are engraved there. For the Egyptians, as for the Yahuds, life was but a passage to reach the celestial world. In the same way, the pyramid of Djoser, a building of six steps, recalls the "works" of Pharaoh. Jacob's ladder, then, harks back to Pharaoh's ladder. Jacob, like Pharaoh, had tests or "works" ahead of him.

Symbol of the celestial ladder in the pyramid of Pepy I.

The Biblical legend of the rock and of Jacob's ladder are reflections of the trials that Pharaoh had to undergo after death. The scribes wanted to preserve a tradition profoundly anchored in ancient Egypt: Pharaoh's last voyage.

♀ ♀ ♀

After wrestling with an angel, God told Jacob that henceforth his name would be Israel. "Israel" was considered an honorific title, linked to his triumph over the messenger of God, who is here identified with the Elohim. "He [the messenger of God or the Gods] said, 'Thy name will no longer be Jacob, but instead, Israel,[21] for thou hast struggled with the Elohim, and thou hast triumphed'" (Hebrew Bible, Genesis 32:29).[22]

The story repeats itself later in Genesis 35:10, when the Elohim appear to Jacob to say, "Thy name is Jacob.[23] But thy name, henceforth, will no longer be Jacob. Thy name shall be Israel."

Jacob's victory over the Elohim is a reflection of Amenhotep IV's victory over his father, for which he too changed his name. Akhenaten had engaged himself against men and the gods. He caused Aten to triumph over the other gods (Elohim) of the Empire, the gods of his father. He had seduced the priests and princes of Egypt (the sons of the Elohim) by attracting them to his capital. There, he had himself acclaimed by all the people on the royal avenue of Akhet-Aten. He was the Father of Nations, the Son of Re, the Living God.

♀ ♀ ♀

Early in the story of Jacob he cheated his brother Esau out of his birthright and fled from his home country. Years later, when Jacob and his family returned to the home country, he anticipated his meeting with his brother Esau, from whom he had been separated for many years. He was concerned that Esau would wish him harm. "Jacob, raising his eyes, saw Esau, who was coming accompanied by four hundred men. Jacob divided his children among Leah, Rachel, and the two maid servants. He placed the maids with their children in the first row, Leah and her children behind, and Rachel and Joseph last. As for himself, he stepped in front of them and prostrated himself seven times before approaching his brother" (Hebrew Bible, Genesis 33, 1-3).

Prostration before Pharaoh was customary in Akhet-Aten. Letters from El Amarna mention this practice frequently. Here is a call of distress from Rib-Hadda, Prince of Gubla:

> *Rib-Hadda says to his Lord, the great king, king of all countries, "I fall to the feet of my Lord, the king, seven times and seven times. Gubla, since ancient times, has been a city loyal to my lord, the Sun of all countries, and I am a footstool for the feet of the king, my lord, and his loyal servant. Now, as for Sumur, the war against it is very rough, and it is rough against me. Sumur has now made raids even to thy gate. They have been able to raid, but have not been able to capture it." (EA 141)*[24]

The seven-fold prostration before the God-King was probably instituted by Akhenaten. The Amarna Letters employ the formula of politeness, "I fall to the feet of my Sun, seven times and seven times." Jacob's ritual is a recollection of the Atenian tradition. In this case Jacob's older brother is a substitution for Akhenaten's father.

♀ ♀ ♀

"Jacob lived in the land of Egypt seventeen years. The days of Jacob, the years of his life, were a hundred forty-seven years" (Genesis 47:28). The 17 years of Jacob's life mentioned here correspond to the 17 years of Akhenaten's reign.[25] The number 17 also appears in the 175 years of Abraham (Genesis 25:7).

The exaggerations in the longevity of Biblical characters stretch over the entire story. Adam is claimed to have lived for 930 years (Genesis 5:5), Noah 950 years (Genesis 9:29), Terah, Abraham's father, for 205 years (Genesis 11:32), Sarah 127 years (Genesis 23:1), and Moses 120 years (Deuteronomy 34:7). This immoderation allowed the scribes to establish the book of the generations in the Biblical tale, and thus spread the story of Akhenaten and the exodus from Egypt over several hundred years.

"These are the generations of the heavens and the earth at their creation (*Beh-heh-baram*)" (Genesis 2:4). Albert Soued shows the relationship between the generations and Abraham:

"Behibaram" is a word in the verse written in a strange manner. The character Heh is miniaturized: by an inversion of the letters Aleph and Heh, the sense of "in Abraham" is obtained. Thus the generations were created within the word Abram thanks to the Heh.[26]

As is demonstrated in more detail in Chapter 22, the Hebrew letter Heh ֹה is the analog of the hieroglyph "the Great God" (i.e., the creator of the heavens and the earth).

☥ ☥ ☥

Akhenaten engraved a vow to his god Aten on some 14 border stelae of Akhet-Aten. This vow may be a territorial and religious compromise between him and his father Amenhotep III, between Atenian and Amunian Egypt. Thus, the two co-regent rivals promised that each would not broach the limits of their respective territories.

This truly is my oath, that my heart pronounces and that I will never betray. The South stela, that is on the mountain east of Akhet-Aten, is the Stela of Akhet-Aten that I shall establish in its place. I will never trespass this southern limit.[27]

Subsequently, Akhenaten solemnly swore by his god Aten never to go beyond the limits of the stelae to the south, west, east and north of the new capital. The oath was marked by sacrifices and an immense banquet.

The parallels with Akhenaten's actions here and the compromise between Jacob and his father-in-law Laban are striking:

Laban said to Jacob, "Behold this heap [this stela]. I have set up this pillar between thee and me. May this heap and this pillar be witness that I will not go beyond them to thy side to do thee harm, nor wilt thou go beyond them to my side to do me harm. May the God of Abraham, and the God of Nahor, the God of thy father, judge between the two of us." So Jacob swore in the name of his father Isaac. He slit the throats of animals as a sacrifice there in the hill country and invited his relatives to the feast. After they had partaken, they spent the night on the mountain. (Genesis 31:51)

The Bible insists that the conflict between Laban and Jacob was of a politico-religious character. The 14 stelae erected delimit the territory of Akhet-Aten, separating Atenian Egypt and Amunian Egypt. Rashi (Genesis 32:3) mentions two camps separating Jacob and Laban. "Mahanaïm. Two camps [two sacred territories, but of different callings], those of the stranger who had accompanied him there and those of the Holy Land that he had happened upon."

♀ ♀ ♀

The seven-times prostration, the seventeen years Jacob was in Egypt, the omnipresence of Abraham from the creation of the world, the solar worship of Jacob, and especially the oath never to trespass the limits of his sacred territory, all show a strict relationship between the Bible and Egyptian history at the time of Akhenaten.

Notes

1. Maurice Bucaille, *Moïse et Pharaon*. Seghers, 1995. See also Henri Lhote, *Le chameau et le dromadaire en Afrique du nord, Sahara*. Groupe Média International, Paris.
2. Richard Lebeau, *Une histoire des Hébreux*. Tallandier, 1998.
3. Cyril Aldred, *Akhenaten, King of Egypt*. Le Seuil, 1997, p. 59.
4. John Adams Wilson, *Egypt. Life and Death of a Civilization*. Arthaud, 1961, p. 203.
5. Christian Jacq, *Nefertiti et Akhénaton*. Perrin, 1996, p. 81.
6. In Year Four according to Gabolde, in Year Twelve according to Aldred. History allows the supposition that Akhenaten's iconoclasm took place in Year Four, but was renewed in Year Twelve. Marc Gabolde, *D'Akhénaton à Toutankhamon*. Institut d'Archéologie et d'Histoire de l'Antiquité, Université Lumière-Lyon 2-CNRS, 1998.
7. Pierre Grandet, *Hymnes de la religion d'Aton*. Le Seuil, 1995, p. 13.
8. Nicolas Grimal, *Histoire de l'Ancienne Egypte*. Fayard, 1988, p. 299.
9. Translation from Cyril Aldred, *Akhenaten*, p. 58.
10. Christian Jacq, *Nefertiti et Akhénaton*, p. 81.
11. Marc Gabolde, *D'Akhénaton à Toutankhamon*, p. 24.
12. Joyce Tyldesley, *Nefertiti*. Le Rocher, 1998. p. 39.
13. While the two individuals were known as Abram and Sarai early in the Biblical story, the translators have consistently referred to them as Abraham and Sarah to avoid confusion.
14. Adolphe Erman and Hermann Ranke, *La civilisation égyptienne*. Paris, 1948–1994, p. 210.

15. According to Phillip Vandenberg, Nefertiti would have been Taduheba, daughter of Tushratta, king of the Mittani. The king gave her to Amenhotep III, which provoked the jealousy of Amenhotep IV – Akhenaten.
16. Cyril Aldred, *Akhenaten,* pp. 155–6. Sekhmet was the goddess of plagues.
17. Christian Jacq, *Nefertiti et Akhénaton*, p. 160. Also, for Smenkhkare and Tutankhamun, see Joyce Tyldesley, *Nefertiti*, p. 150: "There are strong reasons to believe that Kiya bore at least two sons to Akhenaten," and p.184: "More than Nefertiti, it is Kiya who seems to have been the mother of the two princes." Gabolde has demonstrated that Tutankhamun was Nefertiti's seventh child.
18. Adam and Hava (Eve) are buried in the same site (Makpela) as Abraham and Sarah.
19. Adolphe Erman and Hermann Ranke, *La civilisation égyptienne*, p. 244.
20. Christian Jacq, *Tradition primordiale de l'Ancienne Egypte selon les textes des pyramides*. Grasset and Fasquelle, 1998, pp. 125, 166, 292.
21. Israel means "he struggles with God."
22. There is a one-verse discrepancy between the Hebrew Bible and English Bible in this chapter. The English numeration is given here.
23. Jacob means "grabs the heel" in Hebrew, which is an expression for "betrays or deceives."
24. According to the Amarna Letters, one prostated oneself seven times on one's stomach and seven times on one's back.
25. Joyce Tyldesley, *Nefertiti*, p.196.
26. Albert Soued, *Les symbols dans la Bible*. Jacques Grancher, 1995, p.236.
27. Christian Jacq, *Nefertiti et Akhénaton*, pp.82, 83.

CHAPTER 14

☥

Joseph and Ay

Joseph was Jacob's second youngest son. When he was still young, he was sold by his older brothers to Ishmaelites passing through on their way to Egypt.

> *Joseph was brought down to Egypt [by the slave traders]. Potiphar, one of Pharaoh's officers, captain of the guards, a man of Egypt, bought him from the Ishmaelites and put him in charge of his domestic staff. Yahwe was with Joseph and he fared well, when he was admitted into the house of his Egyptian master ... Yahwe blessed the house of the Egyptian. (Genesis 39:1, 5)*

While in Potiphar's service, Joseph had an experience that landed him in prison. His master's wife attempted to seduce him. Joseph rejected her advances (Genesis 39:9), with the pretext that he did not want to sin before the Elohim, and found himself imprisoned as a result of Potiphar's wife's denunciation of him.

While Joseph was in prison, Pharaoh became displeased with his major-domo and sent him to prison. Happily, it was to the prison where Joseph was languishing. When he was in jail, the major-domo had a dream, which he did not understand. In Genesis 40:11, he described his dream to Joseph: "I had Pharaoh's cup in my hand. I gathered the grapes and pressed them into Pharaoh's cup and placed the cup in the king's hand." Joseph was a soothsayer who interpreted the dream correctly. The royal baker was also in prison at the same time; Joseph correctly interpreted his dream too.

The cup of Pharaoh. Akhenaten, standing, engaged in the ritual of the fruit of the vine.

Akhenaten's cup (Karnak talatate*).*

The bread and wine introduced in these verses are reminders that the consecration of these foods had its roots in ancient Egypt. Research on the *talatates* (bricks) of Karnak shows an engraved picture of Akhenaten holding his cup towards Aten as a wine offering. The monotheistic prayer over the fruit of the vine has its origin in ancient Egypt, the first country to consecrate the "drink of the gods," and Judaism and Christianity employ bread and wine as essentials in religious ceremonies to this day.

Two years later, the pharaoh of Egypt was having nightmares. His dreams were about seven fat cows that were eaten by seven thin cows, and about seven ears of good grain that were swallowed by seven ears of bad grain. The major-domo had been restored to the palace by then, and told Pharaoh about Joseph. Pharaoh sent for Joseph to interpret the dreams.

Joseph came to the royal palace and interpreted the dreams to mean that there would be seven years of good harvests followed by seven years of famine. In Egyptian terms, those would be seven years of a beneficent Nile and seven years of the holy river withholding its blessings. Pharaoh was impressed by Joseph's interpretation, and by Joseph himself.

Modern research casts doubt upon the likelihood that Pharaoh would be so impressed by Joseph's soothsaying. Christiane Desroches Noblecourt[1] reveals that the pharaohs of the Eighteenth Dynasty knew perfectly well the myth of the seven fat cows. They were known and represented in the tomb of Nefertari, the first wife of Ramesses II. Seven "good Niles" followed by seven "bad Niles." Pharaoh had no need of Joseph to interpret his dream.

Wall painting from the Tomb of Nefertari, first wife of Ramesses II.

Desroches Noblecourt goes on to say:

> *So Pharaoh could be unaware of some things, but he could not be*
> *unaware of the meaning of the seven thin cows and the seven fat cows.*
> *If one goes to the Cairo or Louvre Museums and is permitted to open*
> *The Book of the Dead, the book of magical formulas that would allow*
> *the dead person to pass to the "other side" without meeting too many*
> *demons or obstacles, one would find there illustrations among which*
> *are the seven fat cows.*

The story of the dream interpretation appears to be a literary device to get Joseph out of his prison and into the position of power where he historically belonged.

Joseph, who had been major-domo in Potiphar's house became major-domo in Pharaoh's house as well. He now held a position of great power in Egypt. Pharaoh gave him Asenath in marriage (Genesis 41:45). She is identified as the daughter of Poti-Phera (or Potiphar). Since Potiphar translates as "powerful pharaoh" there is reason to believe the scribes are referring to Pharaoh's daughter. Asenath, in Hebrew, is rendered by four letters that are the traditional contraction for Ankhensenamun,[2] Akhenaten's daughter, wife of Tutankhamun and Ay.

Rashi's interpretation of this verse is interesting: "Poti-Phera is Potiphar. He was called Poti-Phera because he was castrated for having conceived an impure desire for Joseph." Since Rashi indicates that the two Biblical names (Potiphar and Poti-Phera) belong to a single person, it demonstrates that, before the archeological discoveries confirmed it, it was known that there was a unique pharaoh represented as both male and female: Akhenaten.

Reading between the lines, the scribes, in writing the story of Joseph, are engaged in telling about the hero of the Yahuds – Ay. Philipp Vandenberg[3] reported that Ay married Ankhensenamun twice, the first time in Akhenaten's reign, and a second in order to succeed Tutankhamun. A ring[4] on which are inscribed the names of both Ay and Ankhensenamun, attests to the link between the two of them in marriage. At first, Ankhensenamun refused to marry for the second time a man she considered a servant, and too old. She wrote a letter to Suppiluliuma, king of the

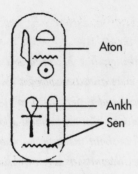

A-S-NA-T   *Asnat (Joseph's wife) and Ankh-Sen-Aton (Ay's wife).*

Hittites, to send her his son Zananza. "My husband is dead and I have no son. It is reported that you have many sons. You could give me one of your sons, who would become my husband. I wouldn't want to take one of my servants as a husband."[5]

Prince Zananza was killed in an ambush, which is attributed to General Horemheb. It would seem that the Divine Father Ay, the primary beneficiary of the intrigue, had manipulated Queen Ankhensenamun to attain his own ends.

Taking Joseph as representing Ay, we see him take as his wife Pharaoh's daughter Ankhensenamun/Asenath. Although not yet a pharaoh himself, he was well on his way by marrying into the royal family.

♀ ♀ ♀

Years later, Joseph's brothers all came to Egypt because famine had hit their land and they had heard that there was grain in Egypt. Joseph, now in charge of the Egyptian economy, had set up storehouses for Pharaoh during the seven good harvest years and saved the excess grain for the bad years to come. Joseph's brothers came to Joseph, but did not recognize him as the brother whom they had sold into slavery. He revealed to them that he was their brother. They expected him to take vengeance on them for their perfidy.

His [Joseph's] brothers came to prostrate themselves before him saying, "Behold, we are thy slaves." Joseph answered them, "Fear not. Am I in the place of the Elohim? As for you, you planned evil against me. But, the Elohim brought it all together for good so that what has happened today would come about, that many people should be kept alive. So, now, fear not. I shall provide for you and for your families." (Genesis 50:18-21)

Joseph pardoned his brothers making them understand that evil had been transformed into good, permitting the saving of the Egyptian people. He did not seek vengeance.

Ay also pardoned the priests who had fraternized with foreign women. He allowed them to continue their worship of the One God outside of Egypt, carrying with them all the wealth of the capital. The teaching of these verses is that Joseph, the ruler of Egypt under Pharaoh, represents Ay, the holder of the same position.

☥ ☥ ☥

That the Biblical Joseph is a representation of the historical ruler Ay is confirmed when we examine Pharaoh Ay's cartouche, which contains the two Yods, shown as reeds. In the engraving shown below, the hand of Ay takes the place of the Yod lacking in his name. He raises his hand (Yad in Hebrew), and identical to the "Yod," symbol of oneness. This is confirmed not only by the royal cartouche, but also by the Aramaic Bible: "Ay is the God of the Yahuds" (Exodus 3:18). He is the hidden pharaoh, uncontested master of Egypt.

The deified Ay takes the place of Amun (or of Re). His raised hand takes the place of the Yod.

The ritual striking of Egypt's enemy by Tutankhamun.

Ankensamun, Tutankhamun's wife, and later the wife of Ay.

ד׳   י׳

Yod hieroglyph and sign of God of the   Yad (hand) or the Hebrew Yod.
name of the Divine Father Ay.

The two reeds are nothing more than the symbol of the powerful hand of Joseph. Joseph, or Yosseph in Hebrew, is composed of a first Yod, the powerful hand (Yad) of God. The second part of the name is an anagram of reed – "suf". Yosseph can thus be interpreted as "the hand is the reed." Therefore, "Joseph" (Yosseph) conceals the double Yods of the name of the Divine Father Ay – Yod-Yod.

Like Joseph, Ay was recompensed by Pharaoh. Akhenaten gave Ay golden necklaces, linen vestments, gloves, probably a golden ring, and a striped coat. One engraving shows Ay, represented as the "Father of the God," on a royal chariot. In another depiction, acclaimed by the jubilant crowd, he holds out his gloved hands to the priests who are praying towards him.

A scratch on the glove could represent the royal ring, which would have been placed on Ay's hand after he put on the gloves, like the golden finger ornaments on the hand of Tutankhamun's mummy. To wear a golden ring on a gloved hand was traditional for kings and religious dignitaries. So, it is quite probable that the Divine Father Ay showed to the people the ring that had been given to him by Pharaoh, as shown on the engraving on gold foil. The priests prostrated themselves, as if Ay had the status of Pharaoh.

In effect, whether seen as Joseph or Ay, the personage depicted was, in fact although not in title, the king of Egypt.

Pharaoh said to Joseph: "Behold! I put thee in charge of the whole of the land of Egypt." And Pharaoh took his signet ring from his hand and placed it on Joseph's finger. He dressed him in robes of fine linen and placed the gold chain around his neck. He had him ride in a chariot as his second-in-command. Men shouted before him, "Abrek,"

"Make way." And he installed him in charge of the entire land of Egypt. Pharaoh said to Joseph: "I am Pharaoh. But unless you order it, no one will lift hand or foot in all Egypt." (Genesis 41:41)

An effigy engraved on Ay's tomb clearly illustrates the Biblical story. After being decorated by Akhenaten with seven gold chains, the Divine Father Ay took his leave and was acclaimed by the masses. He wore the "striped tunic" (linen robes), the royal gloves, as well as many presents (chariots, other necklaces, and fine jewelry, etc.).

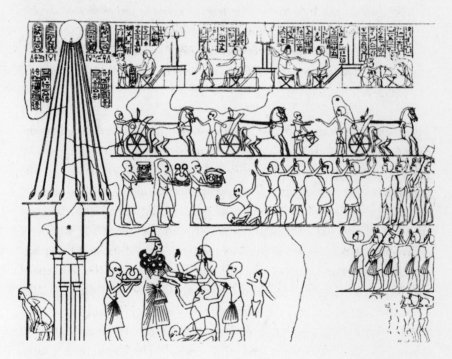

Ay honored by Akhenaten.

Since Joseph had no actual historical reality, the Biblical scribes revealed through him the most extraordinary figure of ancient Egypt – the Divine Father Ay, the forgotten pharaoh.

☥ ☥ ☥

"Now Joseph was thirty years old when he appeared before Pharaoh, king of Egypt. Joseph went out from Pharaoh's presence and traveled over the entire country of Egypt. The earth during those seven fertile years produced abundant harvests" (Genesis 41:45-47).

Joseph's age – 30 – corresponds to the approximate age of Ay when he was decorated by Pharaoh. During Akhenaten's reign, Ay traveled all over the land of Egypt, and the wealth and produce of the country flowed toward Akhet-Aten, the holy capital.

> *When all the country was famished, the people cried out to Pharaoh for bread. And Pharaoh answered the people, "Go to Joseph. Do whatever he tells you." As the famine reigned over the whole face of the earth, Joseph opened all the warehouses, and sold the wheat to the Egyptians. From every country, they came to Egypt to purchase wheat from Joseph, because the famine was severe everywhere. (Genesis 41:55-57)*

These verses indicate that the Egyptian economy was centralized in the capital, as during Akhenaten's reign. Having become governor of Egypt, Ay visited the country ceaselessly, taking account of the miserable state of the population. Ay could scarcely recognize his country, afflicted by the monotheistic megalomania and consequent catastrophe. The dramatic situation of the rest of Egypt contrasted with the enormous wealth of Akhet-Aten and Akhenaten's passivity concerning the distress of his vassals (highlighted in the Amarna Letters). These were the factors that influenced the Divine Father in the actions he took to save Egypt. According to Claire Lalouette, "Ay possessed a complete authority which is notably figured on a stela mentioning a gift of real estate, discovered near the Pyramid of Cheops (Khufu). Then Ay stayed at Memphis."[6] The Divine Father crisscrossed Egypt, redistributing lands and property, and relocating the population, in actions similar to Joseph's. "Joseph, having left Pharaoh, traveled throughout Egypt. During the seven abundant years, the land produced plentifully" (Genesis 41:45). "And he [Joseph] moved the peoples of the cities from one end to the other of the borders of the land of Egypt" (Genesis 47:21).

The degree of power exercised by Joseph is exemplified in Genesis 47:23-26:

*And Joseph said to the people, "Behold! This day I have bought you
and your land for Pharaoh. Here is grain for you. Sow the land with
it. After the harvest, you will give one-fifth to Pharaoh. The other
four-fifths will serve you for re-seeding the fields and for your nourishment, and for that of your homes and for the nourishment of your
children."*

The people of Egypt thanked Joseph for his compassion, and offered
themselves as slaves for Pharaoh. This troubling verse shows the extent to
which they had elevated him, since they called him, Adon-Ay, identifying
Joseph with Pharaoh. Gratefully, they proclaimed, "We offer ourselves as
Pharaoh's slaves."

The common people of Egypt who were not part of the new religion
were sorely afflicted, as the story of Joseph demonstrates. The story agrees
with the historical facts about Ay and with the Stela of Restoration. Joseph,
wearing Pharaoh's ring, was considered as Father of the King in the territories outside the sacred capital, which was most of the country of Egypt. In
exactly the same way, Ay was welcomed as liberating the people from their
afflictions. Joseph and Ay are one and the same person.

☥ ☥ ☥

As the Book of Genesis draws toward its end, Jacob (Israel) dies in Egypt:

*Joseph rushed to his father's face, and cried over him and embraced
him. Joseph ordered his servants, the physicians, to embalm Israel. It
lasted forty days, for that is how long it takes to embalm. The
Egyptians wept for him for seventy days. Joseph went up to bury his
father. All of Pharaoh's servants, all the elders of his house and all the
elders of the land of Egypt went up with him. Also all of Joseph's house,
his brothers' and his father's house went up. Only their children with
their flocks and herds remained in the Land of Goshen. There also
went up with him chariots and horsemen. The convoy was quite large.
(Genesis 50:1-9)*

The Bible describes an immense Egyptian crowd, accompanied by the
army, going to bury an important personality in the land of Canaan. The

scribes reconstituted the story of the historical exodus in relation to Jacob's burial. The story may be dealing with information about Akhenaten's sarcophagus, which was never found, and which was probably carried with the people of Akhet-Aten during the exodus. That would explain the Biblical mourning of seventy days, corresponding exactly to the mourning period for the pharaohs of Egypt. In addition, in Hebrew, the word "*Aron*," sarcophagus, also means ark (Genesis 50:26). This double meaning raises the following questions. Did the Ark carried by the Yahuds contain the Tablets of the Law or Akhenaten's mummy? Were there several arks?

Most of the mummies of Akhet-Aten have never been found. Some Egyptologists deduce that the nobles simply returned to anonymity. Rashi explains that the people of the Exodus bore away with them not only Joseph's body, but also the bodies of the nobles: "And you shall bear my bones from here with you. It was concerning his brothers that he made the oath. We deduce that they bore away with them the remains of the heads of all the tribes, since he said 'with you' (at the same time as yours)" (Rashi, Exodus 13:19).

According to the Bible, Joseph (like Ay) was buried as "Pharaoh of Egypt." "Joseph died at the age of a hundred and ten years; he was embalmed and placed in a sarcophagus in Egypt" (Genesis 50:26).

Genesis ends with Joseph and his grandchildren. In Genesis 50:23, it states that they were born on his knees, meaning he was dandling them on his knees. This image recalls the classical pictures of Akhenaten, dandling his children on his knees.

Joseph makes an appearance again in the Book of Exodus, Chapter 13, Verse 19. "And Moses took Joseph's bones with him [on the Exodus out of Egypt]. For Joseph had exacted a promise from the people. He said, 'The Elohim will come to help you. Then, you must bear my bones away from here.'"

♀ ♀ ♀

"Joseph" had no historical reality. But the Biblical scribes revealed through him the most extraordinary figure of ancient Egypt – the Divine Father Ay, the forgotten pharaoh.

Akhenaten and Nefertiti dandling their children "on their knees".

Notes

1. Christiane Desroches Noblecourt, *Amours et fureurs de La Lointaine.* Stock-Pernoud, 1997, pp. 67–77.
2. Akhensen-Aten is also called Ankhensen-Pa-Aten. "Pa" is the article.
3. Philipp Vandenberg, *Nefertiti.* Pierre Belfond, 1987, p. 274.
4. Anneau Blanchart, note 535, in Marc Gabolde, *D'Akhénaton à Toutankhamon.* Institut d'Archéologie et d'Histoire de l'Antiquité, Université Lumière-Lyon 2-CNRS, 1998, p. 60.
5. Cyril Aldred, *Akhenaten, King of Egypt ,* Le Seuil, 1997, p. 224. Marc Gabolde, *D'Akhénaton à Toutankhamon,* pp. 206–26.
6. Claire Lalouette, *Thèbes ou la naissance d'un empire.* Flammarion, 1995, p. 571.

☥

CHAPTER 15

The Exodus

In the Book of Exodus, Yahwe inflicted plague after plague upon Egypt because Pharaoh's heart was hardened against letting the Hebrews leave the country. Just before the last and most dreadful plague, Pharaoh became enraged at Moses.

> *Pharaoh said [to Moses], "Leave from before my face! Take care! Do not seek to see my face [panay in Hebrew] again. For on the day thou seest my face thou wilt die." To which Moses said, "I will never again seek to see thy face." (Exodus 10:28-30)*

Twenty-three chapters later, in the Aramaic version of Exodus, we read of Adon-Ay saying something remarkably similar: "He [Adon-Ay] said, 'Thou shalt not see my face. For no one can see my face and live.'"

The similarity of these verses is revealing. It demonstrates one of the fundamental attributes of Pharaoh. The king's face, protected by the uraeus (and the vulture) could not be seen by the people. The Hebrew word *panay*, "my face", is a homonym for fear (*pen*). The face of a powerful person inspires respect and, above all, fear. To stare at Pharaoh without his permission constituted a grave offense.

This tradition is found again in the clergy and nobility of ancient Egypt, following Ptahotep's teaching:

> *If thou art called to sit at the table of a grandee, take [only] what is offered thee [and] when it is placed under thy nose. Thou shalt look at what is in front of thee. Do not look all over the place. Because that*

kind of offense is an abomination to the host. Let thy face remain
lowered until he addresses thee. Only then shalt thou speak. Laugh
after he, himself, shall have laughed. And that which thou mightest do
will be agreeable to his heart.[1]

Pharaoh's heart had been hardened after each of nine dreadful plagues were
imposed on Egypt. Moses and Aaron were sent away from before Pharaoh's
face.

After the death of all the firstborn of the Egyptians, Pharaoh did allow
Moses and Aaron to see his face again. He called them in the middle of the
night and urged them to lead their people out of Egypt. "Arise, go away
from my people. Take your flocks and herds, and leave. And bless me, also"
(Exodus 12:30-33).

So the Hebrews made their escape in the middle of the night. There
was total chaos.

☥ ☥ ☥

The Biblical Exodus is a masked narrative of the actual exodus of the
monotheists. In the capital of the Egyptian empire, in the middle of the
night, chaos reigned. The whole population, urged by the Egyptian army
under the orders of Generals Horemheb and Ramesses, prepared to evacuate the sacred city, the eternal city. In the numerous common bakeries
that served the Great Temple of Aten, bakers bustled about preparing
loaves. Urgency prevailed. The army was pressing them to get under way.
The sacred bread destined for the temple would not have time to leaven.
It was necessary to bake the dough and join the rest of the crowd. (Note
Exodus 12:39: "They baked unleavened bread for they were thrust out of
Egypt and could not tarry.") The cries of the women, the dazed children,
and the bewilderment of the elderly, plunged the population into a
nightmare. How does one resign oneself to leave the Egypt of one's
ancestors, to abandon the holy city, the homes, the way of life, the past?
The Divine Father had cursed this land that had previously been sacred.
The exiles would have to leave the terrestrial paradise forever. They were
aware of the presence of the army, an army driving them out. The
Biblical scribes state it in Exodus 12:39, "Because they were thrust out of
Egypt …"

In the trek from Akhet-Aten, the people proceeded northward, along the Nile in the direction of Ramesses, a city for re-provisioning cited in the Bible. Egyptian logistics required that the itinerary begin in such a manner to insure the survival of such a large group of both civilians and soldiers. It was necessary to provision everyone.

The exodus of the monotheists toward the northern provinces was part of Ay's political and military strategy. His political ambition was to repopulate the new holy land of Canaan with a subject people, assuring a security zone between Egypt and the enemy to the north.

His military objective was a punitive campaign against the Hittites and Philistines who were occupying the province of Canaan.

The itinerary taken by the Egyptian monotheists was identical to the description in the Bible of the path of the Exodus. The following Bible verses describe the route: "The Children of Israel journeyed from Ramesses to Succoth" (Hebrew Bible, Exodus 12:37), and "Adon-Ay spoke to Moses, saying, 'Speak to the Children of Israel, telling them to turn back and camp before Pihahiroth, between Migdol and the sea – in front of Baal-zephon [an Egyptian fortresses], on the opposite side make your encampment'" (Aramaic Bible, Exodus 14:1).

Pharaoh's army was not pursuing the people as the Bible reports. It accompanied the exiles. During Tutankhamun's reign, Ay, *generalissimo* and uncontested master of Egypt, ordered his army to accompany the deportees, as is detailed in the Aramaic Bible. The route took the large migrating group past various forts, from where they could acquire fresh provisions and thus avoid certain death in the arid desert of Sinai.

The Bible story has the exiles wandering in the Sinai desert for forty years. "And the anger of Yahwe burned against Israel, and he caused them to wander in the desert for forty years" (Hebrew Bible, Numbers 32:13).

Historically, the exiles from Akhet-Aten were not able to colonize Canaan immediately. A letter from Rib-Hadda imploring aid from Akhenaten shows the seriousness of the situation. The Egyptian army had first to clear the way.

Behold, I am a loyal servant of the king, and the king has no servant equal to me. Previously, at the sight of an Egyptian, the Canaanite kings fled before him. But now, the sons of Abdi-Ashirta [king of

Amuru, whose son, Aziru, had ties to the Apiru] give the Egyptians the runaround.

The army had to engage the nomadic Apiru, in battle. The campaign was a success, and it was easy for Ay's armies, cited several times in the Bible, to recapture the Canaanite cities occupied by the Apiru. The Amarna Letters[2] sent to Akhenaten tell that a hundred Egyptian soldiers and fifty chariots were sufficient to cause the terrorized Apiru enemy to flee.

"Any one of you men can rout a thousand, because it is Adon-Ay, your god, who fights for you, as he promised you" (Aramaic Bible, Joshua 23:10).

Behind the defeated Apiru were two mighty military forces, the Hittites and the Philistines. The Hittite presence had held back the Egyptian army, although it had moved up as far as Qadesh. Ay was far-sighted enough to avoid an open war with the Hittites at that time. The Bible (Exodus 13:17) indicates that the Philistines were also close, and that war against them would not be successful.

The setbacks of Moses at the outset of the exodus correspond to the historical reverses of the Egyptian army commanded by Generals Horemheb and Ramesses during the first year of Tutankhamun's reign. Cyril Aldred explains that the foreign military expeditions had failed. As to the prayers and supplications, they remained without any response.

On the Stela of Restoration is written: "If an army is sent into Phoenicia to enlarge Egypt's frontiers, it does not bring any success. If we pray to a god to obtain anything, he does not answer at all."[3]

Since the military campaign had failed, the exiles had to wait in the Land of Moab until an Egyptian army would come along strong enough to conquer the Promised Land.

♀ ♀ ♀

An intriguing story is told in the Bible about the Parting of the Waters of the Red Sea.

"Moses extended his hand over the sea, and Adon-Ay forced back the sea. The Children of Israel entered into the middle of the sea dry, and the waters were for them a wall to their right and to their left" (Aramaic Bible, Exodus 14:21-22).

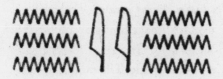

Hieroglyph of the waters. The waters are separated by the two Yods, *symbol of the creative force.*

The Red Sea is a name given by the Hellenists in their translation of the Hebrew Bible. In the Bible, the body of water is called the Sea of Reeds (*yam suf*). The story of the crossing is a message of the scribes to restore one of the basic teachings of ancient Egypt. The Pyramid Texts relate that Pharaoh had the power to separate the waters, forming a space between them, in order to allow the light to illuminate the land.[4]

The Sea of Reeds in Egyptian mythology was the ocean of the pharaohs, the Nun. It was the primordial waters of Creation. Just as the god Amun separated the waters of that Sea of Reeds, the Divine Father Ay triumphed over Akhenaten and Smenkhkare, the monotheistic pharaohs. The separation of the waters represented the rupture between Amun and Aten, between Egypt and its priests.

The Bible, in agreement with the Pyramid Texts, says that the event happened during the night. Several expressions that are present in the Creation of the World (Genesis 1) are found in the Red Sea episode:

> *And a cloud and darkness stood between them [the Hebrews and the Egyptian army pursuing them], and the column of light lit up the night, so that all night the one group could not approach the other. Moses extended his hand over the sea and Yahwe drove back the waters of the sea, all night long, with a strong east wind, and it turned it to dry land, and the waters were divided. (Exodus 14:20-21)*

The separation of the waters of the Red Sea or Sea of Reeds, added to the different symbols (war, darkness, sea, tempest, night, light), recalls the Creation story, where there is found the *tohu-bohu*, the Divine Breath, the light, the separation of the waters (Genesis 1). The miracle of the Sea of Reeds symbolizes a new creation of the world, a new start, the beginning toward another life, the passage from an old world towards a new one.

A second message contained in the Biblical episode concerns the nocturnal rivalry that permitted God to be the conqueror in broad daylight. The Egyptians believed that during the darkness of night, after the god Re died (as he did at sunset each day), Pharaoh journeyed through the dark, fighting the malignant forces of darkness. In the conflict between the two divinities of darkness and light, the Egyptians knew that Pharaoh was sailing over the celestial waters, combating the forces of evil for them, all night long. This image is visible in the tomb of Ramesses I. Sunrise was interpreted as a rebirth of the victorious pharaoh. Light had triumphed over darkness, as life shall triumph over death.

The mythological meaning of the Exodus was that the death of the God of Light was followed by rebirth. And, on the earthly plane, death of the old pharaoh was followed by the enthronement of a new king of Egypt, Tutankhamun, the symbolic son of Ay, as the tomb of the young king confirms. Ay, who crowned the new king, became the first divinity of Egypt, repeating the miracle of Amun by separating the waters and creating the heavens and the earth.

☥ ☥ ☥

Those are the symbolic or mythological interpretations of the Exodus story. But behind them was the remembrance of an historical exodus, which developed in two phases.

In the first phase, there was the reconquest of part of the Canaanite and Moabite territories situated away from Phoenician influence, three days' march from the Biblical city of Ramesses.[5] A limited victory over the Apiru made it possible to avoid a confrontation with the Hittites. Egypt, in a period of complete political and religious reorganization, could not risk conflict with the powerful forces of the Hittites backed by the Philistines. At the end of the Amarnian period, at the beginning of Tutankhamun's reign, the weakness of the Egyptian army was confirmed historically.[6] A Hittite victory would have probably meant an eventual return of the monotheists. Ay was strategist enough to know that the best course would be to avoid hostilities and hold the exiles in the Land of Moab until Egypt could launch a successful campaign in Canaan. It took forty years before such a campaign could be successfully waged.

In the second phase of the exodus, forty years later, the period in which the scribes projected in the scriptures the long wait in the desert, Sety I undertook the second campaign into Canaan at the beginning of his reign.

His victories allowed the repopulation of the north of the country and the recapture of the citadel of Qadesh from the Hittites.

The Biblical Exodus took place during the forty-year wandering of the Children of Israel in the desert between Egypt and Canaan. The forty years actually represent the time between the military campaigns waged by Egypt to regain control of its province of Canaan. With the victories of Sety I, the Exodus was over, and the monotheistic Yahuds entered triumphantly into their Promised Land.

Notes

1. John Adams Wilson, *Egypt. Life and Death of a Civilization*. Arthaud, 1961.
2. *Les letters d'El Amarna*. Le Cerf, 1987, EA 132.
3. Claire Lalouette, *Thèbes ou la naissance d'un empire*. Flammarion, 1995, p. 550.
4. Christian Jacq, *La tradition primordiale de l'Ancienne Egypte selon les textes des Pyramides*. Grasset and Fasquelle, 1998, pp. 46, 107: "Pharaoh takes what belongs to Atum, for whom he separates the heavens from the earth and primordial energy [the "Nun", the celestial ocean]."
5. Exodus 8:23.
6. Christiane Desroches Noblecourt, *Vie et mort d'un pharaoh*. Hachette, 1963, pp. 205–6.

☥

CHAPTER 16

Aaron and Horemheb

Moses is clearly the central hero of the Book of Exodus. He is portrayed as the leader of the Children of Israel in their struggle for liberation from slavery and as their guide into the Promised Land. We are told that he had an older brother, Aaron, who was second-in-command of the operation. Since the Exodus story is based on an event in Egyptian history, Moses' brother Aaron presumably is an historical character.

The Hebrew Bible contains enough hints to allow us to determine who the scribes were masking in the character they called Aaron. The Aaron whom acts as the person second-in-command in the Exodus, historically, was General Horemheb, a son-in-law of the Divine Father Ay and, later, a pharaoh of Egypt.

A major discovery concerning three names inscribed in Horemheb's cartouche – those of the three Biblical characters Aaron, Miriam, his sister, and Hor, Miriam's son, confirm that Aaron was indeed Pharaoh Horemheb.

Part of this discovery was that the name of Horus, the falcon god, the bird of light, was of Greek rather than Egyptian origin. According to Pierre Grandet, the true Egyptian pronunciation of Horus is "Hor": "Several intermediary examples are known of the name of Aten, where Horus' name (Hor) is written phonetically, thus avoiding writing it by means of the picture of a falcon."[1]

According to Claude Vandersleyen, Horus (Hor) was Horemheb's proper name. "His will to pursue concrete reforms reveals itself in his name – Horus (Hor): In effective plans (Hornung, 1971, 49, 50)."[2]

So, Horus is pronounced Hor, like Aaron's nephew in the Bible, and like Aaron himself (A-Horon). These various phonetic coincidences are not due to chance, because the scribes provided other elements that unveil Aaron's true identity. Aaron's sister was named Miriam.[3] The name of Miriam also figures in Horemheb's cartouche in the form of the hieroglyph Meri-Amun (beloved of Amun). Miriam is a contraction, according to strict Biblical and Egyptian traditions, marking Horemheb's affiliation with Amun. As with Abraham, whom the Bible scribes composed from Ab-Rah-Amun, Father of Rah's and Amun's people (Exodus 17:4-5), Miriam is the contraction of Meri-Amun. Miriam, the mother of the people, the metaphor for Isis.

The right side of Pharaoh Horemheb's cartouche (shown below) contains by itself the names "Aaron," "Miriam," and "Hor," associated with the theme of the festival that is none other than the festival of the Golden Calf.

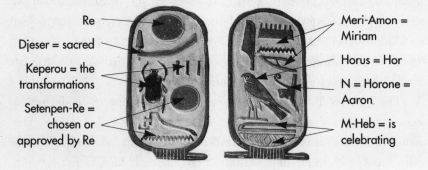

Re

Djeser = sacred

Keperou = the transformations

Setenpen-Re = chosen or approved by Re

Meri-Amon = Miriam

Horus = Hor

N = Horone = Aaron

M-Heb = is celebrating

Horemheb's cartouche. (Left) Sacred are Re's transformations (Right) Horus is celebrating, beloved of Amun.

The phonetic writing of the right-hand side of the cartouche is pronounced Hor-on-m-heb. The sense of the name Horemheb, in Egyptian Hor-n-m-heb, recalls the Biblical story of the Golden Calf. The crown (N) is the symbol of gold, and Horemheb's coronation name is "Golden Horus, the powerful bull."

In the Bible, the god Hor is hidden under various names: Nahor and Haran (Abraham's brothers), Naharim, Horeb, Horma, etc. According to Rashi,[4] Hor would be Miriam's son. He appears briefly in the Bible, disappearing after the episode of the Golden Calf. The relationship "Aaron, brother of Miriam who is the mother of Hor" is illustrated by an effigy in Horemheb's tomb: Pharaoh is placed between Isis and Hor (Horus). Isis, "the sister of Horemheb," is the mother of Hor.[5]

Horemheb and Horus, son of Isis (Tomb of Horemheb).

☥ ☥ ☥

According to the Book of Exodus Aaron bore the responsibility of tax collection and of combating corruption. During the reigns of Akhenaten and Tutankhamun, the Divine Father Ay placed Horemheb in charge of overseeing the fiscal administration of Egypt. Claude Vandersleyen describes this: "By Horemheb's decree, it is known that corruption prevailed among the tax collectors and the judges. Horemheb emphasizes that he traveled all over the country to know it to its depths. Akhenaten, himself, doubtlessly did not travel about. So it is reasonable to expect that he neglected the general management of his nation."[6]

We see Aaron in the same role in the Bible. "Adon-Ay said to Aaron, 'Behold! Here I have given thee the keeping of the contributions which have been made to me, all the holy goods of the Children of Israel. I have given them to thee and to thy sons, as assigned to thee for all time to come'" (Numbers 18:8).

Vizier Ay entrusted his general and tax collector with the responsibility of escorting the Yahuds out of Egypt and into the provinces. Horemheb had a fellow officer who shared the responsibility, a general by the name of Ramesses.

☥ ☥ ☥

With the historical Egyptian drama in mind, let us look at the way the scribes of the Bible relate the story.

When the Children of Israel arrived in the desert, they became disgruntled with conditions and with the leadership. Some of their revolts were more open than others. But, the going was not easy for either the people or for their leaders, Moses and Aaron.

The first revolt of the people driven out of Egypt was against Moses. They reproached him for having led them into the desert without hope of return. The Children of Israel had been participants in a great miracle – the parting of the Red Sea or Sea of Reeds. The revolt took place despite that miracle. The awesome parting of the waters did not seem to have much impressed the exiles. They were more concerned with their discomfort:

> *The entire community of the Children of Israel began to murmur against Moses and against Aaron in the desert. And the Children of Israel said to them: "We wish we had died by the hand of Adon-Ay in the land of Egypt, seated by the meat kettles and eating bread to the full. Because you have brought us out into this desert to kill all the people by starvation." (Aramaic Bible, Exodus 16:2)*

This incipient revolt was solved by the miraculous appearance of food. Manna fell on them from heaven, and game birds appeared on the desert along with other meat. But, all was not well yet in the wilderness.

In the next chapter in the Book of Exodus (17:3), a new revolt was brewing: "The people were there, thirsty, and they murmured against Moses and said, 'Why hast thou brought us out of Egypt to die of thirst, me, my children, and my herds?'"

Moses caused water to flow from a rock and the complaints stopped.

In the Aramaic version of the Bible, in Numbers 21:5, the people have a new complaint, which they direct to Moses: "And the people complained to Adon-Ay and to Moses, 'Why did you drag us out of Egypt to cause us to die in the desert? Because here there is no bread, no water, and we are tired of this miserable food.' So Adon-Ay sent out fiery serpents who bit the people, and a multitude perished."

The snakes who attacked the complaining Children of Israel put a finishing touch to the revolt about the terrible food and living conditions. Yet, there were more revolts in store. There were problems concerning the leadership. People were complaining that Moses had become too dictatorial. The person who spearheaded this revolt over Moses' leadership was Korah.

The episode of the revolt of Korah (Numbers 16:1), of the tribe of Levi (Yahuds), reveals the spirit of rebellion that grew progressively among the priests and the nobility during the sojourn in the desert. The Yahuds reproached Moses for wanting to keep power without sharing it. Their words are angry, ironic, and inflammatory:

> *We do not want to come up [to the land of Canaan]. Is it such a small matter that you have caused us to come up from a country which flows with milk and honey [Egypt] to kill us in the desert, and that you still want to make yourself prince over us, completely? This land into which you have led us really is scarcely one flowing with milk and honey, and has not given us a heritage of fields and vineyards. Do you want to put out the eyes of these men? We do not want to come up! (Hebrew Bible, Numbers 16:12-14)*

These people were no longer in favor of going to a promised land. They wanted to return home to Egypt. The people then reproached Moses and Aaron mightily: "The next day, the Children of Israel began to murmur against Moses and Aaron, saying, 'You are the ones who have caused the people of Adon-Ay to die'" (Aramaic Bible, Numbers 16:41).

Moses quelled the revolt by ordering a massacre of 250 of Korah's priests. "And the earth opened its mouth and swallowed them, they and their households, as well as all the people who were part of Korah's group, and all their belongings. And they went down alive to Sheol [Hell], they and all that they owned, so that they disappeared from the midst of the congregation" (Numbers 16:32).

Tomb of Sety I. The wells of Hell where the damned descend.

Following the execution of the priests of Korah, the exiles suffered a terrible chastisement: "Those who died from the plague mounted up to 14,700 plus those who died because of Korah [the 250 priests]. When Aaron finally returned to Moses, at the entrance to the Tent of Meeting, the plague had ceased" (Numbers 16:49-50).

The scribes here let us know that Aaron had been on the side of Korah's rebels. It was Aaron who finally put an end to the revolt. Since he ended the troubles he must have been part of the dissident group. There was a leadership crisis in the Exodus. The question was whether Moses or Aaron would be in charge of the people. However, both Moses and Aaron realized that open conflict would be counterproductive. A compromise had to be reached between the two brothers (generals). They shared power until the exiles reached Mount Sinai. It was there that events took a new turn, with the matter of the Golden Calf.

☥ ☥ ☥

After the many complaints and rebellions of the people, the group arrived at the foot of Mount Sinai. The events that occurred at that point in the story are among the most dramatic in the Bible – the receiving of the Ten Commandments and the worship of the Golden Calf.

The episode of the Golden Calf is a critical point in the battle for leadership of the people of the Exodus. When Moses was gone from the people for forty days, having gone up Mount Sinai, Aaron constructed a golden calf for the people to worship. When Moses returned, he was enraged. The relationship between the two brother leaders had reached critical mass.

At this dramatic point in the Bible story, let us consider the historical situation it was reflecting.

The Divine Father Ay was the actual ruler of Egypt. King Tutankhamun had died aged 18. There was no direct blood-line leading to a new pharaoh for the Eighteenth Dynasty. The Divine Father, Vizier Ay, assumed the crown. Before becoming pharaoh, he had sent generals Horemheb and Ramesses north to lead the monotheists to the province of Canaan. While the deportees were languishing in Moab, waiting for the Egyptian army to liberate Canaan for them, Pharaoh Ay died.

Again, there was no lineal descendant of Ahmose, the founder of the Eighteenth Dynasty. It was unclear who would become pharaoh of Egypt.

Ramose, a powerful vizier, was a possible claimant for the throne. Horemheb, who had control of the army, returned to Thebes to claim the throne for himself. He was as successful a politician as a general and bureaucrat and easily edged out the competition for the crown, and became pharaoh of Egypt. As such, he was intermediary between the people and Amun. Horemheb had now become both pharaoh and priest.

Now, back to the Bible story, in which Moses and Aaron are still in contention for leadership of the people.

At the foot of Mount Sinai, we are told that Moses went away, up the mountain. "Moses went inside the cloud and went up the mountain. And Moses remained on the mountain forty days and forty nights" (Exodus 24:18).

Does this verse refer to the mourning period for an important person? Remember, Pharaoh Ay, a person who was of great importance to the leaders of the Exodus, had just died. Forty days is the time period required to embalm a person in the Egyptian manner, as revealed earlier in Genesis: "Forty days elapsed. For it takes that many days for a person to be embalmed. The Egyptians cried [for Jacob] for seventy days" (Genesis 50:3). Moses would have been absent to fulfill his religious obligations for the death of Pharaoh Ay.

The Bible tells us that during Moses' absence, Aaron collected gold from the people and cast it into an idol, a golden calf: "Aaron told the people, 'Remove the earrings from your wives, from your sons and daughters, and bring them to me'" (Exodus 32:2).

> He [Aaron] took it [the gold] from their hands, formed a cast, and made a metal calf. And they said, "Here are thy gods, O Israel, which have brought you out of the land of Egypt." Aaron saw it [the golden calf] and set an altar before it. And Aaron proclaimed, "Tomorrow there shall be a feast for Ay [Adon-Ay]." They arose early the next day and presented burnt offerings and brought peace offerings. The people sat to eat and drink, and then arose to carouse. (Aramaic Bible, Exodus 32:4-6)

Aaron here is showing his sympathy for the return to the gods of Egypt. He is displaying his agreement with the Yahuds who wish to return to Egypt. Aaron's commitment is not to carrying monotheism into the promised land, but to reverting to the worship of Amun and allowing the people to return to Egypt. The people celebrate Aaron's leadership and readily worship the Golden Calf and engage in a feast in honor of Amun, Aten, Ay, and the Elohim, pharaohs of Egypt, as we shall now see.

According to Christian Jacq's translation, the Pyramid Texts attest that the Golden Calf symbolizes the birth of Pharaoh merged with the sun-Re. It is the ancient Egyptians themselves that give us the secret of the great enigma of the Golden Calf.

The king's mother is the celestial cow who rises towards the heavens and who does not leave him behind on earth. Pharaoh joins himself to her, the great wild cow in the heavens. She suckles him and does not leave him without strength. After having conceived him and placed him on earth, she places him within her wing that she may cause him to cross over a lake and a canal. And it is in the form of a Golden Calf that Re is born in the heavens.[7]

Thus, the Golden Calf symbolizes the birth and coronation of a new pharaoh.

Aaron is celebrating – Horemheb is celebrating. The celebration symbolizes the return of the Yahud people to the freedom of the previous cult, the return to Amun, materialized in the feast of the Golden Calf.

The episode of the Golden Calf is a representation of the attempt of Horemheb, who had just become the new pharaoh of Egypt, to finally resolve the Amarnian crisis. He granted amnesty to those who had gone out of Egypt by allowing them to worship the ancient gods. In contrast, Ramesses' commitment was to settle the land of Canaan with the monotheists.

When Moses returned from his forty days' sojourn, he was mightily displeased at the turn matters had taken. Surprised by the coronation of Horemheb (Aaron), Moses attacked the people directly. He ordered a bloodbath.

Moses addressed the Levites (the army of the priests): "He said to them, 'Thus spoke Adon-Ay, God of Israel. "Let each man strap on his sword, go back and forth from gate to gate in the camp, and let each one slay his brother, his friend, relative"'" (Aramaic Bible, Exodus 32:27).

Three thousand were killed.

The return of Moses from Sinai provoked a conflict that menaced Aaron's power. The two brothers arrived at a compromise, condemning and chastising the innocent people. The three thousand who were killed satisfied Moses, and Aaron backed down in order to keep the peace.

Now, let us look at what history tells us about this period.

At the beginning of his reign Horemheb continued the policy of his father-in-law, Ay, re-establishing the old gods in the whole land. Horemheb had numerous golden statues sculpted all over Egypt,[8] and reintegrated into their respective temples, as well as many altars.

Although crowned more than ten years after the exodus from Akhet-Aten, Horemheb was angry at the departure of the priests and sages of Egypt. The Stela of the Return indicates that the land needed priests. The new pharaoh did not want to deprive himself of the intellectual elite. He had to give the deported clergy a chance to reintegrate into their fatherland and participate in the process of restoration.

The refusal of General Ramesses to let the people return to Egypt shows his radical determination to repopulate Canaan, in accord with the mission entrusted to him by Pharaoh Ay. So Ramesses had the ability to oppose Horemheb without being sanctioned. A civil war seemed imminent. A compromise was reached between Ramesses and Horemheb after a series of massacres. Horemheb understood that the Yahud priests, with their ancient traditions, represented a potential vital resource for Egypt. However, the only possibility left, then, for the new pharaoh was to recruit future priests from the families of the class of nobles.

Horemheb's retreat from his previous position could explain his consequent hostile behavior towards the memory of his father-in-law Ay because of the dismissal of the priests. He usurped his name on some statues. He did the same on monuments and stelae (for example the Stela of the Restoration) engraved in Tutankhamun's name. On the list of the names of the pharaohs of Egypt he banished the name of the Amarnian kings (Akhenaten, Smenkhkare, Tutankhamun, and Ay), making it appear that he himself was the true son of Amenhotep III.

Horemheb's action created a novel situation for Egypt – the problem of Akhet-Aten and monotheism being sent towards the desert of Moab, near Canaan. Upper and Lower Egypt returned to the old traditional

Amunian gods. However, in the wilderness the Yahuds and the *erev-rav* (the common people) were committed to the monotheistic cult that was held responsible for Egypt's decline. They deified Ay as the "symbol of the name" of the One God in place of Aten. Horemheb took care to annihilate the Atenian cult, and tried hard to neutralize every form of the cult of the Divine Father Ay in the two lands.

♀ ♀ ♀

Horemheb had been promoted to governor of the kingdom by Tutankhamun (under Ay's aegis); he was depicted in the vestments of High Priest, carrying the vase of the oil of unction. He received the golden necklaces, the shawl or sacred vestment, as well as another vase of holy oil. The priests acclaimed him and prostrated themselves before him.

In like manner the Bible depicts Aaron as high priest of the Children of Israel:

> *Aaron said all the words that Adon-Ay had addressed to Moses, and he worked marvels before the eyes of the people. And the people had faith in him. They understood that Adon-Ay remembered the Children of Israel, that he had taken consideration of their misery, and they bowed their heads and prostrated themselves. (Exodus 4:30-32)*

The status of High Priest attributed to Aaron allows us to understand why Moses never punishes him in the Bible story. The description of Aaron's sacred vestments and his priestly function place him above Moses in any hierarchy.

Horemheb was Ay's interpreter and scribe. He was also a man committed to reconciliation and desirous of bringing back the Yahud priests to Egypt.

The policy of extreme centralization in Akhet-Aten, associated with the abandonment of traditional values, had caused dysfunction, anarchy, and corruption at all levels of the administration. The desire to re-establish order was an urgent necessity at Akhenaten's death. The Divine Father Ay, an effective politician and precursor of the return of the ancient religion, was the person who inspired the reform. Horemheb usurped his paternity, as he did on most of the monuments and stelae. He saw himself as the champion of the return of Amun, mercilessly eliminating the memory of his adversaries, mainly Ay, venerated and then detested. Claude Vandersleyen[9] recognized in Horemheb the author of the malfeasances perpetrated in Ay's name in the Temple of Karnak:

> *From Horemheb's attitude when he succeeded Ay, it can be deduced that those four years [of Ay's reign] were not lacking in tension. The temple raised at Karnak by Ay in memory of the young dead king [Tutankhamun] bore both their names. Tutankhamun's was respected everywhere, whereas Ay's names were most often destroyed and the surface prepared to receive a new inscription (Schaden 1984, 46–48, Eaton-Krauss, 1988, 4–5, 10–11). Only Horemheb or Ramesses could have ordered these mutilations since these blocks were finally buried in the second pylon needed for the building.*

Afterwards, Horemheb and Ramesses usurped some monuments and statues that were attributed to Tutankhamun. At the foot of the tenth pylon of the hypostyle room of the Temple of Karnak, there is a stela decreeing the return of order in the land, like the edict of restoration of the Stela of Tutankhamun. Nicolas Grimal believes Horemheb is at the heart of the reform:

> *He [Horemheb] put judges and regional tribunals in place, and reintroduced local religious authorities. The juridical power was divided between Upper and Lower Egypt, between the vizier of Thebes and the vizier of Memphis. The duality of the country is found again in the army where the military units were recast and dispersed into two military districts, one in the north, the other in the south.*[10]

Another vizier, Ramesses, had charge of the eastern territories (Canaan and Moab), applying Pharaoh's laws and organizing the settlement of displaced populations. The vizier who administered these provinces was quite separate from Upper and Lower Egypt, but powerful enough to accede naturally to the throne after Horemheb's death.

Notes

1. See J. Samson, *Mrna, City of Akhenaten and Nefertiti*. Aris & Phillips, 1978, pp.101–3.
2. Claude Vandersleyen, *Egypt and the Valley of the Nile*, Vol. 2. Nouvelle Clio, 1995, p. 488.
3. Cf. Exodus 15:20; Numbers 12:1, 20:1, 26:59.
4. Exodus 17:6, 17:12
5. Alberto Siliotti, *The Valley of the Kings*. Gründ, 1996, p.47.
6. Claude Vandersleyen, *Egypt and the Valley of the Nile*, p. 436.
7. Christian Jacq, *La tradition primordiale de l'Ancienne Egypte selon les texts des Pyramides*. Grasset and Fasquelle, 1998, p.264.
8. For the gold statues and their altars, cf. Cyril Aldred, *Akhenaten, King of Egypt*. Le Seuil, 1997, p. 288.
9. Claude Vandersleyen, *Egypt and the Valley of the Nile*, p. 483.
10. Nicolas Grimal, *Histoire de l'Ancienne Egypte*. Fayard, 1988, p. 297.

☥

CHAPTER 17

Moses and Ramesses I

In his tomb Ramesses I, under the watchful eye of Atum, brandishes his rod over Apophis. Apophis is a twelve-coil serpent surging out of the primordial ocean. This is a sketch of the nocturnal combat between Pharaoh and the forces of evil. A bit further along is an unusual picture representing the ocean, the Nun, separated into two parts. Apophis is pressing back the waters, and twelve goddesses represent the hours of the night. These elements are at the origin of the legend of the nocturnal expulsion of the twelve tribes of Israel and the crossing of the Red Sea, the Sea of Reeds.

Ramesses I hunts the serpent Apophis (Tomb of Ramesses I).

Apophis flees to the middle of the open sea. The dozen goddesses of the night extend their hands towards the sea.

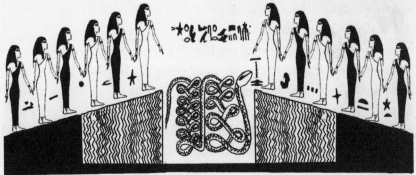

"Moses extended his hand over the sea, and Adon-Ay drove back the sea, all night long, with an east wind drawing them back. And he made the sea dry, and the waters were divided" (Exodus 14:27).

The legend of Moses, a prince saved from the waters, was borrowed, like so many others, from Mesopotamia,[1] and Egypt.[2] It was necessary for the story to have Moses be born a Hebrew and miraculously become an Egyptian, raised by Pharaoh's daughter. Moses then became the head of Pharaoh's house and a student of all the wisdom of Egypt. Later, to affirm before the king his pride in belonging to the Hebrew people, Moses revolts against the supreme authority.

The Hebrew Bible states in Exodus 2:6: "She [Pharaoh's daughter] had pity on him and said, 'It is a child of the Hebrews.'" In the Aramaic Bible, the same verse says: "She had pity on him and said, 'It is a child of the Yahuds (*yehudaeh*).'" So Moses was a Yahud by birth, a son of the Elohim, belonging to the Egyptian nobility, probably the son of one of Pharaoh's daughters.

"This woman conceived, and bore a son [Moses]. She saw that he was beautiful, and kept him hidden for three months" (Exodus 2:2). The reference to keeping Moses hidden in a cradle for three months appears to be taken from the Egyptian temple service where the priests hid Amun (the hidden god) within the sanctuary to have him reborn into the light every three months.[3]

"Not being able to hide him any longer, she prepared for him [Moses] a cradle of bulrushes [*Teva*]. She placed the child in it and set him among the reeds on the bank of the river" (Exodus 2:3). In the same way the Pyramid Texts place Pharaoh's birth in the Lake of Reeds. "In the Lake of the Reeds, Re, Shu, and Pharaoh purified themselves. This place of water and light is similar to the celestial paradise that is shown in the form of the 'fields' that Pharaoh crosses."[4]

Etymologically, in Hebrew the Nile is written as the river of light. So Moses is depicted as a prince, luminous, sailing on an ark among the reeds in a river of light, which conforms to the Pharaoh in the Pyramid Texts. Moses' birth, combined with the appearance of divine light, is associated with the waters of the Nile, the River of Light. Rashi's commentary states: "How beautiful he was. When he was born, the entire house was filled with light."

Although the legend of Moses saved from the waters had been assumed, the symbol of the "divine child" saved from the Nile was an integral part of Egyptian religion. Christiane Desroches Noblecourt confirms this. "Every New Year's Day, the flood brings back the divine child, the solar child who is associated with the young king who, apparently, renews himself every year."[5]

The following two points are of interest. The divine child, Pharaoh's son, mentioned by Christiane Noblecourt is called "Mes" or "Messess" in Egyptian, because symbolically it derives from "slave of the world." In the Bible, the Hebrew word *"Teva"* designates both "the cradle of Moses" and Noah's Ark. Since Pharaoh, Moses, Mosheh, the Messiah, arrive on an Egyptian Ark to save the Hebrews from slavery, the *"Teva"* is the Divine Ark in which God's emissary saves humanity.

"Now Pharaoh's daughter went down to the river (Yeor) to bathe, with her companions following her. She saw the basket among the reeds" (Exodus 2:5). According to the following illustration, and Plutarch,[6] Isis, like Miriam, hid her son Horus (the symbol of light) among the reeds.

Isis, bearing the Re-disk, gives life to the divine child in the papyrus marsh (sea of reeds), assisted by Amun and Thoth, as well as by the two foster mothers who hold the "serpent rod," symbol of life and power.

"The child grew, and she [the nurse] brought him to Pharaoh's daughter. And he became her son [*Leben*]. She named [*Vaykra*] him Moses, saying, 'Because I drew him [*Masheti-oo*] forth from the waters [*Min A-Maim*]'" (Exodus 2:10).

This is surely the most important message in the Bible: Pharaoh's daughter, the image of Isis, pronouncing the sentence justifying Moses' name. An attentive examination of the above verse, in parallel with the Egyptian, makes the attributes of the cartouche of Ramesses I opposite crystal clear; since the cartouche is in Egyptian, the true honorific name of the pharaoh becomes apparent: "Because from the waters [*Min-A-Maim*] I drew him forth [*Masheti-oo*]."

"Min" מִן symbolizes the divine emanation, corresponding with the "Mem" and the "Nun" contained in the cartouche of the throne name of Ramesses I. Min (or Mnévis) recalls the "powerful bull" inscribed in the name of Horus of Amenhotep III.

     Min (who emanates from).

"Maim" מַיִם ("the waters") corresponds to the "Nun," the primordial waters where the pharaohs were born. In the Pyramid Texts, Pharaoh is "made flesh" from the waters of the heavens and of the earth. "Thy water and thy cool water are the abundance that emanate from you." Min and Nun form the principal component of Amun, the hidden god who surges from the primordial waters.

∿∿∿∿   *Hieroglyph of the primordial waters.*

"Masheti-ou" מְשִׁיתִהוּ ("I drew him forth"), contains the Egyptian root MST, that Pierre Grandet[7] translates as "giving birth," "child bearing," "delivery." The root SWT in Egyptian means bullrush, emblem of the king of Upper and Lower Egypt, as the cartouche of Ramesses I indicates. The last part, "Oo" ("he"), is depicted below by the bird hieroglyph – "oo."

Hieroglyph for Moses, Moseh, or Mosheh, born by God or by Isis.

Hieroglyph "oo" (he).

Sut or Nesut (symbol of the king of Egypt).

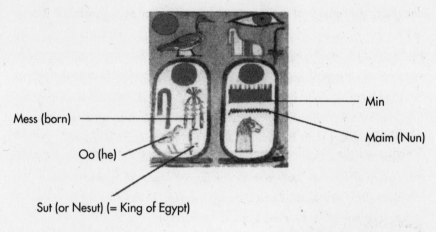

Mess (born)

Oo (he)

Min

Maim (Nun)

Sut (or Nesut) (= King of Egypt)

Cartouche of Ramesses I.

This parallel allows us to make clear the actual Egyptian words of Pharaoh's daughter: He became for her the son of Amun, and she named him "'divine child,' because with Amun, the celestial waters, I bore him."

Thus she admits being Moses' mother and that he was born through the god Amun. Moses is Yahud (heir), son of Levi (lion) and the future Ramesses I, one of the pharaohs of Amun's return. In the historical context, Moses would be the son of a secondary wife of Amenhotep III, perhaps from the harem of Min.

☥ ☥ ☥

Sety I, acting under order of his father Ramesses I, affirms having sent the "dissidents" into the desert, pursuing the mission that Ramesses had undertaken under Tutankhamun's reign and following Ay's orders. During the period of reorganization of Pharaoh Horemheb, Ramesses, who was both a general and the governor of the North, reigned as absolute master over his territory. The words of Sety I, son and co-regent of Ramesses I, according to the translation of Dominique Valbelle,[8] mentions the duties of which he was in charge prior to his coronation. The figure of Moses is realized in this description of the deeds of Ramesses I:

I speak of what I did [what I became] until I was the master of the two shores. I came from the womb [of my mother] like the Bull of Maat [Emet in Hebrew], impregnated by good counsel and teachings.

When he [Ramesses I] was Re, I was with him as a star at his side
[...]. I [subjugated] the lands of the Fenekhu, I drove out for him the
dissidents [the Yahud monotheists of Akhet-Aten] into the desert
country. I organized his monarchy like Horus on the throne of
Unennefer. I chose Maat for him every day, and I bore him on my
bosom [...] in his name Mehenyt. I assembled his army and gave him
a single heart [Lev in Hebrew: the army of the Levites]. I sought for
him the subsistence of the double land and I placed my arm in the
service of his close protection in the foreign lands the names of which
were [still] unknown. I was a courageous hero in his presence in order
that he might open his eyes upon my perfection.

☥ ☥ ☥

If Ramesses I and Moses represent the same person, the Ten
Commandments originated in ancient Egypt. Apart from the prohibition
against having many gods, of fashioning graven images, and of rest on the
Sabbath, Egyptian writings show that the commandments existed in
Egyptian wisdom literature. The "forty-two proclamations of Osiris'
death" contained in the Book of the Dead were considered as commandments before the celestial tribunal. An Egyptian had to justify his
irreproachable conduct, which included upholding seven of the ten
Biblical commandments (called the "seven laws of Noah" or "Noah's laws"
in the oral tradition).

Ramesses I and his son, Sety, accompanied the "dissidents" with the
symbols of the monotheistic religion, as well as the name of Akhenaten
engraved on a double stone tablet. The first and last word on these tablets
(now in Turin Museum, and reproduced on page 145) form "Ankh Aten,"
the living Aten or Anokh Aten, Akhenaten's name, in perfect accord with
the first Biblical commandment "Anokhi Adonay." Before naming the
"ten" commandments, the Bible speaks of "the" commandment:

"Yahweh said to Moses: 'Come up to me, on the mountain, and stay
here. I will give you the stone tablets, the law and the commandment that
I have written for their instruction'" (Exodus 24:12).

Rashi explains that the "six hundred and thirteen commandments are
included in the Ten Commandments," they themselves are contained in
the first. Thus the commandment could correspond to the stone tablets of

Akhenaten consisting of a single commandment: the name of Aten, or Adonay in the Bible. The commandment given to Moses would then be a transmission of the pharaonic power of the sacred name. It signifies the heritage of the pharaonic monarchy, a heritage that had to be due to Moses and not to Aaron.

The "divine characters" are hieroglyphs, since written Hebrew did not exist at the time of the Exodus. The inscriptions of the Amarnian period, particularly the name of Aten, are read in two ways. Rashi, Exodus 32:15: "From one side to the other. The letters could be read from both sides. It was a miraculous work."

Stone cartouches representing the name of Aten (Turin Museum).

In the cartouche of Ramesses I, a lion is depicted (see the illustration on page 143). Biblically the lion is the symbol of Judah: the Lion of Judah. The tribe of Judah was Moses' army (the Levites), who had the same objectives as the leaders of Egypt, the submission of the Canaanite territories. In Hebrew, lion is pronounced "lavi." Moses was the son of Levi, or son of the lion, "Ben-Levi." This symbol of power is found in the royal cartouche of Ramesses I and in the family name of Moses.

The Lion of Judah first appears when Jacob/Israel was foretelling the future of his sons. He had the following to say about Judah: "Thou art a young lion, Judah, my son, who returneth with thy prey. He croucheth as a lion. Who dares to rouse him?" (Genesis 49:9).

♀ ♀ ♀

When Moses became an adult, he had an experience that was to change his life: "A messenger from Adon-Ay appeared to him in a flame of fire, from the middle of a bush. And behold the bush (*seneh*) was on fire. However, the bush was not consumed" (Aramaic Bible, Exodus 3:2). Did the scribes want to hide Re, the sun god represented by the luminous disk, by the image of the burning bush? The verse can be translated: "The fire was within the luminous sphere of Re, the sphere (*seneh*) was on fire, however, it was not consumed." Moses' bush is translated by *seneh*, and Fabre d'Olivet gives the following explanation: "The symbol of the visual sphere (*seneh*), and of everything that is luminous."[9]

Ay is represented in the scribes' retelling of the story both by Joseph and Jethro. Moses hid himself at Jethro's (Ay's) house after the murder of an Egyptian. Then, according to Fabre d'Olivet, Moses came upon the luminous sphere (Re). According to the Aramaic Bible, he met a messenger from Ay. After the miracle of the bush, the words of God, addressed to Moses, were the following: "Ay spoke to Moses saying unto him: 'I am Ay. I appeared to Abraham, Isaac and Jacob, as an all powerful [*El Shaday*] God, and by my name of Ay. I was not known by them" (Aramaic Bible, Exodus 6:2-4). Abraham, Isaac and Jacob, that is the monotheistic pharaohs, had not known that Ay, the Divine Father, was scheming to become pharaoh himself. Ay was upset that his way to the throne was blocked by the royal lineage.

Rashi's commentary on this passage deserves close attention: "I have not made it known, but I have not been known. I have not been recognized by them in my attribute of truth, for which reason my name is called The Eternal. That is to say, faithful in making my words true. Because I have made promises to them, and I have not yet fulfilled them."

The two attributes of "truth" and "fidelity in making my words true," correspond exactly to the symbols described in the cartouche of Pharaoh Ay: the sign of Maat, and that of the kneeling man, dispensing the sacred word.

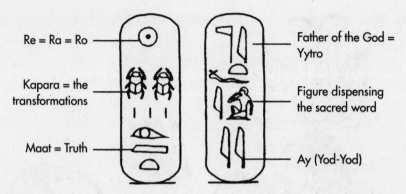

Re = Ra = Ro			Father of the God = Yytro
Kapara = the transformations			Figure dispensing the sacred word
Maat = Truth			Ay (Yod-Yod)

The royal cartouche of Ay containing the figures of Maat (Truth) as well as the symbol meaning "fidelity in making my words true."

The indicative "Father of the God" or "Father of the King" is written as *Ytro* in Egyptian. Ay must actually have had the name Ytro, for Ytro is the Hebrew name of Moses' father-in-law, Jethro. That is Jethro's secret. Thus, Ay's cartouches contain simultaneously the attributes of Joseph (called Abrekh, or Father of the King by the people) and Jethro. Following this reasoning, it seems most likely that Joseph and Jethro were one and the same person: Pharaoh Ay.

☥ ☥ ☥

"Adon-Ay said to Moses: 'Go to Pharaoh. For I have hardened his heart and the hearts of his officials, so that I may place my signs [*Cheteh otot*] in their midst'" (Aramaic Bible, Exodus 10:1).

In this verse, *cheteh* and *tot* mean two. "I place my signs," "*cheteh otot,*" can thus be translated as "my two signs." These could be the uraeus and the vulture that Tutankhamun would wear under Ay's supervision, or equally the two attributes of the word and the truth belonging to the Divine Father.

☥ ☥ ☥

The Biblical texts describe the magic that Moses and Aaron performed before Pharaoh and the royal magicians. The text refers to ancient beliefs about the power of Pharaoh. In the Pyramid Texts the rod is a symbol of power and eternal life.[10] The rod, represented by the scepter, incarnates unity, authority, the justice of Maat and the wisdom of Thoth.

Thoth gives life to the dead Sety I (Temple of Sety I).

When Moses appeared before Pharaoh and his magicians, his rod turned into a serpent. Even by itself the rod inspired fear and discipline, as well as representing transformative magic. The Egyptians believed that magic came directly from God,[11] assuring Pharaoh protection and the power of divination. The serpent, according to the Pyramid Texts, was the intermediary between the world here below and the heavenly world. It is the god Horus' eye of light, which, by incorporating and sublimating itself into Pharaoh's likeness, made him truly a divine being having power over life and death. The story of Moses' brass serpent, which healed the rebels in the desert who were bitten by the venomous snakes (Numbers 21:5-9), represents Pharaoh's serpent, associated with the concept of punishment and its consequences. "Adon-Ay said to Moses: 'Make for thyself a brass serpent, and place it on a pole. Whosoever shall have been bitten, when he beholds it, he shall live!'" (Numbers 21:8).

The legend of the rod turning into a serpent makes sense in this way: it is a sign of defiance toward the authority of Pharaoh. Equipped with the same powers as Pharaoh's, Moses' rod swallowing up Pharaoh's serpents – represents the historic victory of Ay, Horemheb and Ramesses I over the monotheistic pharaohs.

The serpent-rod of Moses and Aaron figures in the tombs of both Ramesses I and Horemheb. Pharaoh on Re's boat is painted with the head of a ram surmounted by the luminous solar disk. All the functions attributed to the rod are related to the power of Pharaoh.

Tomb of Ramesses I. The dead pharaoh shown with the head of a ram and holding his rod is facing the serpent Mehen (an identical picture is shown in Horemheb's tomb).

The Pyramid Texts tie the rod to Pharaoh's word. Moses and Aaron present themselves before Pharaoh with the sacred rod, the power allowing Ay to negotiate: "Adon-Ay said to him, 'What hast thou in thy hand?' He said, 'A rod.' He said, 'Cast it to the ground!' He cast it to the ground and it became a serpent" (Aramaic Bible, Exodus 4:2).

There is another clue tying Moses to Pharaoh: "And the Children of Israel saw the face of Moses, because the skin of Moses' face shone [he had horns], then Moses replaced the veil over his face" (Exodus 34:35). Moses' shining face is a sign of one of Pharaoh's major attributes, a being of light.

Pharaoh Sety I described his father Ramesses I as a shining being of light: "While he was Re, the sun shining at dawn, I was at his side like a star from the earth."[12]

The Yahud priests transposed into the Bible the memories of the serpent, the rod, the horns and the rays of light (Re), which are found in the tombs of Horemheb and Ramesses I. Moses' veil recalls Amun, the ram god hidden under the sacred shawl during the processions. His face hidden, shining and provided with horns, reveals that at the end of his life, he had become Ramesses I, pharaoh of Egypt, as shown in the mural in his tomb in the Valley of the Kings.

☥ ☥ ☥

In the Aramaic Bible, Ay, desiring to assume power, was careful to validate his authority before the people. He sent two generals to negotiate with Pharaoh to let the monotheistic people go. "And I will harden the heart of the Egyptians and they will enter after them [in the Sea of Reeds]; And then I shall be glorified above Pharaoh and his entire army and his chariots and his cavalry" (Aramaic Bible, Exodus 14:17). "The Egyptians shall know that I am Adon-Ay when I am glorified above Pharaoh and his chariots and his horsemen" (Aramaic Bible, Exodus 14:18).

By the repetition introduced in these two verses, the scribes show their real motivations, as well as the personality of Ay. The expression "I shall be glorified above Pharaoh," employs the Hebrew word *kevod* and should be read, "I shall receive honors from Pharaoh, from his cavalry and his army, and I shall be recognized [as God] by all of Egypt."

The second meaning of these two verses is the following: Either the Egyptians recognize in Ay the Atenian One God and accept monotheism, in which case the exodus is useless. Or, instead, they remain Amunians and recognize the Divine Father Ay as the one who brought back the old gods. If the old gods were to be brought back, Ay would have to organize an exodus of the monotheists.

The message of the Biblical scribes was that Ay, clever politician that he was, played both sides, the Amunians and the Atenians, against each other.

When he could deport the inhabitants of Akhet-Aten, he would finally be recognized by the Egyptian people as Pharaoh, and by the Yahuds as the One God. Even though the child Tutankhamun reigned at the beginning of the Exodus, Ay was still revered and glorified as a god after Akhenaten.

"Adon-Ay had found favor for the people among the Egyptians. That man, Moses, also, was very highly considered in the land of Egypt, in the eyes of Pharaoh's servants and in the eyes of the people" (Aramaic Bible, Exodus 11:3).

The text placed between the ninth and tenth plague of Egypt shows that the first objective of Ay and Moses was to increase their own standing with the Egyptian people, who apparently were not very much affected by the ten plagues. Quite to the contrary, it was the monotheists who were called "stiff-necked people," restive and obstinate (Exodus 32:9; 33:3-5; 34:9). This expression recalls the Amarnian art showing popular or royal people with stiff, elongated necks. The sacred art of ancient Egypt is always present in the subconscious of the Biblical scribes.

In history, as in the Aramaic Bible, Ay sought consideration, recognition and honor from the servants of Pharaoh, from the army, the cavalry, the charioteers, the whole of Egypt. The expression, "I shall be glorified above Pharaoh" (Exodus 14:17-18) reveals the intention of the Divine Father to manipulate the pharaohs Smenkhkare and then the child Tutankhaten (Tutankhamun). He was determined to be recognized as God by both Amunian and Atenian Egypt. Claire Lalouette mentions that there appears to have been a co-regency of Tutankhamun and Ay, as shown in the royal cartouches in the Temple of Karnak.[13]

With the death of Tutankhamun, the Eighteenth Dynasty was extinct. Pharaoh Ay prefigured the Nineteenth Dynasty. He was associated with the return of the Amunian orthodoxy and with the accession of Horemheb and Ramesses I.

☥ ☥ ☥

Upon Akhenaten's death, his son Smenkhkare ascended the throne. Smenkhkare was opposed to exiling the people of Akhet-Aten. Ay's objective was to drive the monotheistic priests out of Egypt. In the Biblical telling of this matter we read, "Adon-Ay said to Moses, 'Now you will see what I am going to do to Pharaoh [Smenkhkare]. Because with a strong hand he will let them leave, and with a strong hand he will drive them from his land" (Aramaic Bible, Exodus 6:1).

Later, after Pharaoh's refusal, Ay shows the strength of his authority to Moses and Aaron: "Moses and Aaron went to Pharaoh and said to him, 'Thus saith Adon-Ay, god of the Yahuds [Yahudaeh], "How long wilt thou refuse to humiliate thyself before me? Let my people go that they may worship me"'" (Aramaic Bible, Exodus 10:3).

The story is dealing with a power struggle between the Divine Father Ay, governor of Egypt, and Pharaoh Smenkhkare, enthroned then at Thebes. For the health of Egypt, and to avoid a war between Amun and Aten, the Exodus was inevitable.

♀ ♀ ♀

According to the Bible, Moses and Aaron did not enter the Land of Canaan. The location of their tombs remains unknown (Deuteronomy 34:6). In Deuteronomy, God tells Moses he will die on Mount Nebo. "Thou shalt die on the mountain where you will be reunited with thy people, just as thy brother Aaron died on Mount Hor and was reunited with his people" (Deuteronomy 32:50). Outside of the Sinai (Desert of Sin,[14] symbol of the moon, and of Ay), the archeologists have never been able to locate Mounts Hor, Horeb, and Nebo.[15]

Did Moses and Aaron really die on the sacred mountain, "united with their people"? Why did they disappear?

Pharaoh Horemheb (Aaron) died about two years before Ramesses I (Moses). This coincidence between Bible and history shows why the Yahud scribes could not go any further without revealing the true identity of Aaron and Moses.

Aaron, the older brother of Moses, died on Mount "Hor," which was Horemheb's name (Deuteronomy 32:49-50). Shortly afterwards, Moses followed him in death on a mountain called "Abarim" and Mount Nebo. "Abarim" has as its root *"ever,"* meaning "passed over to the other side." Translating it all then, we arrive at: "Moses and Aaron returned to their past."

The Egyptian word Neb, "Lord," accompanies most of the titles of the pharaohs of Egypt. Moses would have died on the mountain of Nebo, "his Lordship." Hor[16] (Horus) and Nebo are names attributed to Pharaoh. Mountain in Hebrew, *"Har,"* is pronounced phonetically *"Or,"* light.[17]

To say that Moses and Aaron "died on the mountain" should be translated as a symbolic ascension toward the light of eternity.

The Pyramid Texts affirm that Pharaoh is a being of light. The expression used at the time, "Pharaoh mounts and rises towards the heavens,"[18] explains the importance of this theme in ancient Egypt. Moses acceded to the light of Adon-Ay, and Aaron to the light of Horus.

⚲ ⚲ ⚲

At the death of a pharaoh, there was a funeral chant dating back to the Old Empire that began this way:

> *To navigate on the waters*
> *In the most beautiful of all lands*
> *To climb the mountain of the field of rest.*

The mountain theme is taken up in the Bible, as we have observed before: "Moses went inside the cloud and went up the mountain. And Moses remained on the mountain forty days and forty nights" (Exodus 24:18).

Our previous speculation was that the verse alludes to the mourning period of an important person: "Forty days elapsed. It takes that many days for a person to be embalmed. The Egyptians cried [for Jacob] for seventy days" (Genesis 50:3).

At Ay's death, Ramesses and Horemheb were both pretenders to the throne of Egypt. In the Bible, Moses accompanies Aaron and the seventy elders of Israel:

> *Moses and Aaron went up, accompanied by Nadab, Abihu, and the seventy elders of Israel. They beheld the Elohim of Israel. Under their feet was a pavement of sapphire, like the sky in appearance and in clearness. And against the leaders of the Children of Israel, Yahwe did not raise his hand. They contemplated Adon-Ay, and they ate and drank. (Aramaic Bible, Exodus 24:9-10)*

Are the scribes describing a traditional funeral dinner? The seventy elders and the forty days' absence of Moses correspond to the ritual of embalming[19] in ancient Egypt. The pavement that looks like the heavens corresponds to the stone pedestal described by Cyril Aldred, on which the mummy of the Pharaoh is "admired" before being placed in the sarcophagus and the ceremony of the opening of the mouth[20] made by his successor.

Mummy of Makhetaten on a brick pedestal.

As the story proceeds, Moses stays with Joshua and sends Aaron and the seventy elders back. Then he climbs Mount Sinai, symbol of royal mourning. Did Moses (Ramesses) commit a fatal error when he sent Aaron and the seventy elders back? Could it have cost him the kingdom? "And to the elders he said, 'Wait here until we return to you. Here are Aaron and Hor with you. Whoever of you has problems with another, let him go to them.' Then Moses went up on the mountain and a cloud covered the mountain. The majesty of Adon-Ay settled on Mount Sinai" (Aramaic Bible, Exodus 24:14-16).

The same sequence occurred historically. Ramesses remained for Ay's burial in order to proceed to the rite of the opening of the mouth after Horemheb left. That would explain the absence of Moses (Ramesses) among the Children of Israel, because of his religious obligations at the death of Pharaoh Ay. Moses, honored by his involvement in the opening of the mouth, nourished the legitimate hope of succeeding the dead pharaoh. That hope was thwarted by Aaron (Horemheb), who took over power with the episode of the Golden Calf. The need for priests in the Amunian temples occasioned by the desertion of Akhet-Aten convinced the priests to crown Horemheb. These priests are represented by the seventy elders of the Bible. Ramesses had to wait 25 more years to become Pharaoh Ramesses I.

The entrance to Ay's tomb.

Pictures in Pharaoh Ay's tomb make clear that when the Bible speaks of Mount Sinai, it is, in fact referring to that tomb. In one of these pictures, Ay is hunting quail. A papyrus bush is in front of him. The double cartouches of his name, in the form of tablets, are broken.

Claire Lalouette reports that hunting scenes in the tombs of the kings have a high symbolic value:

> *But in Egypt, hunting and fishing do not have only athletic value. They are magic actions destined to kill in all wildlife the malevolent forces that reside there. For the king, hunting is also an exploit that affirms his strength and invincibility. The wild animals being assimilated into the enemies of the empire. So it is an act of salvation, which contributes to the maintenance of the order of the world, and the cohesion of the country.[21]*

On the wall of the "holy of holies" in Ay's tomb, the twelve quail flying in the same direction,[22] symbolize the twelve tribes of Israel driven out of Egypt. Consequently, the papyrus bush would symbolize Moses' bush.

> *Adon-Ay spoke to Moses, saying, "I have heard the murmurs of the Children of Israel. Speak to them, saying 'In the evening, you will eat*

Pharaoh Ay in a basket hunts the twelve Nile Quail with his boomerang. Fleeing the papyrus bush, they fly in order in the same direction.

> meat [quail], in the morning, you will sit down to bread. And you will know that I am Adon-Ay, your God.'" (Aramaic Bible, Exodus 16:12)

The message of the scribes is: the twelve quail will be a sign of recognition that Ay, the God of the Aramaic Bible and in the Hebrew tradition, is the God of the exodus from Egypt.

☥ ☥ ☥

Was Moses' anger and his breaking the Tablets of the Law a great offence against Adon-Ay? Was this a message from the scribes? Was Ramesses I responsible for breaking up the double cartouches of Ay inside the funerary chamber, the holy of holies of his tomb?

"And Moses' anger flared up. He threw from his hands the tablets [of Adon-Ay], and broke them at the foot [*tahat*] of the mountain" (Exodus 32:19).

Aaron, as high priest, became a favorite of Jethro (Ay) (Aramaic Bible, Exodus 18:12) and succeeded him, inciting Moses' anger. In the same way, in the history of ancient Egypt, Horemheb succeeded Ay, preceding Ramesses I on the throne. This would give Ramesses I a stronger motive to destroy Ay's cartouches than Horemheb: Horemheb hadn't any reason to

Ay's tomb. The king's cartouches are broken.

destroy them, since he had been favored, designated as regent of the kingdom in Tutankhamun's time, he succeeded Pharaoh Ay. Consequently, Ramesses I chiseled out the cartouches bearing Ay's name. Hence Exodus 32:19 – Moses broke the tablets "under" (*tahat*) the mountain.

Hathor (Re), Ay's fiancée, and Ay's rod (Tomb of Ay).

If Mount Sinai and Ay's tomb are one and the same place, where did the historical episode of the Golden Calf occur? We have seen that that event occurred just prior to Horemheb's coronation. History relates that he was consecrated king of Egypt at Thebes, by Horus of Hutnesut[23] and Amun-Re, and not in the desert. Claire Lalouette mentions the words engraved in the temple of Montu at Karnak: "I have been installed king [Horemheb], God bowed his head, we see face to face before the entire earth. That was ordered in the heavens and heard in Karnak."[24]

Funerary chamber with the broken sarcophagus of Ay (Tomb of Ay).

Aaron (Horemheb) and Moses (Ramesses) would have returned to Egypt, accompanied by the artist-priest caste in order to create the funerary articles needed for the royal burial. These were the ark, tabernacle, planks, horned incense altar, chandelier or *sema-tauy*, the golden altar, offering table, tent, curtain, purple and scarlet materials of fine linen, the sacred vestments, the oil lamps, the offering bread, the golden pectoral, the sacred diadem, gold rings, and the robe of the High Priest. These objects are depicted in the second part of the Book of Exodus and agree precisely with the treasures discovered in Tutankhamun's tomb. The Bible even tells of "the basin and its stand" (Exodus 40:11), recalling the granite coffin of the pharaohs.

Horemheb was crowned Pharaoh. Ramesses was named Vizier and High Priest of Egypt. The power struggle was over.

☥ ☥ ☥

After all these explanations, it would be as well to examine the hypothesis of the murder of the Egyptian by Moses and Moses' flight to Jethro, as well as the Burning Bush. The line of reasoning that follows is one recognized by the Cabalists.

The turning point in the life of the young Moses, Prince of Egypt, took place at the murder of the Egyptian. The Biblical tradition suggests that it was a conflict with a foreman who had struck a Hebrew that caused Moses to kill him. Exodus 2:11: "He [Moses] struck the Egyptian." Later, the Bible announces the death of the "King of Egypt": "In the course of those many years the King of Egypt died" (Exodus 2:23).

It is not the same account that is given in the long rabbinical oral tradition, which affirms that it was not a case of just any Egyptian being killed by Moses, but rather of a very important person, perhaps even the pharaoh of Egypt. Moreover, it was because of this murder that Moses did not have the right to enter the Promised Land.

Was Akhenaten the Egyptian struck by Moses?

The Book of the Zohar affirms that the Egyptian killed by Moses was, in fact, an "important man";[25] Moses, called "he who was fetched forth from the waters," seized the Egyptian's spear. The Egyptian was "that important man who was the splendor of the light that illuminateth Israel." Rashi (Exodus 2:14) teaches that Moses struck the Egyptian while pronouncing the Divine Name.[26] It is the only case in the Bible where Moses uses the Divine Name, since he had not yet encountered the revelation of God (Adon-Ay) in the desert. What is the nature of the name formulated by Moses?

According the Midrash,[27] Moses pronounced "the name of the One," (in Hebrew, *Shem Ameyuhad*). This is the attribute inscribed inside the royal cartouche of Akhenaten, "the Oneness of Re."

Although all the monotheistic pharaohs were dead at the time of the mysterious circumstances, only Pharaoh Akhenaten, having Smenkhkare as his co-regent, could be considered the one who "was killed" by the hand of Moses. Consequently, the verses "the pharaoh who did not know Joseph" and "the King of Egypt died" do not speak of the same pharaoh. These verses are the Biblical confirmation of the historical co-regency between

Akhenaten and Smenkhkare – a co-regency which was not approved of by the Divine Father. According to the Biblical tale, Ay's objective was to convince the new pharaoh, Smenkhkare, by tentative complicity, that the only course of action was to drive the monotheistic priests out of Egypt.

> *Ay said to Moses: "Now wilt thou see what I will do to Pharaoh. For with a strong hand, he will let them leave. And with a strong hand he will drive them out of his land." (Aramaic Bible, Exodus 6:1)*

> *An emissary from Adon-Ay appeared to him in a flame of fire, in the middle of a bush. And he beheld that the bush [seneh] was on fire, yet the bush was not consumed. (Aramaic Bible, Exodus 3:2)*

Moses' "bush" is translated from *seneh* סנה – "sun" in English. Fabre d'Olivet gives the following explanation. "The symbol of the visual sphere [*seneh*], and of every luminous influence."[28]

Did the scribes wish to hide the sun god Re through the image of the Burning Bush? The verse can be translated: "The fire was inside the luminous sphere of Re, the sphere was on fire, yet it was not consumed."

Moses took refuge in the house of Jethro (Ay) after the murder of the Egyptian. Then, according to the Hebrew Bible and Fabre d'Olivet, he entered into a relationship with the "luminous sphere (Re)" and according to the Aramaic Bible, he encountered "Ay's emissary."

In historical terms, General Ramesses fled to the house of the Divine Father Ay, after the murder of an Egyptian of very great importance. Would that person have been Akhenaten?

The statement God gave to Moses, "I shall be who I shall be" "*Ehieh Asher Ehieh*" (Exodus 3:14), invoked by Ay in the Aramaic, translates the Divine Father's political and religious determination: I shall be a god of Egypt.

Notes

1. Mainly the legend of Sargon of Akkadia, but also of Gilgamesh, Cyrus, etc.
2. The Egyptian legend of Sinuheh.
3. Lionel Casson, *Ancient Egypt, The Great Ages of Man*. Time, 1969, p. 79.
4. Christian Jacq, *La tradition primordiale de l'Ancienne Egypte selon les textes des Pyramides*. Grasset and Fasquelle, 1998, p. 257.

5. Nicole Maya Malet, *Moïse hébreu, Moïse égyptien*. Revue d'éthique et de théologie morale. Le Cerf, 1997, p. 143.

6. Plutarch, *Isis and Osiris*. Translated by Jean Meunier. La Maisnie, 1992.

7. Pierre Grandet, *Cours d'Egyptien hiéroglyphique*. Khéops, 1997, p. 764.

8. Dominique Valbelle, *Histoire de l'Etat Pharaonique*. PUF, 1998, p. 288.

9. Fabre d'Olivet, *La langue hébraïque restituée*. L'Age d'Homme-Delphica, 1991, p.92.

10. Translation by Christian Jacq, *La tradition primordiale de l'Ancienne Egypte*, pp. 102–17, 146.

11. Albert Soued, *Les symboles dans la Bible*. Jacques Grancher, 1995, pp. 174–6.

12. Christiane Desroches Noblecourt, *Ramses II la véritable histoire*. Pygmalion, 1996, p. 68 (notes): "This text was engraved on the pedestal of a statue of Ramesses I dedicated in the temple of Medamud (south of Luxor)."

13. Claire Lalouette, *Thèbes ou la naissance d'un empire*. Flammarion, 1995, p. 570.

14. The Egyptian root "Sn" means uncle or relative, among other meanings. Ay would be the father or father-in-law of Moses and Horemheb. According to Fabre d'Olivet, "Sn" is also the luminous disk, symbol of Re, "sun" in English. Consequently, Moses' bush (*seneh* in Hebrew) would be the sphere of the sun that burns without being consumed.

15. These words are all Egyptian: Hor = Horus; Horeb = "Horus is celebrating"; Nebo = "His Lord." Mount Nebo is located in the Land of Moab (present-day Jordan).

16. Horus is actually read as Hor in Egyptian. Christian Jacq, *Grammaire égyptienne de Champollion*. Solin, 1997, p. 39.

17. Fabre d'Olivet, *La langue hébraïque restituée*, p. 39.

18. Christian Jacq, *La tradition primordiale de l'Ancienne Egypte*. p. 78.

19. Cyril Aldred, *Akhenaten, King of Egypt*. Le Seuil, 1997, p. 182.

20. The successor to a dead pharaoh approached his mummified body and inserted an instrument into the pharaoh's mouth, which transferred power from the dead pharaoh to his successor.

21. Claire Lalouette, *Thèbes ou la naissance d'un empire*, p. 471.

22. Classical hunting scenes of the Middle and New Empire, as well as in the royal tombs, represent a variety of birds flying in all directions, never in order as in the example in Ay's tomb.

23. Claire Lalouette, *Thèbes ou la naissance d'un empire*, p. 574. Hutnesut is formed from Hoten, meaning father-in-law, and from Sut, king of Egypt. Jethro was the "*hoten*" of Moses.

24. *Ibid.*

25. *The Book of the Zohar, Ten Collected Stories*, Vol. 1. Verdier, 1981.

26. Rashi, *The Pentateuch According to Rashi, Exodus*. Samuel and Odette Lévy, 1990, Appendix p.11.

27. *Ibid.*, p.353.

28. Fabre d'Olivet, *La langue hébraïque restituée*, p.92.

☥

CHAPTER 18

Joshua and Sety I

In Chapter 33 of the Book of Exodus, we meet a young man who becomes one of the great warriors of the Bible. "And Adon-Ay [God] spoke with Moses face to face, as one man speaks with another. And Moses returned to the camp. But Joshua, son of Nun, his young aide, did not leave the inside of the tent" (Aramaic Bible, Exodus 33:11).

Joshua ben-Nun appears to be the character devised by the scribes to tell the story of the Egyptian Pharaoh Sety I. The word "Nun" ties the pharaoh in with the Egyptian creation story.

In earlier chapters dealing with the Egyptian creation story, we encountered the word *Nun*. The Egyptian meaning of the word is found in the Pyramid Texts.[1] It is the primordial ocean, the original place which gave birth to everything, and the cradle where each pharaoh was born: "Pharaoh was conceived in the primordial energy [Nun], before the existence of the heavens and the earth." Like the God of the Bible, Pharaoh existed before the creation of the universe.

Pharaoh Sety I's name also reads as "Seth." The words "Seth" and "Sety" are identical in the Egyptian language. Seth means "great in strength."[2]

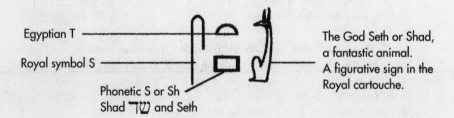

Egyptian T — Royal symbol S — Phonetic S or Sh — Shad שַׁד and Seth

The God Seth or Shad, a fantastic animal. A figurative sign in the Royal cartouche.

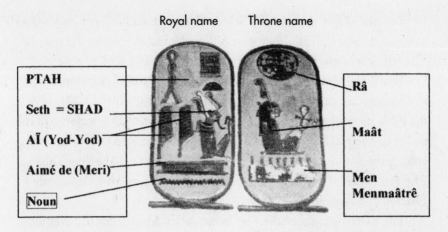

Royal name   Throne name

PTAH

Seth = SHAD

AÏ (Yod-Yod)

Aimé de (Meri)

Noun

Râ

Maât

Men
Menmaâtrê

Double cartouche of Pharaoh Sety I = Shad-Ay (Sety) loved by Ptah and Nun: Men (emanation of) Maat and of Re.

The Biblical scribes give hints here that Joshua son of Nun was in fact a powerful pharaoh, the great Egyptian military hero Sety I.

יהושע בן נון

Yahu-Shua, son of Nun. The Great God Shaday, beloved of Ptah and Nun.

MEN

NOUN

AH-CH-YA

Yahu-Shua ben Nun (Joshua son of Nun).

♀ ♀ ♀

The Bible presents Joshua as Moses' young, loyal aide (Exodus 33:11), having the right to enter the sacred tent, a privilege reserved for Moses and Aaron. Joshua must have had a status superior to that of "just an aide," *eved*, meaning slave in the sense of being dedicated to a cult. Who was Joshua that he could enter the sacred tent? The scribes are indicating that Joshua was Moses' son.

Ramesses I was the father of Sety I. When the scribes described Joshua as the "aide, son of Nun", they were hiding the fact that he was Moses' son. The father-son relationship holds in the historical and Biblical reports.

The Bible relates that Joshua conquered 31 fortified cities (in Canaan and Phoenicia), one of which was named Kedesh (Joshua 12:22). In fact the Bible mentions a number of other cities, indicating that Joshua had the power to conquer the entire region. The cities he defeated were distributed among the twelve tribes of Israel, Judah being granted the "lion's share." The territories of Judah adjoined Egypt, which gave them assurance of Pharaoh's protection.

The campaign undertaken by Joshua after Moses' death corresponds with the historical conquests of Pharaoh Sety I in Canaan and in Phoenicia after the death of Ramesses I. According to Claude Vandersleyen, Sety I, with his son Ramesses II as co-regent, began his Asian Campaign right after his coronation.[3] As reported for Joshua, Sety I attacked Kedesh, a former Egyptian fortress north of Galilee that had been captured by the Hittites. The city was liberated and once more came under Egyptian domination. In the Bible the city was consecrated after its re-capture (Joshua 20:7).

The many cities taken by Sety I during his campaign – Megiddo, Lachish, Beth-Shean, Yenoam, Geder, Tyre, etc. – correspond to those reportedly taken by Joshua.[4] The Book of Joshua declares that until that time, the Hittites were present in the region. According to Claude Vandersleyen, "The kings of Jerusalem, of Hebron, of Jarmuth, of Lachish, and of Eglon were Amorites (Joshua 10:5); Hittites and Amorites are found in the hill country of Judah (Numbers 13:29). This area corresponds to the lands traversed by Sety I and is confirmed by the texts at Karnak."[5] The battle campaigns of Joshua would never have been permitted by the Egyptians unless he was an ally, at the very least.

☥ ☥ ☥

According to John Adams Wilson, Sety I had to confront a coalition of Canaanite kings in the course of his military campaign:

He knew that the princes of Upper Jordan had formed a coalition. Sety's answer was worthy of Egypt's military reputation. "His Majesty *dispatched towards Hamath the first division of Amun, powerful bowmen; the second division of Re, valorous men all, left from the city of Beishan [Beth-Shean], and towards Jenoam, he dispatched the first division of Seth, strong in bows."*⁶

Four of the cities are found close to the Jordan, south of the Sea of Galilee. Sety attacked them before taking Kedesh, thus holding back the Hittite advance.

The campaign led by Joshua was similar. He crossed the Jordan in order to take the neighboring cities from behind. The Bible relates a coalition of the Canaanite kings comparable to the coalition against Sety I: "Adonizedek, King of Jerusalem sent to Hoham, King of Hebron, to Piram, King of Jarmuth, to Jalphira, King of Lachish, and to Debir, King of Eglan, to tell them, 'Come to me and lend me a hand, that we may attack Gibeon, because it has made peace with Joshua and the Israelites'" (Joshua 10:3).

It can be seen that the strength and organization of Joshua's armies were like the Egyptian armies. Joshua, like Sety I, took the city of Kedesh, north of Galilee, using an identical strategy.

♀ ♀ ♀

Sety I had his great military exploits portrayed on a wall of the hypostyle room of Karnak. His exploits are detailed as well on stelae. Two stelae discovered at Beth-Shean confirm his triumph over Canaan.

Joshua also set up stelae; history and the Bible appear to be describing the same person. When Joshua, "separating the waters," led the Children of Israel through the River Jordan, he ordered a memorial of twelve stones to be erected: "If your sons ask you in the future, saying, 'Why are these stones here?' you are to say to them, 'The waters of the Jordan were rolled back before the Ark of the Covenant of Adonay. These stones shall serve as a memorial of this event for the sons of Israel forever" (Joshua 4:6).

At the end of his campaign, before his return to Egypt, Joshua/Sety had a stela engraved:

Then Joshua wrote these words in the Book of the Law of the Elohim. He took a large stone and set it up there, under the great tree which is near the sanctuary of Adonay. Joshua said to the people, "Behold! This stone shall serve as a witness against you if you renounce the Elohim." Then Joshua sent the people away, each to his own inheritance. (Joshua 24:26-28)

☥ ☥ ☥

Whether reading the history book or the Bible, we learn that, either by the military campaigns of Sety I or of Joshua, Egypt extended its borders, with the land of Judah buffering the middle. There was not any war between Egypt and Judah after the settlement of the Yahud priests and the *Erev-rav* (Israel), in the northern territories, in the "Security Zone" against the Hittites, a common enemy. Judah and Israel then were certainly under Egyptian protection.

If the Egyptians were upset with the slaves who had escaped into the northern territories, they could quite easily have avenged themselves by fighting and conquering the people who had miraculously crossed the Red Sea. History demonstrates that the Judahite priests still remained Egyptian subjects. The successors of the Aten pharaohs, the Ramessides, honored the alliances of Ay and Ramesses I, distributing the provinces to the south to Judah (Yahuday) and those to the north to Israel (*Erev-rav*).

After the death of Sety I, his son, Ramesses II, followed his pacification mission in Canaan as far as Kedesh. He also conquered other cities for the Yahuds. An archeological indication found on a pylon of the Temple of Luxor describes how Ramesses II delivered citadels to the Judahites. Christiane Desroches Noblecourt comments on the meaning:

> *And these were the citadels which, according to the Bible, refused passage to the Hebrews. It is interesting to think that Ramesses appeared to attack citadels which did not want to open their doors to the Hebrews, at least, to the so-called Hebrews. So he [Ramesses II] was very interested in having the Hebrews in these citadels. He had allies there who spoke Egyptian.*[7]

(In actual fact, the Yahud priests spoke Egyptian, but the common people, the *Erev-rav*, used the new language, the holy language of the monotheists, Hebrew.)

♀ ♀ ♀

The story of Joshua is always associated with the Battle of Jericho, where the walls came tumbling down when the trumpets were sounded. Trumpets or bugles were part of the military paraphernalia of the Canaan Campaign. "Then Adon-Ay spoke to Moses saying, 'Have two silver trumpets made. Thou shalt have them made of hammered work, and they shall serve thee to summon the assembly and to break [military] camp" (Numbers 10:1).

The Biblical description recalls the Tutankhamun's silver trumpets described by Nicolas Reeves: "In the antechamber Tutankhamun's military trumpets were placed: the first one of hammered silver except for the mouthpiece and for the trim of the bell which were made of curved gold leaf."[8]

Silver military trumpets found in Tutankhamun's tomb.

The trumpets, the military conquests, and the bloodthirsty battles described in the Bible are confirmed by archeology and history. The name of the general, however, turns out to be not Joshua, but Sety I.

Notes

1. Christian Jacq, *La tradition primordiale de l'Ancienne Egypte selon les textes des Pyramides*. Grasset and Fasquelle, 1998.

2. Robert Thibaud, *Dictionnaire de mythologie et symbolique égyptienne*. Dervy, 1966, p. 320.

3. Christiane Desroches-Noblecourt, *Ramses II, la véritable histoire*. Pygmalion, 1996.

4. Joshua 12:21.

5. Claude Vandersleyen, *Egypt and the Valley of the Nile*, Vol. 2. Nouvelle Clio, 1995, p. 300.

6. John Adams Wilson, *Egypt. Life and Death of a Civilization*. Arthaud, 1961, p. 229.

7. Nicole Maya Malet, *Moïse hébreu, Moïse égyptien*. Revue d'éthique et de théologie morale. Le Cerf, 1997, p. 143.

8. Nicolas Reeves, *The Discovery of Tutankhamun*. Thames and Hudson, 1990, p. 164.

CHAPTER 19

☥

The Massai Exodus

A commentary of Rashi regarding the city of Babel tells us: "The language was confounded, the people were dispersed from the valley and were spread out across the entire world."

Was the drama of the city of Akhet-Aten, which was bound to the cult of the One God, an event limited to the Biblical Exodus, or was it a phenomenon with worldwide repercussions? Does archeological data exist which sketches an outline of another exodus? When considering the pyramids of Central America and the sacred writing of the Incas, scholars have hypothesized a migration of people who came from Egypt. They point to the aptitude of the Egyptian sailors at the end of the Eighteenth Dynasty to confront the oceans.

There is a people with traditions going back thousands of years, living in Kenya and Tanzania, who have engraved in their past a story analogous to that of the Bible – the Massai. How did the Massai come to espouse a Biblical monotheism with divine names analogous to those of the Egyptian gods? Are they the forgotten Africans, monotheists driven out of Egypt by the Divine Father Ay? Was there a Massai Exodus?

On the Stela of the Return of Amun it is written: "He [Tutankhamun, directed by Ay] drove out deceit from one end of the two lands to the other. And Maat was re-established; the deceit became an abomination in the land, as it was before." The Stela indicates that the Divine Father directed one exodus to the north and one to the south.

When the venerable Massai priests are asked about the origin of their people, they enter into a kind of trance, looking into the distance, frozen in an ancestral past transmitted from the earliest times. Looking toward the north, they recount how God one day had "driven them out of the Garden of Eden," the paradise lost, the land of the white bird (the sacred ibis) for having eaten the forbidden fruit. God pointed his finger toward the south, designating the Holy Land, and gave them an inheritance of all the cows in the land. The Massai say, "God gave us cattle and grass. Without grass, there are no cattle, and without cattle there are no Massai."[1]

God promised them a land flowing with milk and honey. At the time of that exodus, the people remember having resolutely crossed the cataracts of the Nile. Their legend relates that they climbed up a "sacred ladder" before discovering the holy land and the pastures promised by God. Seeing the fertile lands of East Africa, they sent out scouts, as in the Bible story. The land that flows with milk and honey was there; the divine promise was realized. That legend is revealed by Tepilit Ole Saitoti, an English author of Massai origin:

> *It is believed that the Massai originated from the north and emigrated along the Nile to East Africa, to arrive in Kenya near Lake Turkana (previously Lake Rudolph) around the fifteenth century. The story of their arrival and the extreme difficulties which they encountered doubtlessly constitute the oldest memory that the oral tradition has transmitted through the mouths of the elders.*

In fact, the Massai oral tradition goes back quite a bit further. It is, in every point, comparable to that of the Yahuds. They had to worship their One God, Enkay or Ankh-Ay, in exchange for his protection and blessing. The master of the heavens and the earth, he is not pictured in any drawing or sculpture. Another name for their god is "Motoni," the god who is "male and female,"[2] containing the root Aten. "Aamon" or "Naamoni" appear equally in the Massai language, meaning "I pray." In the Egyptian language "Naamoni" is the symbol for Thebes.

As in the Bible story of Jacob and Esau, the Massai have in their religious stories the tale of the inheritance going to the younger son who was loved by his mother. The younger son received his father's blessing first, to the detriment of the elder brother. Relics of the oral tradition are jealously conserved, since the Massai have no scripture or sacred book.

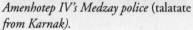

Amenhotep IV's Medzay police (talatate   *Massai warriors with lances.*
from Karnak).

The Massai people have always called themselves "The Elect of God" (or the Chosen People), proudly preserving their heritage and resisting, like the Yahuds, all assaults of other beliefs. They use the Egyptian name of Mess-Ay, "Sons of Ay," which is close to the word *Medzay,* the name of African police of Akhet-Aten. These police assured the maintenance of order in the capital, obedient to their god-king Akhenaten, and forming a monotheistic army feared to the limits of the empire. The Amarna Letters[3] attest to the efficacy of the Nubian troops and of the Kashi soldiers (from the Land of Kush in the south of Egypt) under Amenhotep III and Akhenaten:

> *May my Lord [Akhenaten] send me 100 men and 100 Kashi soldiers and thirty chariots, that I might guard my Lord's land until an important force of bowmen arrive, in order that my Lord can recapture the land of Amuru for himself, and that the people here may be safe. (EA 127)*

The sacred plain where the Massai have established themselves has the name Massay Mara –"beloved sons of Ay," "son of Ay who resides in Ra

(Re)." In Egyptian, the root *masha* means troop or army,[4] which is related to Hebrew "*mass*," head of an army (Exodus 1:11: the *sareh-missim* were the princes in charge of forced labor for Pharaoh). On Mount Lengay, a mountain sacred to God located in Tanzania, in a territory reserved for the priests, the One God of the Massai resides. At the base of the mountain the people come, as in the Bible, to sacrifice a lamb.

The name of the Massai god, Engay or Enkay, comes from the Egyptian *Anok-Ay*, "I am Ay," translated as *Ana Ay* by the Aramaic Bible. *Nan-Ay*, which is in the Massai prayers, means "the Great God" and "the Great Ay" in Egyptian. The common expression of the different names for the name of the god of the Massai, then, is the god of ancient Egypt, the Divine Father Ay.

Following the example of the Yahuds and Egyptians, the Massai are organized into twelve tribes, each one living in its own territory with a chief and a high priest. Their principal nourishment is based on milk and honey. Like the ancient Egyptian priests they have a horror of fish, and do not mix milk and meat.[5] The young men are circumcised at thirteen. The circumcision and the piercing of the ears have a religious meaning, coming from the ancestral tradition of Egypt. The passage to the age of adulthood, including the rights of maturity and responsibilities before God, is accompanied by a new name given by the priest. It is associated with the intensive development of the Massai warrior. After seven years, he shaves his hair (like the Egyptian priests), putting an end to the active period of his youth. He is consecrated from then on to a contemplative and religious life, that of the elders, who are made strong by their wisdom and experience, and will later become the Laibon – Massai priests. The oldest of them receives, again, a new name, parallel with the history of Akhenaten. The meditative ardor of the priests is a source of harmony between the Massai men and the African flora and fauna. This perfect symbiosis between a people and nature finds its origin in the principles of Egyptian wisdom and in the Hymns to Aten.

Red, a color sacred to the Massai, recalls the "red cloth of Upper Egypt" described in the Pyramid Texts,[6] and the red of the crown of Lower Egypt. Visible from afar, it is a symbol of divine protection. Although the Massai warriors are known all over Africa for the fear which they inspire, they are also known for the nobility of heart extended to their guests. Their clothing and jewelry have a practical and religious meaning in relation with Egyptian symbols. The Massai headband is frequently arranged with ornaments in the form of a serpent, like the uraeus of Pharaoh. It is remarkable to observe on most of their ornaments, diadems, and other jewelry, a symbol in the form of a circle pierced in its center, an analog of the hieroglyphic sign of Re. A serpent decorated by pearls and a spread-winged bird sometimes emerges from the circle. The symbolic value of this bird insignia, a sign of Re, recalls the Egyptian god Re Horakhty (represented by a falcon surmounted by the sign of Re). The Massai god has the same name, "bird of prey," in the prayer "God, protect me by thy wings."

Massai woman laden with sacred ornaments. On the headband and the pectoral are symbols of the Egyptian gods. The earrings are in the form of a royal cartouche.

Massai hairstyle, ending in a point like Pharaoh's shawl.

Bracelets are worn in the Egyptian manner on the arms and forearms. The Massai pectoral, made up of various multicolored parts, is reminiscent of Pharaoh's pectoral. The hair of the warriors, carefully braided with a Nubian look, is analogous to that of the police of Akhet-Aten. The hair comes to a point in the back, evoking Pharaoh's shawl. The arms, the lance, the bow, the dagger, the shield of animal skin, the round-edged bludgeon, the Massai sandals, the tools of wood and forged iron are identical to those found in Tutankhamun's tomb.

Medzay warriors and police in Akhenaten's time (talatate *of Karnak). Their hairstyle recalls that of the Massai warriors.*

An ancient legend relates that the god Engay had three sons. To the first, he made the gift of a bow to hunt (like Abel) and he offered to the second a hoe to work the earth (Cain). To his third son, called Natero-Kop (Neter = God; Kop = Khof = serpent), he gave the sacred rod of the shepherd. Natero-Kop became the Father of the Massai.

There is a tradition concerning the sacrifice of a ram at the time of a birth. The midwives pray a psalm in honor of the new-born, beginning with "Na-Amoni Aaay-Ay," "I pray for whom I pray" (Amon-Ay). This custom is similar to the ritual of birthing practiced in the workers' village of Akhet-Aten. As in ancient Egypt and among the Hebrews, red cows are sacred and their sacrifice is reserved for ancestral ceremonies.

The Massai have retained the morning and evening prayer glorifying the morning and evening star. According to tradition, the Massai follow the sun's course. While the officiant presides at the prayer, the assembly listens in silence. It answers with one voice at the end of each blessing, by the sound of "*Heh,*" the Egyptian and Hebrew symbol for the divine breath. The prayer consists of thanking God for the benefits received on earth, and in asking for material goods. But, above all, it is a homage to the beauty of nature and its delight. It is very similar to many contemplative themes in the Hymns to Aten.

The Massai follow an oral set of ethics comparable to the Biblical Ten Commandments. It is forbidden to worship other gods, to kill, to commit adultery, to steal and covet the belongings of others. False testimony and lying are regarded as abominations. Love of truth and respect due to parents are two of the most ancient traditions. The divine presence watches over the elders, particularly over the Laibon priest.

One of the first English explorers of the Massai country, Sidney Hind, reports in his book, *The Last of the Massais* (1910): "The Massai learn very rapidly. Their race is intelligent and can be trusted. And an adult Massai will never steal or lie. He may refuse to answer a question, but once he has given you his word, you can trust it."

The Festival of Eunoto is a ceremony resembling some Biblical traditions, where the warrior must produce a particular trumpet sound on the horn of a kudu. This sound, along with that of bells hanging on the officiant's thigh, produce an effect of exaltation on the assembly. The High Priest of the Jerusalem Temple who sounds the ram's horn or Shofar, wears bells sewed to his vestments.

Although the hieroglyphs conserved by the Massai are rare, they still do exist. Other than the Re glyph traditionally worn on the forehead, there are others in symbolic form. For example, a crossed circle is applied to the cattle as a sign of ownership. This is like the Egyptian pictogram designating a city or a country. Some Massai wear above the Re sign the double line, the symbol of the two lands of ancient Egypt.

Re

Lord

Two lands

The warriors wear a headband displaying the sign of Re and of the two lands.

Protective sign of the Massai warrior.

A protective symbol, identical to the Egyptian royal cartouches, is worn by the warriors at kidney level. The form of this symbol recalls the Tablets of the Law. The name of God is very important among the Massai, as it was among the Yahud monotheists. The two cartouches associated with the belief in a single god come from an ancient memory, that of the two cartouches of the name of Aten.

There are still other symbols on the animal skin shields. The most frequent one is the broken line, the image of the primordial ocean.

As in ancient Egypt, the death of a Massai is considered a great voyage. The dead person carries with him his shepherd staff and his personal effects. As in the Bible, the children mourn for thirty days. The Laibon is buried after the sacrifice of a bull or sheep. His tomb is covered over with stones piled in a pyramid. Tradition teaches that the chief's soul reappears a while after death, in the form of a sacred serpent.

The Laibon High Priest, guarantor of the oral tradition, has the duty of transmitting the teaching of the fathers. Every day, the elders instruct the youngsters, and it is the school of life and of nature that forms the curriculum. The Laibon, like the Egyptian high priest, is dressed in an animal skin attesting to his social status (like Ay in Tutankhamun's tomb). The rod and the fly-whisk, proudly born by the Laibon, are the two principal signs of his authority. They correspond to the fly-whisks and sacred scepter of Pharaoh. A cylinder represents the royal seal of Pharaoh.

Laibon carrying the fly-whisk and sacred rod of the Massai.

Laibon, which is close to the name Laban, the Biblical name of Amenhotep III, is composed of El (God), Ay, and Amun. Since these elements show an Egyptian origin for the Massai, an in-depth linguistic study would certainly provide additional proofs of the similarities to the ancient Egyptian language.

The Massai, a people not known in the Biblical Exodus, are nonetheless an integral part of the historical exodus. They were present in Akhet-Aten and, like the Yahud priests, had to accept a territorial compromise with the reigning god-king, the Divine Father Ay. The powerful clergy of Akhet-Aten, with its army, would never have accepted leaving the Holy Land. The Divine Father had the idea of separating the people from its police and from its army by a second exodus toward Africa. The new king, Smenkhkare, could not stop the greatest human drama in Egyptian history – the exodus of the monotheists.

Notes
1. Carole Beckwith, *Les Massaïs, Tepilit Ole Saitoti*. Le Chêne, 1980, p. 29.
2. *Ibid.*, p. 20.
3. *Les lettres d'El Amarna, EA 95*. Le Cerf, 1987, pp. 127, 131.
4. Pierre Grandet and Bernard Mathieu, *Cours d'égyptien hiéroglyphique*. Khéops, 1997, p. 764.
5. Carole Beckwith, *Les Massaïs, Tepilit Ole Saitoti*, p. 20.
6. Christian Jacq, *La tradition primordiale de l'Ancienne Egypte, selon les textes des pyramides*. Grasset & Fasquelle, 1998, p. 162.

CHAPTER 20

☥

The Pharaoh of Peace

The pharaoh of the Bible is called only "the pharaoh who had not known Joseph." The first words of this pharaoh merit close attention:

> *He said to his people: "Behold! The people of the Children of Israel are more numerous and stronger than we are. Come, let us strive against them, for fear that they will multiply more, and if war should come, they would join our enemies and fight us, and they would leave the land." (Aramaic Bible, Exodus 1:9)*

According to Rashi, Pharaoh feared being driven out of Egypt himself. Pharaoh, in the situation of being in a minority, wanted to preserve himself and his people from an exodus. The expression "they would leave the land," *veala min aarets,* was translated by the sages of the Jewish Midrash as "we will leave Aretz." This meant we, the minority, the marginal ones, the monotheists, will be driven out of Akhet-Aten. Consequently, Pharaoh warned his subjects, the inhabitants of Akhet-Aten, about the growth of power of another people of the empire, designated in the Bible as "the Children of Israel" (the sons of the god Re).

The majority of the rest of Amunian Egypt were governed by the Divine Father Ay. These Children of Israel were disturbed by the intentions of Pharaoh and the monotheists. The interpretation of the end of the verse above shows that Amunian Egypt began to ally itself with Pharaoh's enemies. The people outside the sacred city were favorably disposed toward the polytheist armies of Ay. Archeological studies show that Pharaoh Smenkhkare, caught in a trap, searched out a compromise with Ay and Amunian Egypt.

"The servants of Pharaoh said to him, 'How many times will he [Moses] be a trap to us? Let these people go, that they may serve Adon-Ay their God. Do you not yet know that Egypt is lost?'" (Aramaic Bible, Exodus 10:7).

♀ ♀ ♀

The many similarities between the Bible, the oral tradition, the commentaries of the sages, and Egyptian history, testify to the existence of a first Hebrew Torah, now lost. It revealed the history of the Yahuds. The Yahuds, so as not to lose the memory of their past, wrote down in their sacred book the tale of the exodus from Egypt as they had lived it in the latter days of Akhet-Aten. Modified from century to century, depending on the dominant kings and gods, the Torah became progressively a Mesopotamian history of the Hebrews.

There were those who complained about this practice: "How can you say, 'We are sages and the Torah of Yahwe is with us?' Yes, but the false pen of the scribes has made a lie of it!" (Jeremiah 8:8).

The original Torah was the history of ancient Egypt, reported by the Yahuds.

Relying on the writings in the Theban tomb of Pauah, a priest of Amun and a contemporary of Smenkhkare, Philipp Vandenberg describes that Smenkhkare began to have a temple built in honor of Amun. "It is possible, also, that the pharaoh [Smenkhkare] had recognized how difficult it was to convert the Egyptian people to a single, unique god. They had been offering sacrifices to their local gods for thousands of years."[1]

Smenkhkare, wanting to perpetuate the monotheistic tradition, was opposed to the departure of the Yahud priests. He ardently searched for a compromise with Amunian Egypt. For that reason, he left his capital, Akhet-Aten, where he lived in security. He made himself vulnerable by going to Thebes, a fiefdom of the Divine Father Ay. Smenkhkare was unaware of the ambitions of the Divine Father and of his "nephews," Generals Horemheb (Aaron) and Ramesses (Moses). Outside Akhet-Aten, political power had for a long time belonged to the family of the Divine Father Ay.

In the Book of Exodus, Pharaoh refuses to let the Yahud priests go, in spite of nine plagues, which symbolize the catastrophic state of Amunian

Egypt left behind by Akhenaten. This situation is described in the Stela of the Return. The tenth plague, which relates to the death of Smenkhkare, the firstborn of Akhenaten, reveals the existence of the plot that was brewing.

Scholars concluded that the journey to Thebes was a sign of appeasement for all the Egyptian people. In the Bible, Pharaoh undertook to regain national cohesion by great construction projects. Amenhotep III is reported to have said, "It is my heart that has inspired me to execute work projects with the best men of my army."[2] Pharaoh's words here sound like the order the Biblical pharaoh gave to Moses and Aaron, telling them to continue the work projects: "Pharaoh said to them, 'Why did you lay the people off from their work? Get back to work!'" (Exodus 5:4).

Egyptologists discovered in Tutankhamun's tomb some headbands that came from Smenkhkare's tomb, from which Smenkhkare's name had been scraped off. Christiane Desroches Noblecourt writes: "Several specialists agree in thinking that his [Smenkhkare's] sepulcher was, a few years later, pillaged by Ay, to Tutankhamun's benefit."[3]

According to Pierre Grandet, Smenkhkare and Tutankhamun were pressured to return to the ancient polytheistic religion,[4] and Howard Carter was intrigued by the subject also: "It appears that the return of Tutankhamun to the old faith was not entirely dictated by conviction."[5]

Since Tutankhamun was around eight years old at this time, it is certain that the intrigue to seize power related to the return of Amunian orthodoxy, could only have been fomented by Ay and his family.

Smenkhkare's cartouche always carries the name of Aten, even though the compromise with Amun had already been concluded. After Akhenaten's death conflict erupted between his successor Smenkhkare and the Divine Father Ay. This conflict was described in the Book of Exodus. The compromise is attested to by Tutankhamun's mummy, which displays the principal symbols of both the Amunian and Atenian religions.

"A new king arose over Egypt, one who did not know Joseph" (Exodus 1:8). Rashi's commentary, as brief as it is surprising, is nonetheless evocative of historical memories. "He pretended he did not know him." Tradition affirms that Joseph was still living in this pharaoh's time, which does suggest that there was conflict between Joseph and Pharaoh.

When the new pharaoh came to the throne, Ay was still considered to be a servant and not a divine being superior to pharaoh. Historically, the deified Ay corresponded with Smenkhkare by way of intermediaries: Generals Horemheb and Ramesses. The conflict broke out when Pharaoh refused to recognize Ay as a divinity of Egypt: "But Pharaoh said, 'Who is Ay that I should be obedient to his voice and send Israel away? I do not know Ay at all. Moreover, I will not let Israel go.' They answered, 'The god of the Yahuds is manifested in us'" (Aramaic Bible, Exodus 5:2).

According to the Aramaic Bible, Moses and Aaron were letting Pharaoh know that Ay was the god of the Yahuds, publicly disavowing the authority of the king of Egypt. After this disavowal, Pharaoh let Moses and Aaron leave again. Why didn't the king of Egypt react to that humiliation?

Did Smenkhkare fall into a trap by going to Thebes?

♀ ♀ ♀

"Moses said to him [Pharaoh], 'As soon as I leave the city I will extend my hands towards Ay. The thunder will cease and there will be no more hail, that thou mightst know that the land [*Aretz* = Akhet] belongs to Ay'" (Aramaic Bible, Exodus 9:29).

Ay ordered Moses and Aaron to claim possession of *Aretz* (Akhet). In which city were the negotiations taking place? Was it in Akhet-Aten or in Thebes? Here is Rashi's commentary: "As soon as I have left the city (Exodus 9:29) … And why was the word of God [to Moses] not given inside of the city? Because the city was full of idols."

Only Thebes, the ancient polytheistic capital of the kingdom, fits in with historic reality. The Theban city had been Ay's fiefdom for a long time, and nothing could stop him from pressuring Smenkhkare to yield and adhere to his cause. Rashi (Exodus 8:17) emphasizes "The Hagada gives a reason for each plague, why there was this one and why another. God attacked them following the tactical plan of a king laying siege to a city. First, destroy the water sources. Then sound the trumpets with loud blasts to frighten them and sow terror."

According to different commentaries, it is probable that, historically, the army of the Divine Father Ay laid siege to Thebes, exercising blackmail and intimidation against Smenkhkare, keeping him hostage. Smenkhkare was unable to act in any way against the generals.

In taking the initiative of going to Thebes, Smenkhkare was an heroic pharaoh, animated by the desire for a permanent peace between Aten and

Amun. It would be beneficial for the people of Akhet-Aten as well as for the rest of Egypt.

The sarcophagus in Tomb Number 55 containing Smenkhkare's mummy has the following inscription at the level of his feet. It is addressed to Akhenaten:

> *Words spoken by [name chiseled out]. May I breathe the sweet breath which comes from thy mouth, may I see thy beauty every day. My wish is to hear thy sweet voice, like the breeze, and that my members might be regenerated to life, thanks to my love for thee. Would that thou shouldst extend towards me thy arms bearing thy spiritual strength, that I might receive it and that I might live therein. Would that thou couldst call me by my name forever and ever! ... Thou who art ... Living eternally, as the solar disk ... The king of Upper and Lower Egypt, living in justice, the master of the two lands ... Thou, the perfect child of Aten, who shalt live eternally.*

Misled several times by the words of Aaron and Moses, Smenkhkare perceived too late the trap into which he had fallen. Moses and Aaron addressed Pharaoh:

> *"It is three days journey in the desert that we wish to go, and we will sacrifice to Adon-Ay our God, as he has commanded us." Pharaoh said, "I shall let you go to sacrifice to Adon-Ay your God in the desert. But be careful not to go too far away. Intercede for me." (Aramaic Bible, Exodus 8:23)*

Why did Moses and Aaron hide the truth from Pharaoh? Why didn't they declare that they were accompanying the people to Canaan?

Pharaoh knew the anarchic situation in the Canaanite territories (testified to by the Amarna Letters). He would not have allowed himself to be duped by Moses and Aaron, who gave the pretext of a sacrifice three days' march away. In Thebes, which was under siege, it was impossible for Smenkhkare to send an emissary to warn his army in Akhet-Aten. That's how the strands of the intrigue and the coup d'état fomented by Ay came together, followed by the exodus of the monotheist population.

The image of the evil pharaoh is contradicted by a verse where he accepts the departure of the Children of Israel, but refuses to let the women and children leave:

> *He [Pharaoh] replied, "May Adon-Ay be with you if I let you go, you and your children. Look how evil* [raha] *is before you [= against you]! It will not be thus! … Go then, you men, and serve Adon-Ay, since you desire to go there." And they were driven away from Pharaoh's presence. (Aramaic Bible, Exodus 10:10)*

The verse employs the word *neged*, which means either "with" or "against." Pharaoh is saying that *"raha* is against you." Smenkhkare was opposed to the exodus, predicting a catastrophe. Rashi's commentary confirms that the pharaoh of the Biblical Exodus fought desperately to avoid just such an outcome:

> *Behold how evil is before us. To translate it like the Targum: The evil that you intended to do comes back against you. Here is an interpretation of the Hagada: There is a star that bears the name of* ra'ha *(evil). Pharaoh said to them, "I study astrology and I see this star approaching to meet you in the desert. It announces blood and slaughter."*

Smenkhkare's prediction was realized in the desert, but also within the Egyptian empire, in which a slow and irreversible decline began with the Amarnian heresy. The decline continued for centuries. By refusing a compromise with Aten, Ay had broken the eternal alliance between Egypt and its priests. During the Babylonian exile, the empire collapsed, dragging down in its fall the Kingdom of Judah, the province of the Yahuds, worshipers of Pharaoh. The last Yahud survivors melted into the *Erev-rav* and were called the Hebrews, preserving through the Biblical tradition the essence of the Egyptian religion.

☥ ☥ ☥

The Holy of Holies of Tutankhamun's tomb comprises three containers that cover the red granite sarcophagus enclosing the royal casket, layered within each other. The first two were in gold-covered wood, while the

184 Secrets of the Exodus

third was made of solid gold. Nine centuries before the discovery of the tomb, Rashi[6] gives particulars about the Ark of the Covenant, which only an oral tradition based in the depths of the ages and jealously conserved by the people who went out of Egypt could reveal:

> In the interior and on the exterior wilt thou cover it. Betsalel[7] had made three chests. Two in gold and one in wood, each one having the four walls and the base, but open above. Then he placed the wooden chest inside the golden one, then the other golden chest inside the wooden one, and he covered the top with gold. The result was that the Ark was covered inside and outside.

The description compares with Tutankhamun's sarcophagus. The Hebrew word *Aron* used in the Bible (Exodus 25:10) is the same as the word for coffin in the stories of Jacob and Joseph (Genesis 50:26). Was the Ark of the Covenant a sarcophagus?

On the lid of each of the three caskets of Tutankhamun were carved two large wings directed towards his head. On the lid of the last sarcophagus, in solid gold, there are two angels, facing each other, wings deployed above and below, like the two angels of the Ark of the Covenant.

After having taken the mummy out of the golden sarcophagus, the archeologists delicately removed the cloth strips to extricate from the young king's body the many precious objects, knives, amulets, golden collars and the golden pectoral. The left forearm of the mummy wore six golden bracelets, with a single one at the biceps[8] and two rings on the left hand; one on the middle finger and the other on the ring finger. The bracelets and rings placed in this way correspond to the position of the phylacteries or *tefillin*[9] of the Hebrew tradition, encircling the left forearm and the two fingers of the hand.

The golden headband[10] on Pharaoh's head displays the uraeus on the front, the vulture and serpent, insignia of Upper and Lower Egypt. It ends by two straps falling on the back of the neck. It evokes both the "*tefillin* of the head," and the phylacteries, formed of a case bearing the divine name,[11] a frontal band and two straps.

"Thou shalt attach [the sacred words] as a symbol on thy arm, and thou shalt wear them on thy forehead between thy eyes" (Deuteronomy 6:8).

In a letter addressed to Akhenaten, the King of Tyre, Abimalich, informs him that he *wears* him on his forehead between his eyes.

> *When the king, my Lord, saith, "Be ready before the arrival of a great army," then the servant says to his Lord, "ia-a-ia-a [Yah, the same name of God as in the Bible], in my forehead and in my back I wear the word of the king." (EA 147)*

The head of Tutankhamun's mummy, wearing a skullcap adorned with golden seals engraved with the name of Aten, seems to be the ancestor of the *kippa* worn by practicing Jews.

The ornaments of Egyptian royalty, worn by Tutankhamun, Pharaoh of Egypt, and the symbols of Biblical monotheism: the *tefillin*, the *kippa*, and the *tallith*, are analogous.

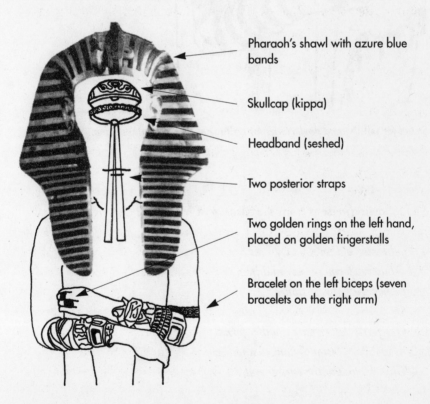

Pharaoh's shawl with azure blue bands

Skullcap (kippa)

Headband (seshed)

Two posterior straps

Two golden rings on the left hand, placed on golden fingerstalls

Bracelet on the left biceps (seven bracelets on the right arm)

Representation of Tutankhamun's mummy. By removing the "pictures of the gods," the principal symbols of the Hebrew religion appear.

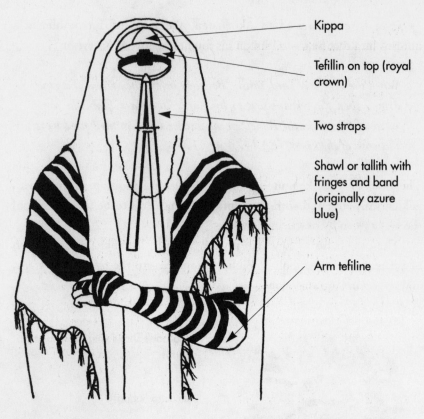

Kippa

Tefillin on top (royal crown)

Two straps

Shawl or tallith with fringes and band (originally azure blue)

Arm tefiline

Shawl (or tallith*) and phylacteries (or* tefillin*) of the Hebrew tradition.*

♀ ♀ ♀

The following verse is from the wisdom of Merykare:

> *Venerate God on thy way,*
> *Whatever form he may manifest,*
> *Be he made of rare stones*
> *Or incarnated in a copper statue,*
> *One form will replace another form,*
> *As one inundation followeth another.*
> *Give thy love to the entire land.*[12]

Notes

1. Philipp Vandenberg, *Nefertiti*. Pierre Belfond, 1987, p. 258.
2. *Ibid.*, p. 87.
3. Christiane Desroches Noblecourt, *Vie et mort d'un Pharaon*. Hachette, 1963, p. 220.
4. Pierre Grandet, *Hymnes de la religion d'Aton*. Le Seuil, 1995, p. 63.
5. Howard Carter, *The Tomb of Tutankhamun*. Pygmalion, 1978, p. 86.
6. Rashi, *The Pentateuch according to Rashi, Exodus*. Samuel and Odette Lévy, 1990.
7. One responsible for artistic works.
8. Christiane Desroches Noblecourt, *Vie et mort d'un pharaoh*, p. 232. The bracelet was a golden band placed just above his elbow.
9. In the Hebrew tradition, for morning prayers the faithful wear (every day except Saturday) leather straps around their left arm (phylacteries in Greek), *tefillin* in Hebrew. This cultural ornament surrounds at the level of the biceps, and continues with seven twists around the forearm. The strap ends by tightly hugging the palm of the hand, then one or two fingers: the middle and the ring. The phylactery or *tefiline* of the head circles the head and divides into two straps, which fall to the back of the neck. The two containers located in front of the head and against the biceps contain the sacred words. The ritual of the embalmers requires that the right hand wear the golden finger ornament and the fist hold gold: "Then thou embalmest thy God. Submerge his left hand so that the fist is in the oil … Place a golden ring on his fingers, and put the gold in his fist." Philipp Vandenberg, *Nefertiti*, p. 141.
10. Called *seshed* in Egyptian. Christiane Desroches-Noblecourt, CD Rom *Tutankhamon*. Syrinx, 1997.
11. Scholars of the Hebrew tradition wear two containers instead of one. Two signs (*Tot* in Hebrew); Rashi explains that *Tot* means "two" in Coptic.
12. Translated by Christian Jacq, *La sagesse vivante de l'Ancienne Egypte*. Robert Laffont, 1998, p. 41.

☥ ☥ ☥

The preceding chapters are a narrative description of the thesis that the Biblical Book of Exodus is derived from the historical events that occurred in the Eighteenth Dynasty of ancient Egypt.

The remaining chapters explore in detail the linguistic and cultural evidence of the relationship between the Biblical and the historical records.

☥ ☥ ☥

☥

CHAPTER 21

Hebrew Writing: An Alphabet of Hieroglyphic Origin

Hieroglyphic texts generally read from right to left, like Hebrew texts. No vowels exist in either language. In Hebrew, no sacred text is permitted to contain vowels; only the oral Hebraic tradition, through memory of the language, allows their introduction among the consonants as you read.

It is the same situation for hieroglyphic texts. Vowels were introduced by Egyptologists in order to facilitate pronunciation and comprehension. Champollion hardly ever placed vowels in his transcriptions[1] due to his concern for honesty and probably in order to leave a bit of mystery intact. Thus, the true language of the ancient Egyptians can never be discovered because their oral tradition has disappeared. The purely conventional translation has to be different from the actual pronunciation of the pharaohs.

Today's pronunciation of the hieroglyphs uses a number of analogies to Coptic, Greek and Latin (particularly for the names of the Egyptian gods). However, a "Hebrew-Hieroglyphic" analogy has never before been detailed.

If one believes that the Hebrews inhabited Egypt for a period of 430 years, as the texts indicate, it is inconceivable for their language not to hold affinities with that of the pharaohs. The similarities, correspondences, and analogies between the two languages are in fact numerous, and quite often flagrant: the common words, the articles, the prepositions, the grammatical formulas, the prefixes and suffixes, the proper names, the numbers, the names of kings, gods, etc. We have to remember that the longest period of Biblical history took place in ancient Egypt, during the age of the New Kingdom – Pharaoh is an important actor in the Bible, even if his name is never divulged. Considering the number of references to Egypt, the Bible should be considered a work of Egyptology. Consequently, it would be useful to take advantage of the numerous cases of ancient Semitic pronunciation (Arabic-Hebrew) of at least two thousand years ago, and compare them with current pronunciation.

A comparative study of Hebrew letters and hieroglyphic characters confirms that the people who left Egypt during the Exodus were inculcated with Canaanite and Phoenician culture. The people of the Exodus returned to the principle of an alphabet, which simplified the immense problem of writing, while still conserving the sacred character of the hieroglyphic form. The Phoenician alphabet comprises 22 letters, while hieroglyphic writing has around three thousand characters. It took ten years of study to learn hieroglyphics, while a few weeks were enough to learn to read and write the Phoenician alphabet.

♀ ♀ ♀

After making comparisons between the Hebrew and Phoenician alphabets, researchers hastily concluded that Hebrew writing was derived directly from Phoenician. But, while it is certain that the number of letters (22) is the same for each of the alphabets,[2] it is difficult to perceive a similarity of forms between them, other than to a very limited degree, as the following table shows:

א	Aleph = mute vowel	&#10230;	K
ב	Beth = B or V	&#10230;	ঽ
ג	Gimel = G	&#10230;	∧
ד	Daleth = D	&#10230;	△
ה	Heh = expirated H	&#10230;	⅂
ו	Vav = V or vowels u or o	&#10230;	Y
ז	Zain = Z	&#10230;	I
ח	Het = aspirated H	&#10230;	𝐁
ט	Tet = T	&#10230;	⊗

Hebrew	Name		Symbol
׳	Yod = Y	⟶	𐤉
כ ך	Khaf = K or Kh	⟶	𐤊
ל	Lamed = L	⟶	𐤋
מ ם	Mem = M	⟶	𐤌
ס	Samekh = S	⟶	𐤎
ע	Ayin = guttural H	⟶	O
פ ף	Peh or Feh = P or F	⟶	𐤐
צ ץ	Tsadel = Ts	⟶	𐤑
ק	Kof = K	⟶	φ
ר	Resh = R	⟶	𐤓
ש	Shin = Sh or Sin = S	⟶	W
ת	Tav = T	⟶	X
נ ן	Nun = N	⟶	𐤍

An evolutionary theory that states that during the "archaic" period of Phoenician writing, the letters developed, bit by bit, into Hebrew, has never really been proven. The Phoenician symbols and the Hebrew have only a very limited correspondence.[3]

On the other hand, the evidence of direct analogy between Hebrew letters and hieroglyphs shows in their phonology, their form, and often in the symbolic value associated with Egyptian numbers, divinities, and beliefs. Each of these analogies is important and reveals direct relations between the people called "the Hebrews" and the civilization of ancient Egypt.

Hebrew writing is an adaptation of Egyptian writing. It is an "Hebraic-hieroglyphic" alphabet, in which certain letters were never transformed from their true hieroglyphs.

The Hebrew Alphabet and Egyptian Hieroglyphs

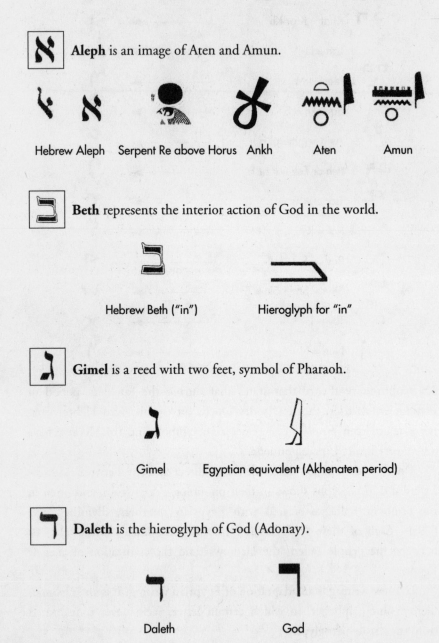

Aleph is an image of Aten and Amun.

Hebrew Aleph   Serpent Re above Horus   Ankh   Aten   Amun

Beth represents the interior action of God in the world.

Hebrew Beth ("in")   Hieroglyph for "in"

Gimel is a reed with two feet, symbol of Pharaoh.

Gimel   Egyptian equivalent (Akhenaten period)

Daleth is the hieroglyph of God (Adonay).

Daleth   God

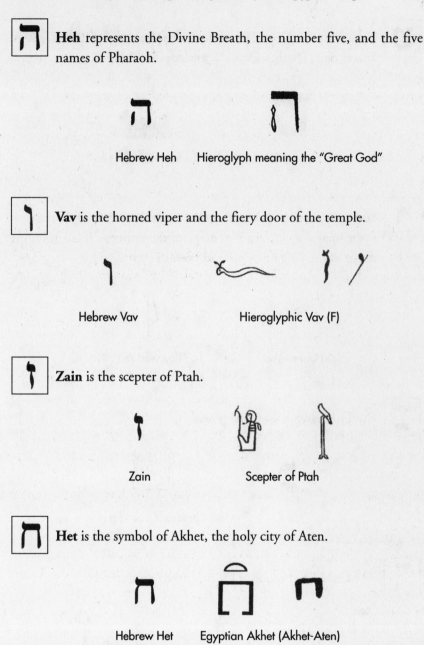

Heh represents the Divine Breath, the number five, and the five names of Pharaoh.

Hebrew Heh   Hieroglyph meaning the "Great God"

Vav is the horned viper and the fiery door of the temple.

Hebrew Vav   Hieroglyphic Vav (F)

Zain is the scepter of Ptah.

Zain   Scepter of Ptah

Het is the symbol of Akhet, the holy city of Aten.

Hebrew Het   Egyptian Akhet (Akhet-Aten)

Tet is the sacred ibis. The white bird is the image of Thoth, god of knowledge (Thoth = Daat = knowledge in Hebrew).

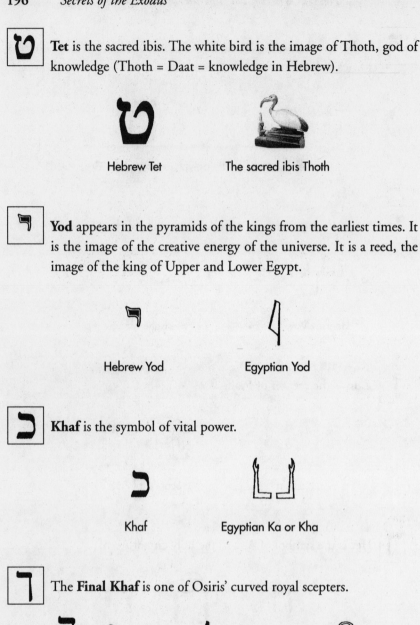

Hebrew Tet   The sacred ibis Thoth

Yod appears in the pyramids of the kings from the earliest times. It is the image of the creative energy of the universe. It is a reed, the image of the king of Upper and Lower Egypt.

Hebrew Yod   Egyptian Yod

Khaf is the symbol of vital power.

Khaf   Egyptian Ka or Kha

The **Final Khaf** is one of Osiris' curved royal scepters.

Hebrew final Khaf   Cursive final Khaf   Pharaoh's scepter "Heka"

Lamed is the uraeus and the headband of Pharaoh.

Lamed   Egyptian "L"

Mem is a vulture, the goddess Mut, Amun's wife.

Hebrew Mem   Egyptian "M" – Mouth

Nun is the primordial ocean or birthplace of the gods.

Nun   Final Nun   Egyptian "N"   Nun

Samekh is a serpent, the cycle of day and night.

Samekh   "S" symbol

Ayin is the image of Ptah holding his scepter.

Hebrew Ayin

Ptah

 Peh is the mouth of Ptah, where the sacred word emerges.

Hebrew Peh   Egyptian Ptah   Egyptian Peh

 Tsadeh is the image of Akhenaten kneeling or standing in prayer.

Hebrew Tsadeh   Akhenaten praying before Aten   Egyptian Tsadeh

 Qof (Kof) is the primordial serpent, an image of God.

Kof   Egyptian "K"

Resh, like Daleth, is the sign of God. It is a caricature of Re, the sun, from whom life on earth emanates.

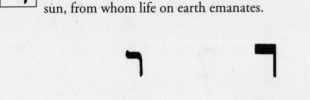

Resh   Egyptian God

Shin is the field of reeds, linked to the creation of trees and plants.

Hebrew Shin   Egyptian Shin   Shin from the   Three Shins in the
                                Habakkuk Papyrus   Hymn to Aton
                                (Dead Sea Scrolls)   (Tomb of Ay)

Tav is the image of Hathor, the cow that nourishes Egypt.

Hebrew Tav   Hieroglyphic Tav   Hieratic Tav   Sign of Hathor

Notes

1. Christian Jacq, *Grammaire égyptienne de Champollion*. Solin, 1997.
2. *L'aventure des écritures, Naissances*. Bibliothèque nationale de France, 1997, pp. 90–5.
3. See the Dead Sea papyrus containing the tetragram Yahwe in archaic letters; Miller Burrows, *The Dead Sea Scrolls*. Robert Laffont, 1973, p. 256.

CHAPTER 22

Letters and Hieroglyphs

The Mystery of the Aleph א

Aleph is the most enigmatic letter of the Hebrew alphabet. It has contained a secret for more than three thousand years.

According to linguists, the Hebrew *Aleph* represents the head of a bull, the first letter of the Phoenician alphabet. However, when the Dead Sea Scrolls are examined, the Hebrew *Aleph* seems more like a combination of hieroglyphic signs:

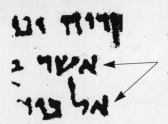

The ancient א is composed of three parts: the upper right flag in the form of a *Yod* י, the oblique bar, and the rounded left foot.

The hieroglyphs were transcribed into hieratic writing, "which permitted rapid writing on papyrus or shell with brush and ink … a writing with many abbreviated marks which can be traced in a single sweep of a brush."[1]

It is mainly in the hieratic writing used in the Eighteenth Dynasty, in the time of Akhenaten, that the correspondence between Egyptian and Hebraic writing should be researched. The similarity between the two forms of writing – the Hebrew square manuscript and Egyptian writing – is evident.

The *Aleph* logically corresponds to the hieratic union of the four hiero-glyphic signs forming the word Aten:

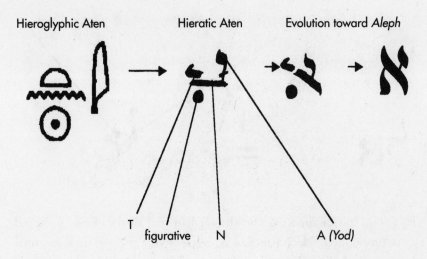

Hieroglyphic Aten   Hieratic Aten   Evolution toward *Aleph*

T   figurative   N   A *(Yod)*

In the Hebrew tradition, Aleph *represents divine unity (numerical value = 1).* Yod *represents the return to unity (value = 10), as in the numerology of the Pyramid Texts.²*

In order to represent the name of their god Aten, the Yahuds who fled Egypt fashioned the *Aleph* in Aten's image, giving it the first place in the Hebrew alphabet. They created a symbol of divine unity, with the numerical value of one. Its form, with its solid base, gives it those attributes of power and stability that are found in Akhenaten and Aten. Note the commentary of Fabre d'Olivet concerning the *Aleph:*

> *As a symbolic image, it (the* Aleph*) represents universal man, the human race. The dominant being of the earth [Akhenaten = Aten]. In its hieroglyphic sense, it characterizes unity, the central point, the abstract principle of one thing [Re, the Sun God]. Employed as a sign, it expresses power, stability, continuity.³*

The lower part of the *Aleph* is generally rounded, forming a foot.

In some verses of the Hebrew Bible (Exodus 16:2) and the Aramaic one (Genesis 14:18), the *Aleph*, lacking its base, reads as "El," meaning God. For example, the word "Israel" is normally written ישׂראל. But it can also be written in the following manner (Exodus 7:2): ישׂרﭏ.

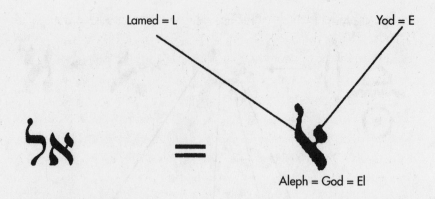

The *Lamed* has disappeared and the median part of the *Aleph*, stretched up, is pronounced "L." The *Yod* above is read "E" – giving the final pronunciation "El." This phenomenon, frequent in the Hebrew and Aramaic Bibles, shows that the Hebrew *Yod* has several values of pronunciation, as was true for the Egyptian Yod, according to Champollion's table.[4] The illustration below is from the temple of Kalbasha in Upper Egypt, where the tail of the serpent takes the form of the *Aleph* at the interior of the Re circle. Thus, the *Aleph* is the figure of Re.

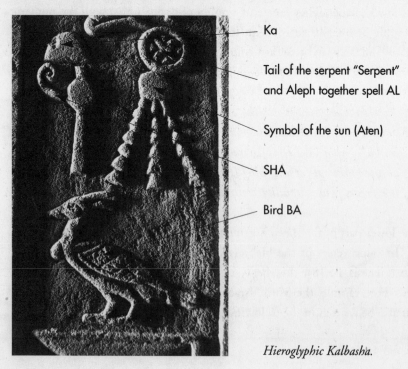

Hieroglyphic Kalbasha.

Additionally, the Hebrew "El" **אל**, like the Aramaic (Chaldean) "Elah" **אלה**, contains the *Aleph* **א**, the sign of Aten, and the *Lamed* **ל**, representing the uraeus or sacred asp, and the headband of Pharaoh.

Aleph = Re = El

The Samaritans followed a religion nearly identical to that of the Hebrews. Their writing consisted of 22 letters of Phoenician origin, and the Samaritan *Aleph* has a form similar to the Hebrew *Aleph* – except that it carries two *Yod*s instead of one, recalling the name of Ay, the word for God in the Aramaic Bible:

 Samaritan Aleph *with its two* Yods = *Unity* = *Adon-Ay.*

These similarities provide evidence that words of the ancient Egyptian language have affinities with numerous Hebrew words, both in sense and in pronunciation. Such words presage the Hebrew language, despite the tendency of time to make changes. This concept would support the idea of a hidden hieroglyphic language that has concealed the true history behind Biblical legend.

Fabre d'Olivet has made this a principal theme in his book *La langue hébraïque restituée*: Hebrew writing gives direct proof of its basic Egyptian origin, thus opening up a whole new approach to understanding the historical reality that was dissimulated in the Biblical story. This hieratic writing is both the language of the Bible and the language of the Biblical pharaohs. Consequently, it is necessary to look again at the sacred texts and explain them in the light of archeological discoveries associated with the history of ancient Egypt.

♀ ♀ ♀

The *Aleph* and Ankh

The true origin of the *Aleph* relates to the Ankh. Aten offers the breath of life to Akhenaten in the oblique position of the *Aleph*. Aten's hand is symbolized by the *Yod* (*Yad* in Hebrew means hand). The oblique bar and the foot of the *Aleph* correspond exactly to the hieratic form of the Ankh, formed from the *Nun* and the *Okh*.

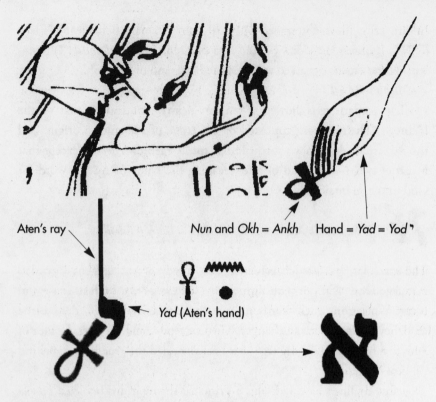

Aten's ray

Nun and *Okh* = *Ankh*   Hand = *Yad* = *Yod* י

← *Yad* (Aten's hand)

A hand, Yad, *borne by Aten's ray, is the breath of life, and the origin of* Aleph.

The *Aleph* and Amun

The form of the *Aleph* also evokes the hieroglyph "Amun" when it is accompanied by the sun Re, present in most of the names of the pharaohs. The Hebrew words *Adon* אדן and *Amun* אמן both begin with an *Aleph*. The *Daleth* ד has the form of the hieroglyph "only one God,"[5] and the *Mem* מ represents the goddess Mut, Amun's wife, mother of the gods. Both of these words ends with a *Nun*, a sign also present in Aten. The *Nun* is the primordial ocean where divinities and Egypt's pharaohs were born. The *Aleph* thus symbolizes Amun, the Multiple God, or Aten, the One God.

Amun-Re   Aleph   El

In this case, El would signify Amun-Re. The Hebrew *Lamed* ל is the figure of the uraeus of the god. In Egyptian, L and R are the same letters. This Hebraic-hieroglyphic rapprochement allows us to discern through the symbols inscribed in the cartouches of certain pharaohs, the Biblical Hebrew names of Abraham, Aaron, and Moses, and thus discover the true identity of the Hebrew patriarchs.

☥ ☥ ☥

Beth ב

The letter *Beth* has not been transformed from its Egyptian homologue. Its form is identical in ancient Egyptian and Hebrew. Its perfect analogy is found in the double cartouche of Aten, in which it figures four times, after the Re sign (shown six times). These two signs express the preposition "in," and, by extension, "inside," "within," "of."

For Fabre d'Olivet, the *Beth* is the hieroglyph of interior action. The *Beth* accompanied by *Aleph* בא (*Ba*), is a symbol of power, an image of continuity at the root of the verb "to come," or "to come to a central point." The Egyptian *Ba* evokes life after death, the departure of the soul toward the other world in the form of "the *Ba* bird," which the Hebrews call the *Olam Aba* העולם הבא – the world to come.

Hieroglyph "in" (M). Agreement in form and grammatical function.[6]

There is another analogy with the letter *Beth*: the first letter of the first verse of the Bible concerns the creation of the world, "In the beginning [*bereshit* בראשית] the Elohim created the heavens and the earth." The *Beth* is a sign binding the heavens and the earth.

Hieroglyph of heaven and earth.   *Hebrew* Beth.

As the Egyptian symbol defines and as it shows in its form, the squared *Beth* ב can represent the elements of creation separated by divine will.

The hieroglyph represents the sacred land, Akhet-Aten, inundated by divine light. The similarity to the Hebrew word *Aretz* אֶרֶץ brings out the Hebrew root *Or* אֹר, the first word of God in the Bible,[7] and equivalent to the Egyptian root *Akh*, also meaning light.[8] The last letter, the *Tsadeh* צ, evokes Akhenaten standing, glorifying the sun, a form equivalent to the hieroglyph *Ts*.

All this gives us, in Egyptian, *Hay-me-Aket*: he who rejoices in the sacred land.[9]

In Hebrew, this is *Hai-Ba-Aretz* חִי בָּאֶרֶץ: he who lives in the sacred land.

☥ ☥ ☥

Gimel ג

The *Gimel*, making the sound of hard "G," is not directly affiliated with an Egyptian god. However, there is a hieroglyphic symbol approaching it that appears in Aten's name. In his cartouche there is a symbol pronounced "yi" in the form of a *Yod* provided with two legs. It is used in the expression "he who comes from the light of Aten," or "he who resides in the light of Aten."

In Hebrew, the verb "to reside" or "to inhabit" is *Gar* גָּר. The two letters of this word find their analogy in the expression "who resides" included in Aten's title. The Egyptian symbol expresses the idea of movement, since it employs two legs. It emanates light and dwells within the solar disk. This concept – stemming from the very heart of Egypt and found in The Pyramid Texts – emphasizes that God and man come from the light and go toward the light.[10]

An analogy of form and symbol.

♀ ♀ ♀

Daleth ⁊ and Resh ⁊

The *Daleth* (D) and the *Resh* (R) symbolize Pharaoh's headband in their horizontal elements. The point that appears on the upper left side is an evocation of the royal uraeus or sacred asp, and the downstroke part the tail of the protector serpent. In the most ancient parchments, the uraeus symbol is always evident. The *Resh* ⁊ signifies *rosh* (head), evoking the head of Pharaoh. The hieroglyph corresponding to it represents the divine serpent united with Pharaoh.

The uraeus symbol in the Hebrew letters

Egyptian "D"

The uraeus, an emblem of power and fear, and a fixed part of the band which surrounded Tutankhamun's head (see page 209), terminates with two vertical straps, like the phylacteries of the Hebrews, which are worn to this day: "And this shall be as a sign upon thine arm and as a frontlet (*totaphot)* between thine eyes, because with a strong hand Yahwe brought us out of Egypt" (Exodus 13:16).

In Egyptian, the royal headband is called *Seshed* or *Seshad*, and is written phonetically as S-Sh-D. The hieroglyph *Seshed* transcribes phonetically into Hebrew with three letters *Shin-Shin-Daleth* שֶׁשֶּׁד, visible on the phylacteries or tefillin (when worn on the head) of the Hebrews. On the left side of the case is the *Shin* with four branches, and on the right side, the classical *Shin*. The *Daleth* is represented by the knot at the back of the head.

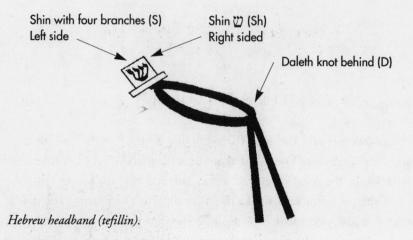

Shin with four branches (S)
Left side

Shin ש (Sh)
Right sided

Daleth knot behind (D)

Hebrew headband (tefillin).

Resh ר is the first letter of the name of Re (or Raha) רע, the king of the gods in ancient Egypt, the supreme principle of creation. That explains why the *Resh* is found in Biblical names like Sarah, Rachel, Abraham, Ruel, Par'oo (Pharaoh), Ytro, Deborah, Rebecca, and in words like *Kapara* (offering), *Barakha* (blessing), etc. As in Egyptian names, it introduces the presence of the god Re.

Hieroglyphic Re   Hieratic[11] Re   Hebrew Resh

The symbolic analogy is described by Fabre d'Olivet:

> *We saw the principal movement acting from the center to the circumference, modify itself bit by bit in light, in fire, in water, in air, in ethereal fluid, according to the roots* אר, רהה, רו, רח, רי: *but, the same movement coming from the root* רו *and degenerating more and more towards the material meaning, to become in the root Re* רע *the emblem of everything terrestrial, opaque, and evil. It is worth noting seriously.* [12]

Hieroglyph for God.

ק ד ר ל ה

The letters Qof, Daleth, Resh, Lamed and Heh contain in their form the hieroglyph for God.

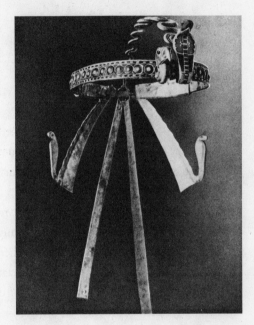

Tutankhamun's headband.

♀ ♀ ♀

Heh ה

The Hebrew *Heh* ה, the fifth letter of the alphabet, is pronounced by breathing from the depth of the throat. Its original meaning is "breath."

In its abstract form the Hebrew ה serves to write the name of God (Hashem), which the faithful are forbidden to utter. Genesis 2:4 reads: "This is the description of the creation of the heavens and the earth. When Yahwe and the Elohim created ..." Rashi comments on the meaning of the ה: "It is with the *Heh* that the heavens and the earth were created," which is to say by the breath of God.

It was the same in ancient Egypt, according to Christian Jacq: "The Texts of the Pyramids affirm in clear fashion the reality of a unique divine power, inaccessible to the human spirit. 'Great God, whose name is unknown …'." [13]

The hieroglyphic sign is graphically identical. Its translation, "the Great God,"[14] is extremely close to the symbolism of the Hebrew "Heh."

Great ————————————— God

Hieroglyph meaning "the Great God," showing the correspondence of form and meaning with the Hebrew Heh.

The *Heh* has a numerical value of five, which corresponds to the five books of the Torah (Old Testament), as well as to the five chapters of "The Great Harris Papyrus."[15] It also recalls the five Great Names of the royal titles of the pharaohs from the time of the New Kingdom.

In the El Amarna Letters from Akhet-Aten, Pharaoh Akhenaten is called "the breath" by his vassals, the Canaanite and the Phoenician kings: "My country and my brothers, servants of the king, my lord, and servants of Tutu, my lord, are delighted when the breath of the king, my lord, arrives." (Extract of a letter from Aziru, Chief of the Amorites, EA 164.)

The *Heh* ⌐⌐, a divine sign, is found in Tutankhamun's tomb:

Hieroglyph meaning "the Great God," identical to the Hebrew Heh, *meaning "the breath of God."*

The sacred writing situated on the east wall of the funerary chamber calls upon the dead king to accede to life eternal. The translation of the three columns of text above is as follows:

Column 1: "O, Nebkeperureh" (Tutankhamun's throne name)
Column 2: "Come in peace"
Column 3: "O, Great God, protector of the earth!"

Twelve priests pulling the cord of the sleigh of King Tutankhamun's mummy.

Below the *Heh* hieroglyph, high dignitaries pull the sleigh of the king. They are the twelve viziers of Upper and Lower Egypt, regional governors. They are distinguished among each other by their tunics and hairstyles. The two viziers with shaved heads are priests; the ten others, noblemen.

These twelve people represent all the provinces of Egypt, and it is a number which one finds again in the Biblical story of the twelve tribes of Israel, composed also of priests and noblemen, and the twelve sons of Jacob transporting the embalmed remains of their father (Genesis 50:12-13).

Rashi's commentary on this is as follows:

> *Jacob had arranged a place for each one, three on the East side and similarly for each of the other sides. Levi [the High Priest] did not need to carry [the sarcophagus] because he was destined to carry the Sacred Ark. Joseph also didn't have to carry because he was king [of Egypt]. In their places, there were Manassus and Ephraim [two sons of Joseph]. (Rashi, Genesis 50:12-13)*

The separation of the twelve bearers of Jacob's sarcophagus into "ten, plus two," mentioned by Rashi, is found in the depiction of the twelve viziers in Tutankhamun's tomb (above). This arrangement can be seen again in the processions of the Ark of Amun, which the king of Egypt and his high priests are involved in carrying.

Twelve priests arranged in four groups of three, bearing the Ark of Amun. Pharaoh and the two central high priests do not carry it, conforming with Rashi's Commentary (From the Temple of Karnak).

From the time of the Old Kingdom, the priests participated in the principal religious ceremonies:

> *It was God they served, everywhere in the North and South, the length of the river, the priests celebrated a morning rite with strict forms which varied hardly at all during all of the Old Kingdom. After a purifying bath in a sacred pond, at dawn, a group of some twelve priests passed through the doors of the temple's enclosure, crossed the open-air court in single file and entered into the actual temple.[16]*

Another hieroglyph closely recalls the Hebrew *Heh* in this form and sound with five sides.

Hieroglyphic "H"[17]   Hebrew *Heh*

It corresponds to the partitive article "of" in the translation of the Egyptian word *Yahudadaha-Malek* discovered by Champollion, and rendered in Hebrew *Yehuda-hamalkhut*.[18] They both mean "the Kingdom of Judah." The *Heh* is also present in the name *Yahu* inscribed on a column of the temple of Amenophis III at Soleb.

Vav ו

The Hebrew letter *Vav* ו, with sounds of "V," "U," and "O," is analogous in form with the hieroglyph representing the horned viper, which conventionally is the sound of "F."

According to Champollion's *Treatise on Grammar*, the third person singular possessive – his, her, its – is represented by the horned viper. In Hebrew as well, the third person singular possessive is represented by the *Vav* ו.

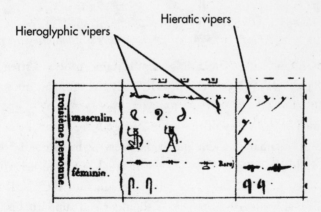

The horned viper is shown standing, like the Hebrew Vav ו.

The Hebrew *Vav* doesn't have the same pronunciation as its corresponding hieroglyph, although they are employed in an identical fashion in both languages. However, according to Fabre d'Olivet, the "V" has the same phonetic value as the "F." Thus *Vav* demonstrates a triple analogy of sound, form, and meaning.

Zain ך

Zain ך recalls the scepter "Uaz" or "Uzer" of the god Ptah, the symbol of creative power and of the divine breath. The hieroglyph represents the letter Z, as does the Hebrew letter *Zain.* The Egyptian Z is found in the Little Hymn to Aten:

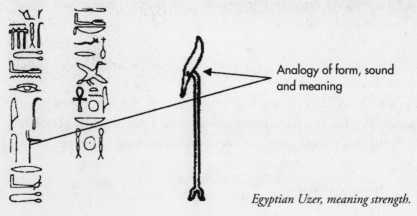

Analogy of form, sound and meaning

Egyptian Uzer, meaning strength.

The Egyptian noun Uzer, "strength," has the same root as "strength" "Ozer" עָזֵר and "Oz" עַז in Hebrew. "He is my strength and my song" (Exodus 15:2).

In the tombs of the Valley of the Kings, the gods represent the ancestors or fathers of the pharaohs. On one of the posts of the tomb of Sety I, the god Ptah holds his scepter "Uaz" facing Pharaoh. On another, Atum symbolizes Ramesses I; the father receiving the son into the Garden of Eternity. Atum places his hand on Sety I's shoulder and supports his arm with the other hand.

> *Moses did as Adon-ay had commanded: He took Joshua and placed him before Eleazar the priest [El-Uzer = Ptah] and all the congregation. He [Moses] placed his hands on him [Joshua] and gave him orders as Adon-ay had said, through the organ [the hand] of Moses. (Numbers 27:22-3)*

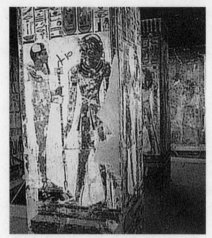

Ptah = El Uzer = Sety I
(God Uzer) = Eleazar

Sety I
Atum

Ptah, facing Sety I, holds the scepter Uaz (from the tomb of Sety I).

Ramesses I (Moses) identified with Atum, welcomes Sety I and places his hands on him (from the tomb of Sety I).

Het 𐤇

The *Het* 𐤇 is pronounced like an over-exaggerated "H," and its corresponding hieroglyph is evident in Champollion's table:

Hieroglyphic *Het* 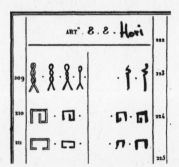 Hieratic (lower case) *Het*

Analogy of sound, form, and meaning: the Hebrew Het *and the hieroglyphic* Het *bear the same name.*

The *Het* ח represents the door of a house or entrance to a temple with its two doorposts and its lintel, just like its Egyptian counterpart.

ያ ያ ያ

Tet ט

Fabre d'Olivet[19] states that there is a connection between the Hebrew letters D and T. Both the name and the form of the *Tet* make one think of the Egyptian Thoth, the god of knowledge and writing, represented by an ibis. The Hebrew *Tet* seen here is certainly a caricature of a fowl.

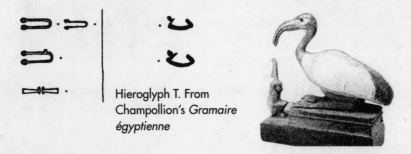

Hieroglyph T. From Champollion's *Gramaire égyptienne*

ט *Hebrew* Tet *compared to the sacred ibis. The ibis represents the god Thoth before the goddess Maat, coiffed with a feather. Note the tail of the ibis pointing up like the Hebrew* Tet.

The Hebrew word knowledge (science) is pronounced *Dahat* דעת, which is phonetically very close to Thoth (*Dahuty*).[20] Thus there is an analogy of name, sound, form, and symbol.

ያ ያ ያ

Yod י

Identical to the Egyptian *Yod* in Tutankhamun's tomb, the Hebrew *Yod* י has the sound "Ye," and can be joined to many vowels (Ya, Yo, Yi ...). It is as frequently used in the Hebrew language as it is in hieroglyphic writing.

Many of the Ancient Egyptian words using the *Yod* are close to the Hebrew, but scholars have always given priority to Greco-Latin sounds, rather than to the sounds of the Semitic languages. Therefore in conventional pronunciation, it is given only the sound "yi." This distorts the language of Ancient Egypt, where it loses meaning in words with yo, yu, and ye, and particularly in ya and ay (the "A" being a majority vowel in Semitic languages). Champollion assimilated the Yod into the letters A, E, Y, AY and EY. For the great Egyptologist, then, the Yod had an understood value, a bit like the Hebrew Aleph.

The *Yod* is the image of the creative faculty, the manifestation of divine power, eternity, etc.[21] Like its hieroglyphic homologue (in Hymns to Aten, for example) it is tied to the concept of God and His creation. Its numerical value, 10, is a symbol both of multiplicity and of unity.

The Hebrew *Yod*, like the Egyptian one, serves to designate the possessive pronouns "mine" and "thine," as well as "my" and "thy."

The Egyptian *Yod* can be written in the opposite direction, still keeping its same meaning.

Hebrew Yod

Fragment of the Psalm of Akhenaten.

Fragment of parchment from the Dead Sea Scrolls.

The illustration above shows a Hebrew *Yod* from a fragment of the Dead Sea Scrolls; the ancient Hebrew writing is very like the Egyptian characters.

♀ ♀ ♀

Kaf (or Khaf) כ ך

The *Kaf* כ, with the sound of "K" or *Khaf*, with the sound of "ch" (as in the Scottish *loch*), is a letter with a double pronunciation. It is called *Kaf* or *Khaf* depending on how the word is read. It looks like a bowl turned on its side. At the end of a word it is called the final *Khaf* ך and has its base elongated downward. The *Kaf*, like all Hebrew letters, has an upward pointing sweep (resembling the uraeus of the king of Egypt). The scepter of Pharaoh – *Kheka* – has a pronunciation that brings to mind the two sounds of the Hebrew *Kaf*.

The scepter *Kheka* of Pharaoh   Hebrew final *Khaf*   Cursive   Final *Khaf*

In Hebrew cursive writing, the *Khaf* is identical to Pharaoh's scepter.

Many Hebrew words symbolizing royalty are written with the final *Khaf* ך. For example *Melekh* מלך, meaning king, *Abrekh* אברך, meaning father of the king, and *Yerekh* ירך, meaning royal lineage.

The Hebrew *Khaf* כ serves as a possessive pronoun designating the second person singular, like the Egyptian "K," which is represented by a kitchen utensil or a plate with a handle. The grammatical correspondences between Hebrew and Egyptian writing constitutes a fundamental base in the concordance of the two languages.

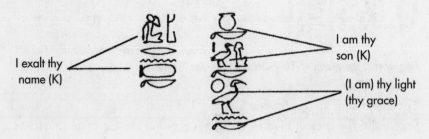

I exalt thy name (K)   I am thy son (K)   (I am) thy light (thy grace)

In this example, "thy light" is *Akhek*, which is very like *Orekha* אוֹר ךְ.

Along the same lines, "I am thy son" – in Egyptian *Anok i shk* [*Anok i shak*] – is close to the Hebrew *Anokhi* (I am), *Ish* (man), *kha* (of thine) [*Anokhi Ishkha*].

The *Kaf* כ is also like the hieroglyph *Kha*, or "vital energy," represented by two arms stretched toward heaven, exalting God.

Hebrew Kaf

Hieroglyphic *Kha* or *Ka*

Analogy of sound, form, and meaning.

Notes

1. Guy Rachet, *Dictionnaire de la civilization Egyptienne*. Larousse Bordas, 1998, p.122.
2. Christian Jacq, *La tradition primordiale de l'Ancienne Egypte selon les textes des Pyramides*. Grasset & Fasquelle, 1998, p. 79.
3. Fabre d'Olivet, *La langue hébraïque restituée*. L'Age d'Homme-Delphica, 1991, p. 7.
4. Christian Jacq, *Grammaire égyptienne de Champollion*. Solin, 1997, p. 35.
5. *Ibid.*, pp. 10 and 115.
6. *Ibid.*, pp. 115, 189, and 210.
7. Christian Jacq, *Nefertiti et Akhénaton*. Perrin, 1996, p. 78.
8. Pierre Grandet, *Hymnes de la religion d'Aton*. Le Seuil, 1995, p. 137. A phonetic translation of the Great Hymn to Aten.
9. *Ibid.*
10. Christian Jacq, *La tradition primordiale de l'Ancienne Egypte*, 1998.
11. *Grammaire égyptienne de Champollion*, p. 173.
12. Fabre d'Olivet, *La langue hébraïque restituée*, p. 123.
13. Christian Jacq, *La tradition primordiale de l'Ancienne Egypte*, p. 98.
14. *Grammaire égyptienne de Champollion*, p. 325.
15. Adolph Erman and Hermann Ranke, *La civilisation égyptienne*. Payot and Rivages, 1994, pp. 380–1.
16. Lionel Casson, *Ancient Egypt, The Great Ages of Man*. Time, 1969, pp. 78–9.
17. *Grammaire égyptienne de Champollion*, p. 45.
18. The "kh" in Hebrew is pronounced like the Spanish Jota "J." When this phonetic sound is applied (for example, to Akhet-Aten), the similarities with Hebrew are intriguing.
19. Fabre d'Olivet, *La langue hébraïque restituée*, p. 55.
20. Pierre Grandet and Bernard Mathieu, *Cours d'Egyptien hiérogliphique*. Khéops, 1997, p. 816
21. Fabre d'Olivet, *La langue hébraïque restituée*, p. 39.

CHAPTER 23

Letter Round-up

Lamed

The *Lamed* ("L" sound) is a slithery letter, like the *Qof* or *Kof* (see page 230). Its form is that of a half raised serpent, ready to bite. This is the uraeus, which writhes in front of Pharaoh's head, protecting him from his enemies.

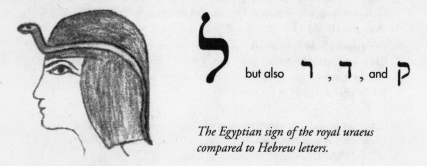

The Egyptian sign of the royal uraeus compared to Hebrew letters.

There are two hieroglyphs similar to the *Lamed*. The first is a serpent in hieratic form (lower case), given by Champollion for the "L" sound. The "mouth" designates the sounds "L" and "R."

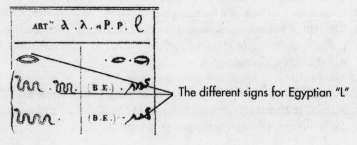

The different signs for Egyptian "L"

The second is a hieroglyph taking the form of the uraeus (serpent) of Pharaoh, and is graphically identical to the *Lamed*:

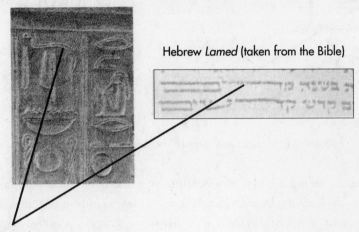

Hebrew *Lamed* (taken from the Bible)

Symbol of the serpent on the left exterior door of the second chapel of the funerary chamber of Tutankhamun.

In the Dead Sea Scrolls, the *Lamed* represents an elongated cobra, upright and swollen at head level.

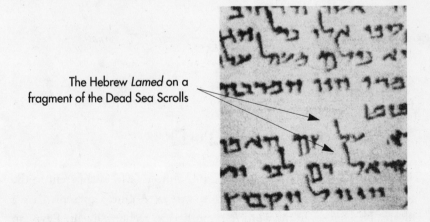

The Hebrew *Lamed* on a fragment of the Dead Sea Scrolls

The serpent, to which convention has given the "D" or "Dj" sound, is found in the expression "forever," which occurs in many religious Egyptian texts. This is *Dataneheh* in Egyptian, and in Hebrew *Lanetsah*.

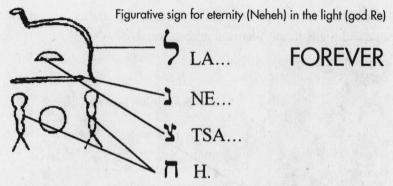

Figurative sign for eternity (Neheh) in the light (god Re)

LA... NE... TSA... H.   FOREVER

Hieroglyph "forever" (Dataneheh) and *"forever" in Hebrew* (Lanetsah).

There again, taking account of a Semitic approach (Arabo-Hebraic), and following the lead of Christian Jacq,[1] the word *Neheh* tends to be translated as "luminous eternity." *Neheh*, like *Netshah*, carries the suffix "Ah," meaning light in Egyptian.

Besides this, the Hebrew *Netsah* (eternal) is close to the Egyptian *Netsher*,[2] which means God. These words are at the root of the Biblical translation for "Eternal."

The god holds in his Hand the Ankh, symbol of eternal life

God in Egyptian: Netsher, equivalent to Hebrew Netsah נצרה *(eternal).*

♀ ♀ ♀

Mem כ or ם

The glyph *Mem* כ or ם (final *Mem*), pronounced "M," is apparent in the hieroglyphic form of the goddess Mut, wife of Amun, represented by a vulture. This figures in the word *Em* (mother) in Hebrew, like its Egyptian homologue *Mut* (mother).

Champollion in his *Treatise on Grammar* gives an insight into the analogy.

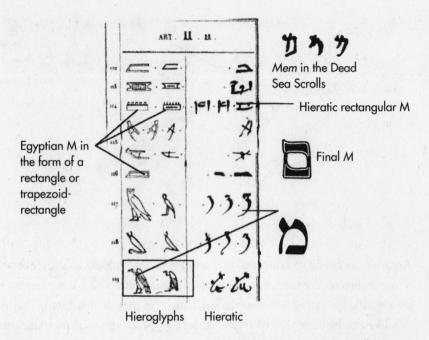

Comparison between the Hebrew "Mem" and the Egyptian "Mem" by analogy in the form of a vulture or owl.

Paleographic studies undertaken on the Dead Sea Scrolls show the evolution of the *Mem*, and let us understand the transformation of the hieroglyphic character and the Hebrew letter, a true caricature of the vulture *Mut*.

Analogy of sound and of form.

The rectangular Egyptian *M* is in the Biblical texts in the form of the final elongated *Mem*.

Hebrew final Mem □
squared or rectangular recalls
the Egyptian M in the Grand
Hymn ▭

Fragment of the Bible in Hebrew.

Another comparison concerns the word "Truth," which sounds out as *Maat* according the conventional pronunciation, and which is represented by a goddess wearing a feather in her hair. The root of this hieroglyph is *Mt*, like the Hebrew word "Truth," *Emet* אמת. In the Biblical tradition, *Emet* is one of the most important words associated with *Amen* – in rapport with truth, justice and faith.

♀ ♀ ♀

The god Aten was called "he who is satisfied by Maat."[3] Because of the importance of this religious concept, employed regularly in the psalms and prayers, the priests of Akhet-Aten suppressed the image of the goddess. They adapted a phoneme for this indispensable word, present in the Great Hymn to Aten.

Here is an example of the analogy between the Great Hymn and a Hebrew prayer recited every day, "*Anokhi Adon-Ay Eloekhem Emet,*" meaning "I am Adon-Ay your God [living in] truth."

Every Hebrew term finds its mate in the Hymn:

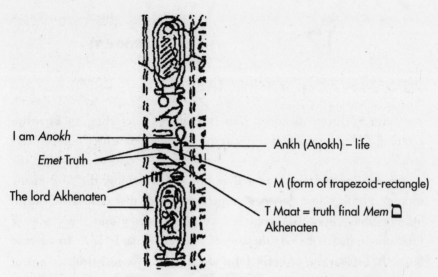

I am *Anokh* — Ankh (Anokh) – life

Emet Truth —

The lord Akhenaten — M (form of trapezoid-rectangle)

T Maat = truth final *Mem* ▢
Akhenaten

"*Nefer-keperu-Re, son of Re, he who lives in truth, the lord of the two crowns, Akhenaten.*" *Third column of the Great Hymn to Aten.* "*Akhenaten, living in truth.*"

The Hebrew *Mem*, in its elongated form, recalls the hieroglyph of the two lands, or "the heavens and the earth." Fabre d'Olivet defines it as "universal expression."

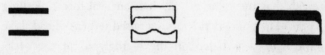

The two lands   The heavens and the earth   Elongated Hebrew *Mem*

The final Hebrew *Mem* ▢ represents the elements of creation separated by Divine Will, as does the *Beth* ⊐ (see page 205).

♀ ♀ ♀

Nun ⊐ Final Nun ⎟

The letter *Nun* is written in Hebrew ⊐. When it is placed inside a word, it doesn't seem to correspond with any hieroglyph. However, when it is at the end of a word, it takes the elongated form ⎟, identical both in writing and in pronunciation with *Nun* in Egyptian. Champollion's design demonstrates this:

Hieroglyph unot[4] *(hour). Analogy of sound and form.*

For Fabre d'Olivet, the final *Nun* is a symbol conferring an extensive meaning: "All that prolongs abundantly, all that extends itself and prolifer-ates."[5]

In the Pyramid Texts, as well as in classical writing, the *Nun* in the form of a broken line **〰** represents things that can extend out to infinity: the primordial ocean, source of all energy and the cradle of Pharaoh. Joshua is called "the son of Nun" (Joshua 1:1). In its hieratic form, the broken line takes the form of a simple horizontal stroke.

⚤ ⚤ ⚤

Samekh ⵔ

The Samekh[6] has the value of "S." It is an oval form, recalling a serpent biting its tail. The point at the top is a raised serpent's head. Like Pharaoh's uraeus, the *Samekh* is based on the hieroglyph for the cycle "day and night."

Champollion's *Treatise on Grammar* shows the Egyptian "S" sign in the form of an oval.

The Egyptian serpent showing the cycle of day and night is present on the north side of the second chapel of Tutankhamun.

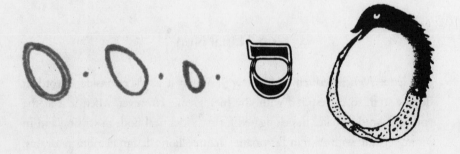

☥ ☥ ☥

Ayin ע

The *Ayin* ע is a guttural sonority deeper than the *Heh*, originating from a deep breath. This articulation, common to Semitic languages, is naturally found in the language of ancient Egypt in the sign of an extended arm, which Egyptologists compare to the Hebrew *Ayin*.[7]

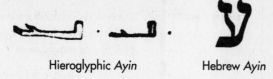

Hieroglyphic *Ayin*   Hebrew *Ayin*

Correspondence of sound.

The *Ayin* seems to represent the god Ptah kneeling and holding the scepter *Uaz,* the scepter of the gods, in his hands.

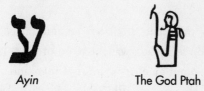

Ayin   The God Ptah

Correspondence of form.

☥ ☥ ☥

Peh or Feh פ

The first letter of the Hebrew word *Par'oo* פַּרְעֹה (Pharaoh) is the letter *Peh* פ, which signifies, respectively, "P" or "F." It has the form of a human head with the uraeus on the forehead. The sacred asp symbolically permits air to penetrate inside the skull, whence it is exhaled and made holy. Fabre d'Olivet says on this subject: "As a symbolic image, it represents the mouth of the man, of whom it paints the most beautiful attribute, that of rending his thoughts."[8]

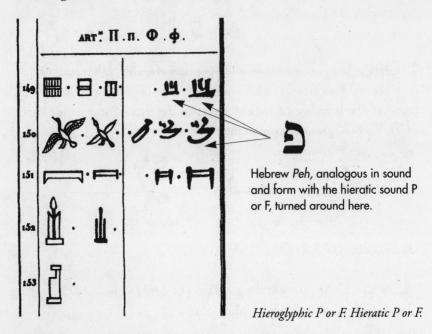

Hebrew *Peh*, analogous in sound and form with the hieratic sound P or F, turned around here.

Hieroglyphic P or F. Hieratic P or F.

For the Egyptians, the organ of speech became sacred, since it dealt with pharaoh. The word of Pharaoh was the word of God. Inspired, he received the teaching in his mouth and repeated it to mankind.

Peh פֶּה, which means mouth, is written with the letter *Peh* and the letter *Heh*, representing the divine breath. There existed in ancient Egypt a mythical city called Peh, located in the delta of the Nile and cited in the Pyramid Texts in connection with Pharaoh's coronation.[9]

Tsadeh צ, Final Tsadeh ץ

The Hebraic letter *Tsadeh* is a double consonant, which is pronounced "Ts." It's the only letter in the Hebrew alphabet having this peculiarity. The question is why did the scribes adopt it, since they already had the sounds of "T" and "S" in the same alphabet? Could there have been a reason of a mystical nature?

The hieroglyphic letter corresponding to the *Tsadeh* "Ts" in the Little Hymn of Akhenaten holds exactly the same phonetic value[10] as the Hebrew "Ts."

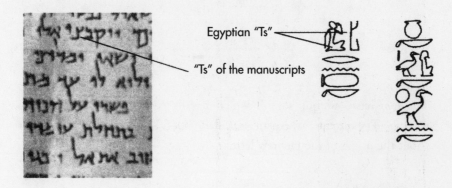

Egyptian "Ts"

"Ts" of the manuscripts

Fragment from the Dead Sea Scrolls.   Fragment from the Little Hymn of Akhenaten.

The Hebrew *Tsadeh* can represent a person in a state of exaltation, standing or kneeling, his arms raised towards the heavens, which is its hieroglyphic homologue. In this case, the person's feet go in reverse, as in the Hebrew *Tsadeh*.[11]

Analogy with the Hebrew Tsadeh.

Christian Jacq states in his book, *Nefertiti and Akhenaten*: "There also exist statuettes representing Akhenaten with a pedestal in the form of an L. In this last case, the king seems to be kneeling and holding his hands in front of him in adoration of Aten at his rising."

The final *Tsadeh* is the analog of the man standing in a state of exaltation.

Figurative symbol of exaltation   Hebrew final *Tsadeh*

The *Heh,* the *Shin* and the *Tsadeh,* as well as the *Yod,* the *Beth,* the *Gimel,* and the *Vav* (compared earlier, see pp. 205–13), are found in the first tomb of Ay, and are archeological evidence that Hebrew is of Egyptian and Amarnian origin.

Qof or Kof ק

The *Qof* has a unique sound, which has its equivalent in hieroglyphic writing. The Egyptian serpent is called "Qof," which leaves no doubt about the origin of the Hebrew letter.

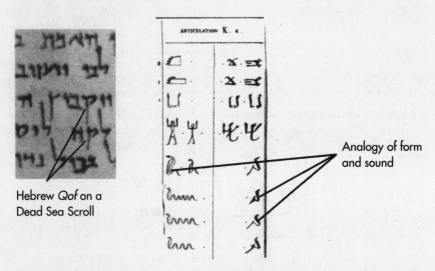

Hebrew *Qof* on a
Dead Sea Scroll

Analogy of form
and sound

According to Champollion's table, the *Qof* is also represented by a man raising his arms, or by two arms extended towards the heavens, forming a square. The serpent is the radiating and joyous spirit of Pharaoh, the heir of the vital strength that issues from Re, called the *Ka.* The *Qof* ("K" sound) is present in Ytshak יצחק (Isaac, Abraham's heir), Yaakov יעקב (Jacob), Cain קין, Cabal קבל (Ka-ba-la, transmission of the divine heritage), as well as in the formula used for the pharaoh of the Exodus, *vaykra Par'oo* ויקרא פרעה containing *Ka* and *Re,* symbols included in Smenkhkare's cartouche.

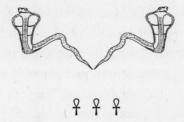

Shin or Sin ש

The Hebrew *Shin* expresses the two sonorities of "sh" or "s."

It's worth noting that the sign figuring in the Great Hymn of Akhenaten has exactly the same form as in the Dead Sea Scrolls, the most ancient texts known in Hebrew.

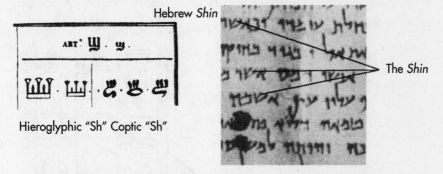

Hebrew *Shin*

The *Shin*

Hieroglyphic "Sh" Coptic "Sh"

Fragment of the Dead Sea Scrolls showing the "Sh" sound in Coptic Treatise of Champollion.

According to Champollion, there is an analogy of form and sound between the hieroglyphic "sh" and the Coptic "sh."

On the other hand, when we consider the Hebrew "sh" which figures in the Dead Sea Scrolls, it is evident that there's an absolute analogy of sound and of form between it and the hieroglyphic "sh" and the Psalm of Akhenaten.

Sekhet hieroglyph: the field, pasture.[12]

The hieroglyphic "sh" (blade of grass) is classified by Champollion as a figure representing the potential growth of vegetation. It symbolizes one of the elements of vegetation. It is found three times in the Hymn to Aten with the translation of pasture, trees, and plants. Just as in the Biblical story of creation *bereshit* ("in the beginning") figures as the first word in the Bible, Christian Jacq emphasizes that the sign *Sha* (three reeds) serves to give the notion of "commencement," by reference to the first manifestation of life, springing forth from the primordial waters.[13] The *Shin* is employed in the words pasturage, vegetation, trees and plants, the grass of the fields: "When no vegetation was yet in the earth and no plants bearing seeds" (Hebrew Bible, Genesis 1:5).

The expression "plants bearing seeds," *esseve asade* עשב השדה, means pasturage. "And the Elohim said, 'Let the earth produce plants yielding seed'" (Hebrew Bible, Genesis 1:11). The word "vegetation" is written *deshe*. And so each of the Hebrew words meaning pasturage contains the *Shin*.

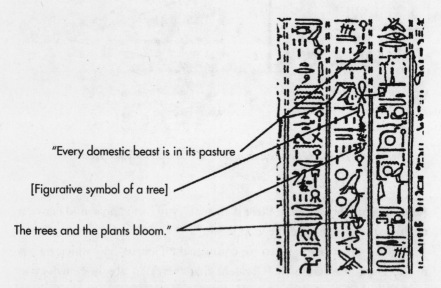

"Every domestic beast is in its pasture"

[Figurative symbol of a tree]

The trees and the plants bloom."

Column 5 of the Great Hymn of Aten. This passage speaks of pastures, trees, and plants (Pierre Grandet's translation).

An analogy between the name of Pharaoh Shishak in the Bible and the name Shechonq I, which is shown below, confirms the value of the hieroglyphic *Sh*.

Cartouche of Sheshonq I

The name of Shishak, the Pharaoh of the Bible

Tav ⊓

Tav, like the letter *Tet* ⊂, represents the Hebrew "T." It is like the Egyptian *Tep*, the heavens.

With the *Tav*, the scribes included a new divine symbol, perhaps of the goddess Hathor or the goddess Nut – Egyptian divinities symbolizing the celestial vault – in an alphabet containing 22 letters.

Nut, Goddess of the Heavens.

Hathor, Cow of the Heavens.

The *Tav* has its analogy in the hieroglyphic and hieratic name of Hathor, the sacred cow that nourishes Egypt, and the image of perfection and abundance. The following hymn is dedicated to the goddess:

How beautiful it is
Thy journey, starting from the horizon
Thou floatest to the heavens joyfully.
Hathor, Lady of Dendara, Eye of Re,
Lady of the sovereign heavens of all the gods,
Who travels the beautiful way without enemies.[14]

Hieroglyphic Hathor   Hieratic Hathor   Hebrew Tav

Analogy between the Tav and the Hathor hieroglyph.

The Egyptian word for goddess[15] written in hieratic writing recalls the Hebrew *Tav* (as drawn by Champollion).

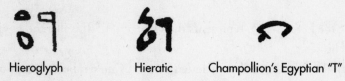

Hieroglyph   Hieratic   Champollion's Egyptian "T"

The sistrum, an Egyptian instrument used in the temples, is related to Hathor in its shape (the head of a woman with ears of a cow). In the Great Temple of Akhet-Aten, Nefertiti and her daughters shake sistra in honor of Aten. In Tutankhamun's tomb, the cow Hathor was discovered in a linen vestment, similar to the vestments covering the divinities, the chapels, and the sarcophagus of the king. In ancient Egypt, Hathor wore the solar disk Re between her horns. Hathor, wife of Horus, means "domain (*Hath*) of Horus (*Hor*)." By extension, she is Pharaoh's wife. Queen Nefertiti, deified as Goddess Hathor, symbolized the living presence of the goddess of love and fertility.

Hathor resided in the sacred domain of the Theban mountains, with the charge of accompanying the dead pharaoh on the celestial road and of nourishing him. The Book of the Sacred Cow was discovered in one of the chapels of the funerary chamber of Tutankhamun.[16] Like the Book of the Dead or the Book of the Doors, it contains funeral incantations as well as the legend of the flight into the desert of those accused of plotting against Re.[17]

The Aramaic word for cow is synonymous with mountain, *Tora* or *Tura*.

The *Tav* is the first letter of the word Torah. It exists in many analogies between Hathor and Torah. As the Hathoric pillars sustain the Egyptian temples, the Torah symbolizes one of the three pillars of the world.

The goddess Hathor, symbol of joy and love, was the protector of the sacred mountain of Thebes. The Torah is intimately linked with that same sacred mountain. The scriptures relate that the Torah was revealed on Mount Sinai after the Exodus from Egypt. The two rolls of the Torah enveloped in a linen cloth are placed in a case holding sistra, which are shaken during the ceremony of Simha-Torah (joy of the Torah). After the ceremony, it is placed in a box shaped like the courtyard of an Egyptian temple.

According to Fabre d'Olivet, the word Torah is formed by "T" ‏ת‎ *Tav*, whose root *To* is a hieroglyphic symbol: "‏ות‎ The whole idea of a hieroglypic sign, symbol, or character: a fable, a tale, a description, a book, a monument, etc."[18] The second part, *Re* ‏רה‎, recalls the great solar god Re, figured in the representations of Hathor wearing the solar disk Re above her head. The Bible is also called the "Torah of Light," a teaching permitting us to surmount the trials of life.

The goddess Hathor, surmounted by the Sun God Re.

The Images of the Gods

The image of the vulture, the symbol of royalty in Upper Egypt, inspired the monotheistic scribes in their transcription of the Hebrew *Mem*. The female vulture protects her young to the death, as *Mut* and the uraeus (vulture and serpent), above Pharaoh's head, protect him. The two symbols inspire fear of the divinity. The Egyptian people were not able to see the face of Amun, the hidden god, just as in the Bible one cannot "see the face of God and live."

The Hebrew letters fit in perfectly with the Egyptian gods. When the monotheistic scribes arrived in Canaan, they were proud of having come from Egypt. They introduced the divinities into the Hebrew alphabet, despite the Second Commandment forbidding the representation of images of the Amunian gods Mut (*Mem*), Thoth (*Tet*), Ptah (*Ayin* and *Peh*), and Hathor (*Tav*). The Egyptians considered their writing to be formed by images of the gods: terrestrial symbols invaded by the waters of the flood and celestial symbols accompanying Pharaoh into the heavens. They never were to go beyond the limits of the Nile. Before leaving the sacred land of Egypt, Pharaoh's letters were translated into cuneiform. Subsequently, the Second Commandment's prohibition concerning the "images of the gods," came down as a prohibition to the Yahuds, deported to Canaan, against using the sacred hieroglyphic writing.

> *Thou shalt not have any other Elohim than us. Thou shalt not make any idol, nor the image of anything at all that is above in the heavens or below under the earth or in the waters beneath the earth. (Exodus 20:3)*

In several places, the Bible alludes to the "gods of your fathers," recalling and blaming the people for having worshiped idols and images representing their culture and ancestral past. That is why they introduced these symbols in the alphabet of the priests and scribes of Judah (Yahuds), which was then called the Hebrew alphabet.

Notes

1. Christian Jacq, *La tradition primordiale de l'Ancienne Egypte selon les textes des Pyramides*. Grasset & Fasquelle, 1998, p. 248.

2. Jacques Champollion, *Lecture illustrée des hieroglyphs*. Le Rocher, 1998, p. 277.

3. John Adams Wilson, *Egypt. Life and Death of a Civilization*. Arthaud, 1961, p. 206.

4. Christian Jacq, *Grammaire égyptienne de Champollion*. Solin, 1997, p. 98.

5. Fabre d'Olivet, *La langue hébraïque restituée*. L'Age d'Homme-Delphica, 1991, p. 87

6. The *kh* is pronounced like the "ch" in Scottish *loch* or German *buch*.

7. *L'aventure des écritures, Naissances,* Bibliothèque Nationale de France, 1997, p. 37.

8. Fabre d'Olivet, *La langue hébraïque restituée*, p. 102.

9. Christian Jacq, *La tradition primordiale de l'Ancienne Egypte*, p. 145.

10. Pierre Grandet, *Hymnes de la religion d'Aton*. Le Seuil, 1995, p. 157.

11. *Grammaire égyptienne de Champollion*, p. 538.

12. Christian Jacq, *Le petit Champollion illustré*. Robert Laffont, 1994, p. 84.

13. *Ibid.*

14. John Adams Wilson, *Egypt. Life and Death of a Civilization,* p. 205.

15. *Grammaire égyptienne de Champollion*, p.122.

16. Nicolas Reeves, *The Discovery of Tutankhamun*. Thames and Hudson, 1990, p. 101.

17. Adolphe Erman and Hermann Rank, *La civilisation égyptienne*. Payot and Rivages, 1994, p. 101.

18. Fabre d'Olivet, *La langue hébraïque restituée*, p. 133.

CHAPTER 24

Gods and Pharaohs

The God Ptah

Ptah is the god of the creation. He created the heavens and the earth by the divine word. He is the creator of the animals, the plants, and all that the earth can produce – everything is created through his commands. Ptah is also the god of "the opening of the mouth," the ceremony designed to render to the dead pharaoh the god's power and his word. In the names of the kings of Egypt, Ptah is represented as a kneeling man, in a meditative state, holding in his hands the scepter *Uaz*, the symbol of power.

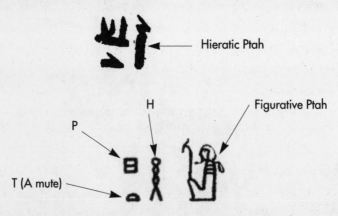

Ptah's hieroglyphic phonetic name (Treatise of Champollion).[1]

The root *Ptah* in Hebrew means precisely "to open," *Poteah*, an extension toward space, or that which is extended, beginning with the letter *Peh* פתח.

The god Ptah holding his scepter Uaz *before Pharaoh Sety I.*

Pharaoh

The name "Pharaoh" has always fascinated mankind. The name's origin has known many interpretations. The interpretation most often assumed by science is that it was derived from the hieroglyphics *Per-Aa*, which means "the great house."

That house would be Pharaoh's domain, his holy place. The Bible speaks of the holy place where the Divine dwells, the *Makom* מקום.

> *Then Jacob awoke from his sleep and thought, "Surely Yahwe is in this place; and I did not know it." And he was afraid, and said, "How awesome is this place! This is none other than the house of the Elohim, and this is Heaven's Gate." (Hebrew Bible, Genesis 28:16-17)*

In Hebrew, the word "Pharaoh" is identical with its Egyptian homologue. Only the pronunciation, *Par'oo* פרעה, is slightly different, taking the vowels into account.

The letter *Peh* פ represents Pharaoh's head and mouth. The *Resh* ר, Re or Reh, the sun, king of the gods. The *Ayin* ע recalls Ptah, the primordial god of the creative word. Finally, the *Heh* ה (Great God), introduces the divine breath of creation.

The Egyptian word for "sun," written in its hieratic form, is close to "Pharaoh" in Hebrew: PER-AA = PAR'OO.

Heh: Great God   ה ע ר פ   Peh (mouth of Pharaoh)

PAR'OO = Pharaoh

PER'AA = Hieratic sun

PER'AA = Hieroglyphic sun

Comparative reading of Pharaoh: The Great God issued from the mouths of Re and Ptah.

The true meaning of the name *Par'oo* is associated with several pharaohs. Consequently, the Biblical scribes usually used the term *Par'oo* to designate Akhenaten (Anoki-Aten), and also to designate Amenhotep III and Smenkhkare. *Par'oo* means the sacred place where the king resides (*Hamelekh*).

In Judaism, the One God is called *Hamelekh* (the king) or *Hamakom* (the place).

Bill Manley affirms that the true origin of *Par'oo* or *Per-aa* (Pharaoh) is found at Akhet-Aten: "The king [Akhenaten] and the court were so intimately linked that the word designating the entire royal institution, *Per-Aa*, (the great domain), became a synonym for king and, through the influence of the Bible, this word came into the modern world in the form Pharaoh."[2]

☥ ☥ ☥

Akhenaten's Name

In the cartouche of Amenhotep IV, as Akhenaten was originally called, the name carries the notion of good (Hotep), peace or integrity.[3] "Hotep" is close to the Hebrew *hatov* הטוב, "good".[4] In the Bible, God acts for good and peace. Hotep is reunited with Re, the divine. The good is located in the divine dimension, where there is no opposition to it. Tov = Salom = Shel Amon, the peace of Amun.

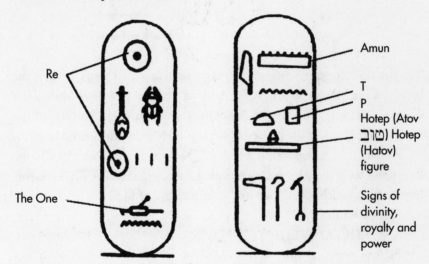

The first cartouche of Amenhotep IV (Amun is in peace), symbolizing the good, peace, satisfaction and oneness of Re, the king of the Egyptian gods.

Akhenaten's name derives from "Ankh Aton," which is composed of five figures and means "The living Aten" – Anokhi Aton.

An'kh Aten, pronounced "Anokh-i Aten."

Anokhi Aton is close to Anokhi Adonay, the First Commandment of the Bible. Akhenaten's cartouche, below, contains seven elements (seven is Akhenaten's number), written from bottom to top – unlike Amenhotep, which is read from top to bottom.

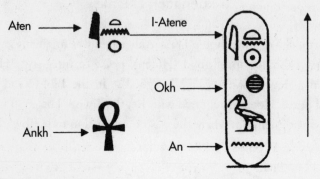

Ankh Aton.   *Akhenaten = Anok-i Aten.*

The divine hieroglyphic sign *Ankh* is present in Akhenaten's name ("the breath of life," Ankh-Aten), in the Amarna Letters,[5] as well as in the First Commandment: "I am your Anokhi Yahwe, who brought you out of the land of Egypt, out of the house of bondage" (Hebrew Bible, Exodus 20:2).

Anokhi is a juxtaposition of *Ani* אני (the Biblical word "I"), the Egyptian *Okh* (the Hebrew *Or*), meaning light, and the *Hai* חי, representing life (that which springs forth): "I am the light of life."

Biblical writing:

ANOKHI YAHWEH: אנוכי יהוה

Biblical pronunciation:

ANOKHI ADONAI: אנוכי אדני

The pronunciation "Akhen-Yaten" proposed by Egyptologists agrees with the holy Biblical name *Anokh-i Adon-Ay*, which is close to *Anok-i Aten*.

The Egyptian *Anokh* or *Anok* means "I am," like the Hebrew *Anokhi*. Egyptologists have translated the phrase as "Living disk" or "Living Sun" – I am Aten = I am the (living) Sun.

This sentence from Akhenaten's psalm is apparent in the First Commandment: *Anokhi Adonai Eloeka*: I am Adonay thy God.

The expression Ankh Aten is contained in the royal cartouches of the god Aten. Ankh is the first word and Aten the last. Conventionally, the two signs mean "Aten, the living," but the Biblical parallel favors the following interpretation, "I am Aten."

Akhenaten's royal cartouche confirms the direct relationship between the Hebrew *Anokhi* אנכי and Akhenaten's name.

The expression *Anokh Aten*, several times engraved in the Hymns to Aten, represents the uniqueness of the living god, symbol of the god-king Akhenaten, the exclusive pharaoh, and Akhenaten's name, "I am Aten," remembered by the Yahud priests and scribes, was introduced into the First Commandment of the Bible.

☥ ☥ ☥

After Ay's rise to power, first as the Divine Father, next as vizier of the empire, then Pharaoh of Egypt, following the ancient tradition, Aten became Aten-Ay (later Adon-Ay in the Bible) for the inhabitants of Akhet-Aten and particularly for the priests. This tradition is largely confirmed by the addition of Ay's name to that of the god Seth (*Shad* in Hebrew), becoming *Shad-Ay*, designated as one of the names of God in the Bible.

Shad-Ay corresponds to the actual pronunciation of Sety I (Seth + *Yod-Yod*), Pharaoh of Egypt, and Cyril Aldred confirms in his book *Akhenaten, King of Egypt*:

> *King Ay reigned briefly, about four or five years, and followed a policy which he had no doubt would have been adopted by his predecessor [Tutankhamun]. The rehabilitation of Amun and the abandonment of the most extreme aspects of the Aten religion were pursued relentlessly. Ay continued his projects in the construction of Karnak, adding his own names to those of his predecessor, without usurping that predecessor's work.*

Maybe Tutankhamun was the son of Ay. Cyril Aldred found the name of the Divine Father Ay near Tutankhamun's name. In the Bible, Ay is associated with different divinities, expressions, or geographic names: Adon-Ay, Shad-Ay, Mordekh-Ai, Sin-Ai …

☥ ☥ ☥

Amun

The god Amun, seated on his throne and wearing the double feather on his head, dominates the cartouches of the Amenhotep pharaohs up to Amenhotep IV. In the fifth year of his reign, Amenhotep IV changed his name to Akhenaten and Amun's name disappeared from the cartouche. It reappeared when Tutankhaten became Tutankhamun.

Amun is the origin of the Hebrew words *Amen* and *Ma Amin*, which mean "to believe," and *Emuna*, meaning faith, or belief. Amun is the emanation of the Nun, the primordial ocean. According to Fabre d'Olivet, the root "mun" or "bun" is associated with that which emanates from the divine.[6]

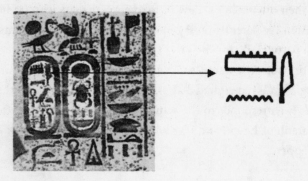

Name of the god Amun in the cartouche to the left of that of Tutankhamun (North façade of Tutankhamun's funeral chamber).

In the illustration above, the rectangle represents the "M" of Amun; the lower waves the "N," and the reed on the right, the *Yod*, represents "A" in the majority of Semitic languages. Ancient Egyptian, a chanted, psalmodic language, had a sound comparable to Semitic languages and dialects like Arabic, Hebrew, and Aramaic.

The presence of the *Yod* (reed) poses a problem in pronouncing the word "Amun." Some researchers have suggested placing the *Yod* in front of Amun. With a single value of "Y," this would give a pronunciation of "Ymun." However, this new pronunciation doesn't take into account Champollion's indications giving the Egyptian *Yod* different values (A, IA, E, I, Y).[7] Thus, in the Semitic pronunciation of the *Yod*, the sound "A" isn't hidden. It can be said "Amun" or even "Amen."

♀ ♀ ♀

Amen

In the Bible, Moses orders the people to answer "Amen" at each of the twelve curses written in Deuteronomy: "Cursed is the man who sculpts an image or casts a statue, a thing Yahwe (Adonay) detests, the work of a woodworker or metal worker, who puts it in a hidden place. Then all the people must answer and say: 'Amen!'" (Hebrew Bible, Deuteronomy 27:15).

The proclamation of Amun by a monotheistic people reveals a major Biblical contradiction. But it was later sidelined by the scribes, who attributed to the word Amun (Amen) the traditional meaning that it still has today. The pronunciation "Amen," meaning "truly," was generalized in the curses and blessings, and then into all the monotheistic prayers.

♀ ♀ ♀

Aten Sacrifices Amun

The pharaohs identified themselves with Amun, a man with a ram's head. This ancient tradition is revealed in the story of Abraham, sacrificing a ram in place of his son Isaac. It is the ram Amun who was sacrificed in Isaac's place. The *shofar*, an instrument formed from a ram's horn used in certain religious ceremonies, symbolizes liberation from the idea that Amun should be considered as an abomination.

The sacrifice of the ram (Amun) is generally interpreted as the end of human sacrifices. However, they continue in the Bible, thus: "'Seize the prophets of Baal.'[8] Elijah had them brought down into the valley of Kishon and slaughtered there" (Hebrew Bible, I Kings 18:40).

♀ ♀ ♀

Aten's Name

Before becoming Akhenaten's god, Aten was written in Egyptian in a brief form, with the figure of the sun, as in Amun's name. This corresponded to the old phonetic writing.

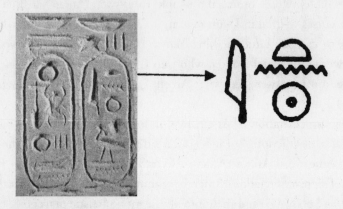

Double cartouche of Akhenaten bearing the (short) name of Aten. The half circle or half-loaf designating the "T" sound; the waves, the "N" sound; the reed to the left, Yod A *(Biblical pronunciation: Adon); and the complete circle (sun) is the symbol which must not be spoken. As explained by Champollion in his* Treatise on Egyptian Grammar.

Linguists are convinced that no relationship between Adon, Adonay, and the sun exists. However, the Egyptian word *Aten* is like the Hebrew *Adon*. As a matter of fact, the Book of Zohar confirms that "Adon is the sun that lights up and floods the earth."[10]

The letter *Yod* is at the beginning of Aten's name, which gives it the pronunciation "Yten" (the Egyptian and the Hebrew *Yods* are similar letters). The Egyptian names Aten and Amun begin with a *Yod* just as the Hebrew words *Adon* אדן and *Amun* אמן begin with an *Aleph* (A). Champollion states in his *Treatise of Egyptian Grammar* that the *Yod* has the values A, E, Y, Ay, Ei, and O. Hieroglyphic writing, like Hebrew, has no vowels. Consequently the Egyptian *Yod* should be considered like the Hebrew *Aleph*,[11] since it represents several vowels.

According to its sense, Aten may mean Lord, God, or Sun, all words that are often used in the El Amarna Letters.[12]

Values in Coptic Letters

Voice Signs

Hieroglyphs	Hieratics	Value

Extract from Champollion's Treatise of Egyptian Grammar. The Egyptian Yod can have several phonetic values (here in Coptic letters).

In the Bible, the Tetragram Yahwe יְהֹוָה is read as Adon-Ay אֲדֹנָי, because it is forbidden to pronounce the name of God. In the Hebrew liturgy, as in the Aramaic Bible, Adon-Ay is also represented by two *Yods* יי, which generally are absorbed into the Tetragram Yahwe יְהֹוָה.

Yahwe יְהֹוָה as *Yod-Yod* יי is read as Adon-Ay too. The prohibition on uttering the name of God is written in the Second Commandment (Exodus 20:7): "Thou shalt not take the name of Yahwe in vain." Tradition however tolerates the pronunciation of the word "Adon-Ay" while forbidding Yahwe and *Yod-Yod.*

What is the origin of the "Adon-Ay" name?

According to Sigmund Freud, there had been an abandonment of the Adon-Ay name in favor of Yahwe. Later, there was a reversal toward the Egyptian roots of the monotheistic religion, reintroducing Adon-Ay as a compromise for Yahwe. According to the Freudian thesis of "The Return to the Father" (Adon-Ay) it occurred in one or two generations. The scribes did not want the name Adon-Ay to be forgotten, so it was understood that it was the name of the original god, the God of the Exodus from Egypt, and the God of the compromise of Aten and Ay.

As Freud said: "If Moses was an Egyptian and if he transmitted his own religion to the Jews, it was Akhenaten's, the religion of Aten." If, according to Freud, the religion of the Hebrews was related to the religion of Aten, the pronunciation of the name of the god Aten could be the origin of the name Adon.

Since many Egyptian names are read with the letter "D" or the letter "T" (Tushratta, Dushratta, Taphne, Daphne, etc.), one can surely affirm that the original pronunciation of Aten was "Adon." The names of gods of Greek origin are generally written with a D: Zeus was pronounced Dzeus, Deu, Adonis, etc., and in the Coptic alphabet,[13] the letter D (*Dau*) is pronounced "D" or "T." From all the evidence, it seems that the Yahud priests, in order to please the Ptolemaic pharaohs (cf. Rashi, Exodus 12:40), adopted the names "Adon" and "Adon-Ay" for their god; names close to those of the Greek god Adonis. In this, they conformed to the old tradition of accepting the god of the conquerors.

As in the case of Akhenaten's name, Aten's didactic name also underwent changes. Engraved on two stone tablets (or cartouches), there is a first naming: "Re Horakhty, who lives and rejoices in the Region of Light (Akhet-Aten), in his name of Shu, which is in the solar disk Aten."

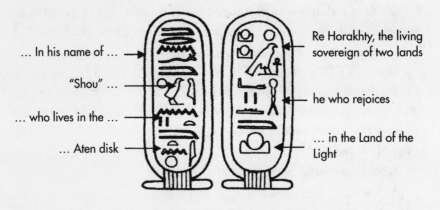

... In his name of ...

"Shou" ...

... who lives in the ...

... Aten disk

Re Horakhty, the living sovereign of two lands

he who rejoices

... in the Land of the Light

Left cartouche   Right cartouche

First didactic form of Aten's name.

The title of the god Aten, or his didactic name, has numerous variants according to the translations of the Egyptologists. But it is never separated from its global context, placing Aten as the Sun god, reigning over the universe and inhabiting the sacred land of Akhet-Aten.

It is interesting that each of the words inscribed in the divine cartouche has its correspondence with Hebrew:

The Ankh, symbol of life or the breath of life.

In the Torah (Bible), when Pharaoh speaks, he says "Anokhi," אָנֹכִי, "I am."

The Talmud says that Anokhi אָנֹכִי is the "word of words,"[14] "the summary of the Decalogue" (the Ten Commandments engraved on the Tablets of the Law), whose origin is Egyptian.

In Egyptian, "I am" is said as *Anok*, a word close in sound to *Ankh*, Life. "I am Life." That attribute conferring to the king the power to radiate light and life about himself, conforms to the usage in the Pyramid Texts.[15]

He who rejoices (Hay).

The indicative "he who rejoices" reads as *Hay* in Egyptian. In Hebrew, "life" reads as *Hay* חַי – a synonym for rejoicing, and with the symbolic meaning of "rejoicing in the holy land."

Akhet

The Akhet horizon or Land of Light.

Phonetic Akhet.

This figure represents the holy land, flooded by divine light, Akhet-Aten. The similarity with the Hebrew word *Aretz* אֶרֶץ is shown in the Hebrew root *Or* אֹר: light – the first word of God in the Bible,[16] and equivalent to the Egyptian root Akh also meaning light.[17] The last letter, the Tsadeh צ, evokes Akhenaten standing, exalting the sun, a form equivalent to the hieroglyph TS.

In Egyptian this gives Hay meh-Ahet: "who is delighted in the holy land,"[18] and in Hebrew, Hai Ba-aretz חַי בָּאָרֶץ: "who lives in the holy land."

Shem

In his name = Meranef   Name (ren)   Egyptian shen
In his name

The expression "in his name," composed of four hieroglyphic signs, approaches the Hebrew *besemo* בִּשְׁמוֹ, "in his name," formed by four letters. The horned viper recalls the Hebrew *Vav* ו, "his/her/its," the third person singular possessive, like the identical *Beth*.

The word "name" in Hebrew is *Shem* שֵׁם, and it is made up of two characters, as is the equivalent Egyptian word *Ren*. Its origin could derive from the Egyptian *Shen*, the little cartouche to the right of the hieroglyph below, meaning "the name."

                                                          Shen

Hieroglyphic Shen.

☥ ☥ ☥

Shu

Shu, the solar fire.

Shu, the luminous fire, is represented by an ostrich plume and is composed of the same root as the Hebrew *Esh* אֵשׁ, also meaning fire.

In Hebrew, *Shemesh* שֶׁמֶשׁ, "sun," is always broken down into two parts: *Shem* שֵׁם, "name," and *Esh* אֵשׁ, "fire." The "name of *Esh*" designates the sun, Shemesh, just as in Egyptian "the name of *Shu*" is included in the title of the sun god Aten.

Furthermore, שָׁם *Sham* translates as "over there." The Egyptians, like the Hebrews, thought that "over there" – in the heavens – fire (*sham-esh*) and water (*sham-mayim*)[19] were to be found.

☥ ☥ ☥

The analogy surrounding the name of Aten allows us to present a case for a concordance between the Hebrew and Egyptian languages. It would, then, be useful to base our argument on Biblical pronunciation, at least for certain words and religious names, if the Bible is to be considered a book of Egyptology.

Aten's name was first used from Year One to Year Nine of Akhenaten's reign, overlapping the Theban and the Amarnian periods. Akhenaten then proceeded to change the didactic form of Aten's name. More precisely, he deleted from the name all images or caricatures referring to the ancient Egyptian gods. The falcon, Re-Horakhty, disappeared from Aten's name, as well as the plume of *Shu*. Both these were replaced by the circle, the phonetic symbol of the god Re who is without image, and still present in the first didactic name of Aten.

The change in the god's name is fundamental for an understanding of the evolution of the religion of Aten. For the first time in Egypt's history, a pharaoh banned the worship of the gods as images and idols. The act recalls the Second Commandment in the Bible: "Thou shalt not make for yourself a graven image, nor the likeness of anything that is in the heavens above, or in the earth beneath, or in the waters under the earth" (Hebrew Bible, Exodus 20:4).

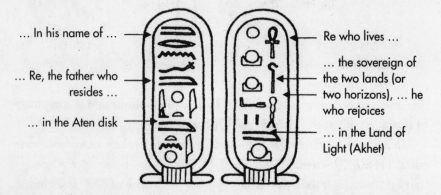

... In his name of ...

... Re, the father who resides ...

... in the Aten disk

Re who lives ...

... the sovereign of the two lands (or two horizons), ... he who rejoices

... in the Land of Light (Akhet)

In the second form of Aten's name the images of Shu and Horus have been replaced by Re (e.g. p. 248).

The Resident Father

The verb *to reside, to inhabit*, is written in Hebrew with two letters, *Gimel* and *Resh* ‏גר‎: *Gar.* The hieroglyph for "reside"[20] (shown above), according to Pierre Grandet, is very like the Hebrew *Gimel* followed by the symbol for Re (circle). In the Hebrew language, the verb *Gar* means both "stranger/foreigner" and "inhabitant." So, Exodus 23:9 could be transcribed as: "Thou shalt not oppress an inhabitant, because thou knowest how inhabitants feel, for ye were once inhabitants in Egypt" (Hebrew Bible, Exodus 23:9).

The scribes used the term "inhabitant" to describe the people. The word came to mean "stranger" only after the Exodus from Egypt, probably in the time of Nebuchadnezzar.

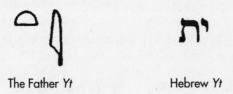

The Father *Yt*   Hebrew *Yt*

The word for father, *Yt*, which figures as an element in Aten's name, is found in the names of *Ytro* (Jethro, Moses' father-in-law), and *Ytshak* (Isaac, "the smile of Father Abraham").

Notes

1. Jean François Champollion, decipherer of the Rosetta Stone.
2. Bill Manley, *Historical Atlas of Ancient Egypt*. Autrement, Collection Atlas/Mémores, 1998, p. 76.
3. Cf. Fabre d'Olivet for the root TB or TV טוב: "All ideas of conservation, of central integrity; this is the symbol of healthy fruitfulness, of a force capable of holding off all corruption." Fabre d'Olivet, *La Langue hébraïque restituée*. L'Age d'Homme-Delphica, 1991.
4. Hatov is close to Hotep symbolically, as in its pronunciation, because of the absence of vowels in the two languages. The Hebrew "V" is pronounced the same as "B," a letter analogous to the "P," requiring the same articulation in the mouth. Compare the Hebrew Beth, symbolizing the heavens, which is the same as Beth and Pet in Egyptian.
5. *Les lettres d'El Amarna*. Le Cerf, 1987, EA 382; EA 403.
6. Fabre d'Olivet, *La Langue hébraïque restituée*, p. 20.
7. For the Yod, cf. Christian Jacq, *Grammaire égyptienne de Champollion*. Solin, 1997, p.35.
8. Baal is a god of Canaanite origin associated with human fertility. The son of El and brother of Anath, together they form a triad.
9. *Grammaire égyptienne de Champollion*, p. 22: "These characters express precisely the object which they present to the eye, an image more or less true and more or less detailed."
10. *The Book of Zohar*, Vol. 1. Verdier, 1981, p.189.
11. Franz Rosenthal, *Grammaire d'Araméen biblique,* translated by Paul Hébert. Beauchesne, 1988, p. 48 and the following chapter. The Hebrew *Aleph* is written with a *Yod* on its upper right part.
12. *Les lettres d'El Amarna*.
13. *Grammaire égyptienne de Champollion*, p.34.

14. Rabbi Chélomo de Lubavicch, *Réflexions sur la vie juive*, vol. 3, pp. 892–5, 2nd edition, 1987, Merkos l'Inoynei Chinuch, Anoki, the "word of words," source *likouté-si-hot*.
15. Christian Jacq, *La tradition primordiale de l'Ancienne Egypte selon les textes des Pyramides*, Grasset & Fasquelle, 1998.
16. Genesis 1:3
17. Cf. Christian Jacq, *Nefertiti et Akhénaton*. Perrin, 1996, p.78.
18. Pierre Grandet, *Hymnes à la religion d'Aton*. Le Seuil, 1995, p.137.
19. Genesis 1:1.
20. Cyril Aldred, *Akhenaten, King of Egypt*. Le Seuil, 1997.

☥

CHAPTER 25

The Culture of the Nile

Music

The musicians of the Eighteenth Dynasty comprised groups of two, three, or four instruments. The harp, double flute, and lyre were accompanied by tambourine. This implies a tradition incorporating tempo, arpeggio, rhythm, and harmony.

The Bible recalls the music of ancient Egypt. "His brother's name was Jubal. He was the father of all who play the lyre and flute" (Hebrew Bible, Genesis 4:21). "… So I could send you away with joy and singing to the tambourine and lyre" (Hebrew Bible, Genesis 31:27).

Three musicians play the double flute, the lute and the harp (Painting from the Eighteenth Dynasty).

☥ ☥ ☥

Slaves or Servants?

"They worked them unmercifully, and made their lives bitter with hard labor, in mortar and brick; and in all kinds of fieldwork; in all their work the Egyptians used them unmercifully" (Hebrew Bible, Exodus 1:13-14).

The commentary in the Maxims of the Fathers concerning these verses teaches that Pharaoh excluded from slavery the tribe of Levi. This tribe, composed of priests and nobles and their families, would have escaped the servitude imposed by the king of Egypt. The Hagadah (the story of the Exodus from Egypt) gives this explanation: "It [the tribe of Levi, the Yahuds] owed its safe standing to the care of the nobles and to ancestral practices, like circumcision and the study of the law."[1]

Rashi's commentary is just as explicit: "The Midrash [Commentary] still says that the tribe of Levi, to which Moses belonged, was never enslaved by Pharaoh."[2]

These explanations, issuing from the oral tradition, mention the presence of Levite priests among the populations of the Biblical Exodus. They could only be representatives of Egyptian nobility and clergy from Akhenaten's era. It simply isn't possible to admit in ancient Egypt a cohabitation between two separate clergies and two nobilities of different origins. Foreigners who entered Egypt had to give allegiance to Pharaoh. As in the case of the Hyksos conquerors, the archeological traces of such an exception to ancestral traditions would have been discovered. Consequently, the monotheistic priests exiled to the land of Canaan carried with them the religion of Akhenaten. Therefore that is how we find in the Bible the agreements and the straight connections with the religious wisdom and traditions leading back to the cradle of Egyptian civilization.

The Yahud priests formed the tribe of Judah, the most important and powerful of the exiled people. It was entrusted with the majority of the Canaan territories (Judah), leaving the remaining people, the multitudes, to colonize the frontiers. Rashi (Exodus 12:37) explains as follows: "A mixture of the converted nations, forming a great multitude." Following the example of Pharaoh Ay, the tribe of Judah created a second buffer zone peopled by the great multitude, the humble people who formed Israel (I Kings 12:19): "Israel has been in rebellion against the house of David ever since."

Rashi affirms that the people of the Exodus from Egypt were the "servants of Pharaoh." The servants of Pharaoh owned slaves themselves (and therefore wealth), and could only be nobles and priests. The *Erev-rav* who followed them out of Egypt formed the multitude.

The Levites were the priests of Akhet-Aten. Not only were they not slaves, they were privileged people of the capital. The oral tradition taught by Rashi makes clear here the true sense of the word *eved*, which means "servant," but also "to offer worship to Pharaoh." This ambiguity in the meaning of certain Hebrew words permitted the scribes to hide the truth within the Biblical tale.

This is how the name of the god Re, the king of the Egyptian gods, is synonymous with the word *ra* meaning "evil" in Hebrew.

     עבדה

Hieroglyph for Het or Akhet (Aket)   Sin: Hatat (Het-At)

"Sin" in Hebrew is *Hatat* (Genesis 4:7), formed by *Het* (phonetically "Akhet") and *At* (the first two letters of Aten). Akhet-Aten is the "City of Sin."

The Egyptian God of gods was demonized by the Biblical scribes, in the same way as the pharaohs of Egypt.

Hieroglyph "STN," a reed designating the king of Upper and Lower Egypt.

The origin of the word "Satan" probably derived from the root "STN" according to Champollion, the representation of a reed used by the Egyptians to designate the king of Egypt.[3] Frederic Portal declares that

*the white crown and the red crown became the crown of the impious
pharaohs, and a crown soiled with blood. The scarab was the apoca-
lyptic symbol of the grasshoppers who issued from the wells of the abyss;
in short, not only would the pharaohs have been impious, but the gods
would be transformed into Satan.*[4]

The common people of the capital weren't subjected to slavery, as they
proved later by revolting against Moses several times, because they missed
Egypt, the land "flowing with milk and honey."

Why did the Biblical scribes use the expression "the Children of
Israel?" It appears that the Bible uses the expression in order to designate
either the Egyptian people (they were dispersed all over Egypt to make
bricks), or the monotheists who left Egypt (priests and nobles of Goshen,
the region spared from the plagues). Christiane Desroches Noblecourt, in a
discussion on this subject, recalls that "everyone in Egypt made bricks."[5]
The scribes' message unveils the origins of the people of the Exodus from
ancient Egypt, and thus confirms the Egyptian meaning of the word
"Israel" – son of Re and of God.

♀ ♀ ♀

The Light of Akhenaten

About sixty years after the abandonment of Akhet-Aten, Pharaoh Ramesses
II managed to have what remained of the cursed city dismantled and
destroyed.

Some hymns to Amun name Pharaoh Akhenaten as a criminal, celebrating his defeat before the polytheistic god Amun: "The criminal has
been rejected from Thebes, 'Misfortune to the one who attacked thee! Thy
city thrives [Thebes], but he who attacked thee has fallen! The light of the
one who knew thee not has gone away, but the light of the one who is with
thee riseth over the temple square.'"

However, Akhenaten was never expelled from Egypt. He was never
rejected from Thebes. He reigned as absolute master of the empire. What's
more, he was buried in the family crypt of the royal family of Akhet-Aten.

Later, when the city was abandoned, his mummy disappeared, as did that of Nefertiti and their daughters. Did Akhenaten's sarcophagus accompany the monotheistic population into exile?

As to that "light" that had gone away, the text makes allusion to the priests who "know Amun not." After their departure, Akhet-Aten, the cursed city, was abandoned to the darkness of Aten's monotheistic cult, which had been responsible for Egypt's decline.

If the Stela of the Restoration of the cult of Amun (engraved on the orders of Ay during the reign of Tutankhamun) does not overtly speak of a massive exodus out of Egypt, the information engraved by the scribes stated it implicitly. There also, one must read between the lines to discover a message over 3500 years old, one of the oldest coded messages: that of the scribes of the Stela of the Exodus.

Fortunately for future generations, over the centuries the scribes remained the bearers of Egyptian culture. They jealously preserved the feeling of a "chosen people," the Egyptian nation. With subtlety, they impregnated the verses of the Bible with their attachment to ancient Egypt, to the terrestrial paradise.

The historical truth hidden in the Bible must be revealed by "holy exegesis," as Champollion recommended.

⚥ ⚥ ⚥

Yahud and Yahwe

The name Yahud came out of ancient Egypt.

"She [Leah, Jacob's wife] conceived again and bore a son. Then she said, 'This time, I will praise [*Hodah* הֹדָה] Yahwe.' So she called him Judah [*Yehuda* יְהוּדָה]" (Hebrew Bible, Genesis 29:35).

Judah is the one who praises, who adores. His name contains the root *Hodah* הֹדָה, praise, and *Yahu* יְהֹ, God. *Yahu-Hodah* are the roots from the names Judah and Judea (*Yehudah* or *Yahudah*), *Yehudi* (an inhabitant of Judea), *Yehuds* or *Yahuds* (monotheistic priests) and *Yahu.*

According to Isha Schwaller of Lubicz,[6] the root *Yahu-Daeh* is found in the Egyptian words *Yahu-Dueh*, meaning adoration, prayer, homage, and giving praise. The Yahuds of the Aramaic Bible, the monotheistic priests who left Egypt, rendered homage to the dawning light. The Great and Little Hymns to Aten begin with the word *dua* (or *dueh*): "Adoration of Re-Horarty ..."[7] The *Yahu-Dueh*, the priests of ancient Egypt, are the *Yehu-Daeh* of the Aramaic Bible, worshipers of the Divine Father Ay, Pharaoh of Egypt and the future Adon-Ay, identified with Re.

The origin of Jehovah, Yahwe, or *Yod-Heh-Vav-Heh* יהוה, is Egyptian. The tetragram can be read as Yahu. The third letter, the *Vav*, reads as a "U," the *Heh*, the fourth letter, being mute. The true pronunciation of the tetragram, consequently, is Yahu-Heh. The monotheistic Yahuds adore *Yahu-Heh*, the divine breath.

There is a hieroglyphic pictogram *Yahut* (or Yahud):[8]

| Y | A | OU | T or D | Symbol for *Yaut* |

Hieroglyphs for Yaut, *which means "divine heritage," "function," "mission."*

Fabre d'Olivet emphasizes that the Hebrew Yahud relates to "the heir" יהוד: "Divine emanation, God-given: that is the name of the Jewish people or the ones from Judah, from which it derives."[9] So, it follows that the Yahud priests are the heirs of the Egyptian tradition. The Yahud symbol is found on the hand of the first of the Yahuds, the high priest, Pharaoh.[10]

The Dead Sea Scrolls, in their commentary on Habakkuk, reveal that the Tetragram Yahwe (Jehovah) יהוה was not initially accepted by all the Yahud priests. The scribes of the Babylonian period decided to give Yahwe's name an inferior or provisional dimension in the sacred writings. The Yahwe name was written in archaic, not representative writing. As Freud explains it, Yahwe was only made acceptable bit by bit, as a compromise. But Yahwe did not replace Elohim, as is generally believed.

In Column 10 of the Commentary on Habakkuk, Yahwe's name is written in archaic or Phoenician letters (The Dead Sea Scrolls, *William Burrows, Robert Laffont*), *although the rest of the manuscript is written in Sacred Hebrew characters.*

Is Yahwe's name, inscribed on one of the columns of the Temple of Soleb[11] in Upper Egypt, the origin of Yahwe? The inscription reads: "The house of Yahu in Shasu land."[12] Shasu is located in the country of Edom, in the south of Canaan, an Egyptian province. Constructed by Amenhotep III, Soleb is a smaller version of the Temple of Karnak. The Shasus, a pastoral, semi-nomadic people of Asiatic (Mid-Eastern) origin, entered Egypt as prisoners of war under Thutmose II. Here, they are represented as worshipers of Yahu. The Amarna Letters show that the Canaanite kings worshiped Pharaoh. Thus, the Shasus, subjugated by the Canaanite kings, could not help but worship Pharaoh. Ahmose, an Egyptian officer, affirms in an inscription to have "brought back from the land of the Shasus innumerable prisoners."[13] Pardoned by Pharaoh, they rapidly adapted to

Egyptian life and thus formed an indispensable workforce for the great work projects of the country.

The presence of the god Yahu among the Shasus and their influence on Egypt, gave rise to the supposition that perhaps they were the people of the Exodus. The evidence supporting this hypothesis – the three letters forming the word Yahu, *YHW* and the way the Shasus dressed – is insufficient. On the other hand, it is quite possible that they were part of the common people of Akhet-Aten (*Erev-rav*), the multitude that had converted to monotheism. According to Claude Vandersleyen, Amenhotep III had built Soleb in order to establish a cult to himself, "the king doth here worship the king."[14] The Shasus, then, worshiped Amenhotep III there, under the name of Yahu. This can easily be demonstrated by observation of the *YHW* cartouche.

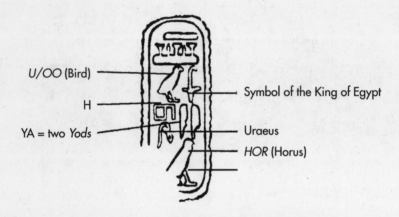

The name of Yahu on the columns of the Temple of Soleb (Amenhotep III).

Several elements indicate that the name Yahu designates Amenhotep III, King of Egypt, who, quite naturally, was deified and worshiped in his Temple of Soleb by his subject Shasus.

The "*STN*" diagram (or conventionally, Nesut) is the symbol of the king of Egypt.

The falcon symbol, Hor, is the name of Amenhotep III.

The double cartouche enclosing the name Yahu, destined exclusively for the king, indicates that the name engraved within is of a divine and royal nature.

His son, Amenhotep IV – Akhenaten – is represented there in the temple venerating his father.

On the line in the middle of the cartouche above is the *Yah* name, comparable to the *Yah* יָהּ of the Bible: "Ya (יָהּ) is my strength and my song ..." (Hebrew Bible, Exodus 15:2). Only the Yahud priests had the authority to write a name like that on the temple columns. The Shasus did not have the right to practice sacred writing. Consequently, Yahu is one of the divine names of the god-king Amenhotep III. *Yah* is written on the two lions of Soleb.

The three hieroglyphs of the nation, discovered by Champollion, *Ya-Hu-Da-Ha Malek*, are present in the cartouche of Amenhotep III at Soleb. Yahu is formed of three hieroglyphs, *YHW*[15] ⟨◌⟩ . Does this word have any connection with the Biblical name Yahwe (*YHWH*) (Jehovah)?

| Y | A | U or OO | Worship *(Dua, Daeh)* |

Representation of worship

Hieroglyph for Yahu.[16]

The Tetragram יְהֹוָה Yahwe is composed of the root *Yahu* יְהוּ, Pharaoh's name, and of הֵ *Heh*, the divine breath.

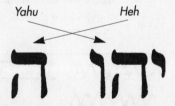

Yahu   *Heh*

Concerning the pictograph expressing worship, *Daeh* or *Dua*, Isha Schwaller of Lubicz emphasizes, "He extends his two arms towards thee in *Iau*."[17] This allows us to understand the interpretation of the name of Yehuda, son of Leah. "Then she said, 'This time, I will praise יְהֹוָה *Yahu-Heh*

ה וֹהְי.' So she called him *Yehu-Da* הד וֹהְיי" (Genesis 29:35).
Consequently, the meaning of the hieroglyph above is a representation of
the *Yahu-Daeh* of the Aramaic Bible, the monotheistic priests who left
Egypt. The pictogram is the representation of the priest (*Dua* or *Daeh*)
offering adoration to Yahu.

The Yahuds certainly couldn't worship the Midianite god of the
volcanos, Jehovah, a stranger to the Egyptian pantheon. They were
worshipers of the great god *Heh*, or *Yahu-Heh*, the One God represented
successively by Amenhotep III, Akhenaten (Aten), Smenkhkare,
Tutankhamun, and Ay: the Elohim or "individual gods" who are none
other than the pharaohs of Egypt.

Yahu is found in many Biblical names: Yehushua, Yasheyaku, Yehuda,
Yeremiahu, Matatyahu, etc. Several centuries after the Exodus, the scribes
in Babylon separated the Yahu god from the Ay god, thus rendering sepa-
rate the Hebrew and Aramaic Bibles. Here again, to mask their Egyptian
origin and to hide Ay's name, they added to the name of Yahu וֹהְי the
divine letter *Heh* ה, as Abram became Abraham (Genesis 17:5). The actual
Egyptian pronunciation of the Tetragram הוֹהְי, then, is "Yahu-Heh".
Adoration of the great god *Heh* took place through pharaoh's picture: "And
God (*Yahu-Heh*) created man in his own image ..." is sung in the hymn of
Amun of Amenhotep III himself.

The Nile and Mitsraim םירצמ (Egypt)

Below is the written word "Nile" which Egyptology translates in part by
Ytru. However, the Semitic pronunciation of this hieroglyph is very close
to *Mitsraim* םירצמ (Egypt in Hebrew).

"Mitrsraim" is
found phonetically
in the Egyptian
hieroglyph for
"Nile."

Nile Hieroglyph.

The Nile, the river that nourishes Egypt, in conventional hieroglyphic pronunciation has the phonetic value *ytru* or *ytro*. In the Bible, Ytro is the Hebrew name of Jethro, the father-in-law of Moses. Ytro is also the symbolic name of Pharaoh Ay, represented as the god of the Nile.

Ay deified as the God of the Nile = Ytru = Ytro (Museum of Fine Arts, Boston).

In Hebrew, "Nile" is *Mitsraim* מצרים.

It is composed of three parts: *Mits* מיצ, which means to spill or spread out, the *Resh* ר, which is the name of Re, and *Yam* י, water. The final *Mem* represents the waters of the Nile: "The god Re has spread out the waters of the river." Egypt is a gift of the Nile, which overflows, mixes itself with the earth and waters the earth, creating a harmony among the elements.[18]

This new meaning teaches us that the people "who came out from Mitsraim" were only expelled from the sacred territory delimited by the Nile, with the obligation to remain in the Egyptian provinces of Moab and Canaan. The "coming out from the Nile," then, would be considered as an internal politico-religious solution.

☥ ☥ ☥

Hebrew Letters and Pharaoh's Uraeus

Five Hebrew letters have the cabalistic function of looking upward toward the heavens. The zenith is represented by the uraeus of Pharaoh, the sacred

Picture on the north side of the funerary chamber of Tutankhamun. The king is lost in admiration before the beauty of Nut, goddess of the heavens, equivalent to the Canaanite goddess Anat עָנָת;[19] his right hand holds the traditional rod and his left hand the sign of power and life, the "Ankh." He wears the headband symbolized by the five Hebrew letters.

serpent he wears on his forehead. The five letters include the hieroglyph for God, ר or ד. Together, the *Heh, Lamed, Resh, Daleth and Kof* ה, ל, ר, ד and ק, symbolize the uraeus, the headband and the two straps located behind Pharaoh's head.

Notes

1. David Berdah, *La Hagada de Pâque*. Alpha Magium, 1986.
2. Rashi, *The Pentateuch according to Rashi, Genesis*. Samuel and Odette Lévy, 1990, p. 368, Chapter XVIII.
3. Christian Jacq, *Grammaire égyptienne de Champollion*. Solin, 1997. The origins of Satan derive equally from the Egyptian god Seth, who was loathed by the Ptolemaic pharaohs.
4. Frédéric Portal, *Archéologie égyptienne*, vol. III Les symbols égyptiens. Editions de la Maisnie, 1985.
5. Nicole Maya Malet, *Moïse Hébreu, Moïse Egyptien*. Cerf, 1997, p.143.
6. Isha Schwaller de Lubicz, *Ehr-Bak disciple*. Flammarion, 1956, p. 347.
7. Pierre Grandet, *Hymnes de la religion d'Aton*. Seuil, 1995, pp. 23, 99. Phonetic transcription pp. 136, 153.

8. Champollion, *Lecture illustrée des hiérglyphes*. Le Rocher, 1998.

9. Fabre d'Olivet, *La langue hébraïque restituée*. L'Age d'Homme Delphica, 1991, p. 60.

10. Christiane Desroches-Noblecourt, *Toutankhamon*. CD Rom, Syrinx, 1997.

11. Guy Rachet, *Dictionnaire de la civilisation Egyptienne*, Larousse Bordas, 1998, p. 244.

12. *Ibid.*

13. *Ibid. Grammaire égyptienne de Champollion*, p. 66.

14. Claude Vandersleyen, *Egypt and the Valley of the Nile*, Vol. 2. Nouvelle Clio, 1995, p. 375.

15. Pierre Grandet and Bernard Mathieu, *Cours d'égyptienne hiéroglyphique*. Khéops, 1997, p. 748.

16. *Ibid.*

17. Schwaller de Lubicz, *Ehr-Bak disciple*, p. 347.

18. Rashi, *Pentateuch*, Genesis 2:11.

19. Andre Dupon-Sommer and Paul Geuthner, extract from the magazine *Syria*, XXXIII, 1956. Sety I established a cult to Anat at Beth-Shean.

The Roots of Ritual

Aten, Atum and Eth אֵת

The first verse of the Bible reads "*Bereshit bara Elohim Eth Hashamaim* (heavens) *veEt Aarets* (earth)." The word *Eth* אֵת (or At), formed from the first and last letter of the Hebrew alphabet, defines everything that unifies the power that exists between God and his creation.[1] In the Bible *Eth* is not only a preposition, but it holds a high symbolic value as well. The first part of the names of Atum and Aten, *Eth* אֵת has the *Aleph* (a hieroglyph corresponding to Aten = Akhenaten), and the *Tav* symbol of the perfection relating to Hathor (= Nefertiti). אֵת, the divine word, as used in the Bible, means "between the eyes," or "symbol" in general.[2] The Zohar[3] defines *Eth* as "my sovereign" (Adon-Ay).

Rashi (Exodus 12:16) explains that *Tot*, "between the eyes," in Hebrew means "two symbols" in Catpi (Coptic). Therefore, the two *Eth* אֵת of the first verse of the Bible tie together the creation of the heavens and the earth, which brings back the image of the vulture hovering in the sky and the serpent crawling on the earth – sacred symbols placed on the headband between Pharaoh's eyes.

☥ ☥ ☥

The Earth: Aretz and Akhet

Earth, אֶרֶץ *Arets*,[4] is phonetically identical to the Egyptian *Akhet*, meaning the "land of light,"[5] a metaphor found regularly in the Pyramid Texts: "Sacred Land," inundated by "Sacred light." "Holy Land" in Hebrew (*Aretz* אֶרֶץ) contains the root of the word " light," *Or* אוֹר, in the same way the Egyptian word Akhet contains *Akh*, which means light. The last letter, the *Tsadeh* צ, represents a standing person making an offering. So Akhet-Aten, the land sacred to the god Aten, is like the Hebrew *Aretz Adon-Ay* אֶרֶץאֲדֹנָי, the land sacred to the Lord Adon-Ay.

The written Hebraic-hieroglyphic *Aretz* אֶרֶץ approaches the name of Aten, "Re, sovereign of the two lands, who is exalted at the horizon of Akhet, in his name of Re, the father who resides in Aten."

צ He who is exalted   ר Re   א Aleph = Aten

"He who is exalted, Re Aten." Hebraic-hieroglyphic reading of Aretz.

☥ ☥ ☥

The Creation of Man

Genesis 1:27 says, "The Elohim created man in their image. It is in the image of the Elohim that they created. Male and female they created him."

Is the image of the Elohim the image of man? Does this verse fit in with notions of anthropomorphism encountered in Egyptian imagery? Most of the Egyptian gods are represented as humans or as people with animal heads. The expression "male and female" in Hebrew is *zakhar unekeva* זָכָר וּנְקֵבָה, which expresses the joining together of masculine

and feminine characteristics in Adam's person, as they are in representations of Akhenaten.

In Genesis 2:4, we read, "This is the description of the creation of the
heavens and the earth. When Yahwe and the Elohim created ..." (*Beheh-
baram* בהבראם). Rashi[6] said about this, "It was with the letter *Heh* ה
that the heavens and the earth were created." *Beheh-baram* בהבראם is
translated by "created by the *Heh*," which is to say by the Divine Breath.
The Hebrew *Heh* is similar to the hieroglyphic *Heh* (the Great God).

Beheh-baram בהבראם is an anagram for *Beh-Abraham* באברהם,
which ties Abraham into the creation of the world.[7] "Then Yahwe and the
Elohim, from the dirt of the earth, formed the man into a living creature by
breathing the breath of life into his nostrils" (Genesis 2:7).

☥ ☥ ☥

The God of Thy Father

"He said [Adon-Ay said to Moses], 'I am the Elohim of thy Father, the
Elohim of Abraham, the Elohim of Isaac and of Jacob'" (Aramaic Bible,
Exodus 3:6).

The expression "thy father," in Hebrew *Abikha* אביך, represents the
triad of Abraham, Isaac, and Jacob as one individual. The expression "thy
fathers" in Hebrew would be *Abotkha* אבותיך. Since the plural is not
used here, the message of the scribes is, "Thy father is, at the same time,
Abraham, Isaac, and Jacob. The three patriarchs form a single person."
Rashi comments, "I shall make of thee [Abraham] a great people. That is
why in the Amida [Hebrew prayer] you say: God of Abraham. And I will
bless you. That is why you say: God of Isaac. And I shall magnify thy
name. That is why you say: God of Jacob" (Rashi, Exodus 3:6).

The three patriarchs of the Bible are the image of Akhenaten, the
father of monotheism.

☥ ☥ ☥

The Jerusalem Temple

The Jerusalem Temple is reminiscent of the temples the Yahuds had left behind in Egypt.

In Deuteronomy, Moses gives indications how the temple should be built once the Yahuds get to Jerusalem. He did not want the temple to be a duplicate of the Egyptian temples, although the people did recall vestiges of the temples of Akhet-Aten. Because of Moses' commandment that the new temple not be identical to the ones in Egypt, the Temple of Jerusalem had neither post nor obelisk. These were replaced by two bronze pillars, placed at each side of the porch. Moses' words were, "Thou shalt not plant for thyself any kind of tree as a sacred post next to the altar of Jehovah thy God. Thou shalt not set up a sacred pillar, a thing which Jehovah thy God truly hateth" (Deuteronomy 16:21).

Yet, the Jerusalem Temple did have the style of Egypt in its overall structure, and it had some similarities to the temples in Thebes. It had a copper bowl borne by a dozen oxen (or a dozen cows) for the holy water, as well as many small basins for the purification of the priests, as in the Egyptian temples. According to the architectural description of the Second Temple, reconstructed with Cyrus' approval, the rectangular form, the common room, the sections, and the Holy of Holies recall the structure and organization of Egyptian temples. The animal sacrifice to God of a "red cow" in Solomon's Temple reminds of the sacrifices of "red oxen" in the Great Temple of Amun. One of the seven fattened cows in the tomb of Nefertari, wife of Ramesses II, was called "the red one."

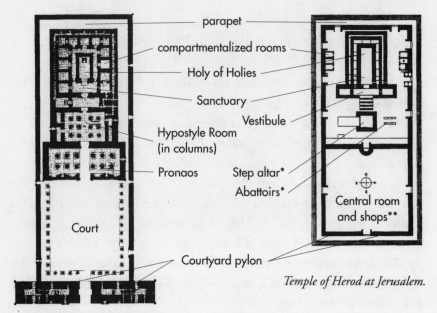

parapet
compartmentalized rooms
Holy of Holies
Sanctuary
Vestibule
Hypostyle Room
(in columns)
Pronaos   Step altar*
               Abattoirs*
Court   Central room
                        and shops**
Courtyard pylon

Temple of Herod at Jerusalem.

Temple of Horus (Edfu).

* The vestiges of a step altar and abattoirs have been discovered in the ruins of
Akhet-Aten at Amarna.
** The columns of the Temple of Jerusalem have not been shown.

Why was Jerusalem chosen by the Yahud priests as the holy city? Letter EA
287 of the El Amarna Letters, in which Abdi-heba, Governor of Jerusalem,
complains about the attacks of the Apiru, says that Akhenaten had placed
his name in Jerusalem: "For your information. Since the king placed his
name in Jerusalem forever, he must not abandon the country of Jerusalem."

Akhenaten made Jerusalem sacred, conferring on it a status superior to
that of other cities. Thebes was called "the city of one hundred doors,"
which is translated into Hebrew as "*Mea Chearim*," a name given to the
religious neighborhood of Jerusalem.

The worship of Pharaoh continued in Judea as well as within the
Temple of Solomon, King of Judah. The Bible mentions the excellence of
relations between Egypt and Solomon, who married Pharaoh's daughter. In
the course of his reign, Solomon continued to worship the Egyptian gods,
building altars to them, so that he was as powerful and respected as a
pharaoh. The kings succeeding him followed his example, in the "temple
of the sun" which was the house of Jehovah:

"Yet the High-Places were not taken away ..." (I Kings 22:43).

"He destroyed the houses of the sacred prostitutes which were in the house of Jehovah ..." (II Kings 23:7).

"He removed the horses that the Kings of Judah had dedicated to the sun at the entrance of the house of Jehovah." (II Kings 23:11).

⚥ ⚥ ⚥

The Candelabra

He [Joseph] said to them, "Please listen to this dream I had. We were binding sheaves in the field. Suddenly, my sheaf arose and remained standing. Yours gathered around it and bowed down before mine." His brothers said to him, "What! Art thou to reign over us? Art thou to become our master?" (Genesis 37:6-8)

Joseph's first dream brings in an essential theme of Egyptian society called *Sema-Tauy*,[8] the unity of the two lands. The twelve bowing sheaves of the Bible, symbolizing the twelve viziers of Egypt, stand for Pharaoh's coronation. The *Sema-Tauy* represents the enthronement by the gods tying the sheaf of papyrus (Lower Egypt) to the sheaf of lilies (Upper Egypt), bowing down before Pharaoh.

Is the *Sema-Tauy* the origin of the candelabra that plays such an important part in Jewish ritual? Egyptian iconography corresponds with the Biblical description of the candelabra in the second part of the Book of Exodus.

And he made a candelabra of pure gold. From one single stone, he made the candelabra. Its base and its shaft, its capitals, its knobs and flowers came out of it. Six branches came up from its sides, three branches on one side and three on the other. Three cups made like almond flowers, each with capital and flower, and three cups also made like almond flowers, each with capital and flower on the other branch. Thus for the six branches that go out from the candelabra. (Exodus 37:17-19)

Sema-Tauy of Ramseses II   Sema-Tauy of Tutankhamun

The sheaves bowing before Pharaoh.

In Hebrew, "candelabra" is *Menorah* מנרה, having Amun and Re for a base: the emanation/illumination of Amun-Re. The central light is called *Shamash*, the sun. Composed of seven or eight branches, it recalls the luminous serpents, surmounted by the solar disk Re, which Pharaoh wears in front of his loincloth. The central serpent wears the name of "Re."

"Name of Re" under the Sun

Tutankhamun's loincloth with nine lights. The central light bears the name Re, the sun god. Temple of Luxor.

Menorah with nine branches, plus the "shamash" (Sun, "name of Esh").

Temple of Amun-Re at Karnak. Loincloth of Sety II.

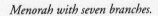

Menorah with seven branches.

The candelabra is a symbol of unity,[9] and also of victory. It celebrates the triumph of Judas Maccabeus over Antiochus Epiphanus (167 BC). On the Arch of Titus, the Romans are shown exhibiting the candelabra (70 BC). Tutankhamun's ceremonial chariot represents the *Sema-Tauy*, sign of victory over Egypt's enemies.

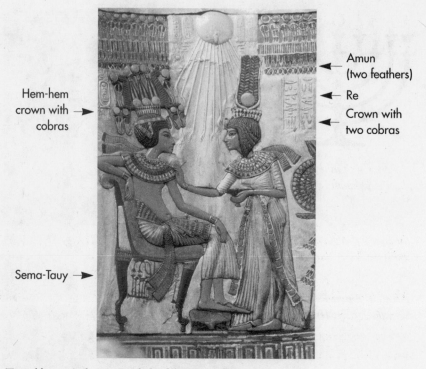

Hem-hem crown with cobras →

→ Amun (two feathers)

← Re

Crown with two cobras

Sema-Tauy →

Tutankhamun's throne. Symbols of Amun-Re (Menorah).

If the Biblical description of the candelabra represents an apparent symmetry, it depicts an emblem of unity and of duality, rejoining the image of the *Sema-Tauy*. Along the same lines, this symbol is omnipresent in the Cobra Crowns and the Hem-hem Crown worn by Akhenaten and Tutankhamun. The cobras adorned with the light of Re and the double feather of Shu recall Amun-Re.

> *He had still another dream, and he told it to his brothers, saying, "I had another dream where I saw the sun, the moon, and eleven stars prostrate themselves before me." He told his father and his brothers. His father reprimanded him, and said to him, "What kind of a dream is that? Indeed! That I and thy mother and thy brothers will come prostrate ourselves to the ground at your feet?" (Genesis 37:9-10)*

Interior panel of one of the ceremonial chariots of Tutankhamun. The Sema-Tauy *is exhibited with Nubian and Asiatic captives (Cairo Museum).*

The second dream hides Akhenaten (the sun), Nefertiti (the moon) and eleven stars that prostrate themselves before him and recalls the twelve viziers, governors of Egypt. Christina Reiche[10] defines Akhet-Aten in this way: "Amarna is, simultaneously, the exact point where the heavens and the earth meet and the privileged place where the 'here and now' meets the 'out there.' So it's the whole cosmos, in which the stars are the sun in the heavens and the royal family on earth."

Pharaoh's Cup

The entourage of Pharaoh – his master cupbearer, his master baker, and ten officers, called *Rav-reveh Par'oo* – are all described in the Biblical account of Joseph's dream interpretations.

In Genesis 40:11, the master cupbearer describes his dream: "I had Pharaoh's cup in my hand. I gathered the grapes and pressed them into Pharaoh's cup and placed the cup in the king's hand."

Research on the talatates of Karnak show a graven image of Akhenaten, holding up his cup towards Aten as a wine offering. The monotheistic prayer over the fruit of the vine has its origin in ancient Egypt, the first country to consecrate the "drink of the gods."

Pharaoh's cup. Akhenaten, standing, practices the ritual of the fruit of the vine. Talatates of Karnak.

♀ ♀ ♀

The Washing of The Hands

The tradition of the washing of the hands (in Hebrew, *netilat-yadayim* נטילת ידים) was practiced by the Judahite priests (Yahuds) and it continues up to the present day in all monotheistic traditions. One hand pours water over the other, each playing the role of servant. The *talatates* of Karnak demonstrate this ritual. They show a servant pouring water over the hands of Akhenaten.

The puzzle formed by the three bricks show a servant (left) pouring water on the hands that Akhenaten extends under the hands of the pourer. Talatates of Karnak.

⚥ ⚥ ⚥

The Washing of The Feet

He [Abraham] lifted his eyes, and behold, three men stood before him. On seeing them, he ran from the entrance of his tent and prostrated himself on the ground. And he said, "Lord, if I have found favor in thy eyes, do not pass by thus before thy servant! Let a little water be brought, and wash your feet, and rest under the tree." (Genesis 18:2-4)

Rashi comments on this verse. "And wash your feet. He [Abraham] thought that they were Arabs who prostrated themselves before the dust of his feet, and he took care not to enter into his home the object of an idolatrous cult."

Rashi was the heir of the oral tradition, and mentions Arab visitors (or *Erev-rav*) in Abraham's time. Thus the word "Arab" refers to the many kinds of people from Akhet-Aten, newly converted to monotheism, and called *Erev-rav* in the Bible (Exodus 12:38). After studying the roots in Hebrew, Arabic, Samaritan, Syrian, and Chaldean, Fabre d'Olivet confirmed the common origin of the words "Hebrew" and "Arab":

> *Everyone knows that both people [Hebrews and Arabs] trace their origin to the patriarch Heber. But the name of this claimed patriarch means nothing more than "what is placed somewhere else, that is far away, hidden, dissembled, deprived of daylight; what passes by, what ends, what is off in the West, etc." The Hebrews derived from it* hebri, *the Arabs* harbi, *by a transposition of letters which is quite ordinary in such a case. But whether it is pronounced* hebri *or* harbi, *both words always express that the people who are called by it always are found "over there" or "far out," or at the western end of a country. So, from the most ancient times, the Hebrews or the Arabs, relative to Asia, were on the western end, what they termed the Land of God.*

Rashi gives another explanation of the word "Hebrew." "Abram the Hebrew. He who comes from the other side (*Heber*) of the River"[11] (Rashi, Genesis 14:13).

The image of Abraham welcoming the visitors resembles Akhenaten receiving the heads of foreign lands in the capital at the annual Jubilee. The vassals prostrate themselves at the feet of the one they call their Lord, their God, their Sun.

Princes and foreign kings prostrate themselves before Akhenaten (Talatates *of Karnak*).

According to Christiane Desroches Noblecourt, there existed in the living room of the houses of Akhet-Aten (especially in those of the priests and nobles) a slab on which the feet were placed when arriving: "A large slab with a slight incline was fastened to the wall. It was there that the purifying fresh water was poured on the feet and hands of the masters and their guests."

Notes

1. Fabre d'Olivet, *La langue hébraïque restituée*. L'Age d'Homme-Delphica, 1991, p. 16.
2. *Ibid.*, p. 17.
3. *Zohar*, Vol. 1, translated by Charles Mopsik. Verdier, 1981, p. 95.
4. The word *Aarets* is also given in the text as *Arets* and *Aretz*. All mean "earth" or "land," and are transliterated into Roman letters according to the pronunciation used in spoken Hebrew.
5. *Akhet* can also be translated as "horizon."
6. Rashi, *The Pentateuch according to Rashi, Genesis*. Samuel and Odette Lévy, 1990 (Genesis 4:2).
7. See Genesis 17:4-5.
8. Christiane Desroches-Noblecourt, *Amours et fureurs de La Lointaine*. Stock-Pernoud, 1997, pp. 67–77.
9. Albert Soued, *Les symboles dans la Bible*. Jacques Grancher, 1995, p. 33.
10. Christina Reiche, 1996, in Marc Gabolde, *D'Akhénaton à Toutankhamon*. Institut d'Archéologie et d'Histoire de l'Antiquité, Université Lumière-Lyon 2-CNRS, 1998, p. 19.
11. Rashi, *Genesis*.

☥

Conclusion

In El Amarna Letter EA4, Kadashman Enlil, King of Babylon, asks for one of Amenhotep III's daughters as his wife. Amenhotep refused, citing the long Egyptian tradition of never giving a princess in marriage to a foreigner, even to a king. After many exchanges, Kadshman Enlil, assisted by his counselors, would have been able to invoke the Biblical past and argue that Abraham, the Hebrew king born in Ur-Kasdim, a Babylonian city, had married an Egyptian queen and princess. The letter testifies that neither the king of Egypt, nor the Babylonian king knew the Biblical legend of Abraham in the fourteenth century BC.

Before Akhenaten's One God, relationships among the Egyptians were fraternal. With the appearance of the "Amarnian monotheistic heresy," the notion of intolerance and of election by a Single God began to take hold in their souls. Akhenaten had promoted his God to the summit of the initiation of the secrets of Egypt, supplanting most of the other Egyptian gods. His father, Amenhotep III, had ordered the separation of the followers of Amun and Aten, a separation that was transposed much later in the Torah, where Egypt was dissimulated through numerous Biblical metaphors. By order of Ay and his successors, the tragedy of the exodus from Akhet-Aten caused a monotheistic movement, certainly hidden, but nevertheless inseparable from long Egyptian tradition.

All through its history, Judea enjoyed its alliance with God, "the support of the reed," that is, the protection of Pharaoh and Egypt. However, the attempts to resolve the Amarnian crises by a massive exodus of the monothiest population are the origins of the religious wars and conflicts that appear to be human destiny.

According to the words of Moses (Aramaic Bible, Deuteronomy 10:17), "The Eternal One [Ay], your God, is God of the Gods."

The Wisdom of Merykare teaches that God is observable through the multiplicity of His creation. This manifestation takes place in everyday life, where the Creator, not distinct from His creation, arouses respect and compassion through the gods present in Nature.

Whether this God is one or many, visible or invisible, He is the same manifestation in the Bible as in ancient Egypt. The Universal God does not concern Himself with rivalries. At the origin of Creation he has stood for goodness, for love among humanity. By invoking His name, Pharaoh had the duty to establish peace among the people over the land of Egypt. As Erik Hornung[1] demonstrates, the many was the one, the one was many.

Thus, the hypothesis of the Egyptian origin of the Hebrews is only at a beginning. Studies will permit other treasures hidden in the immense Jewish culture to become unveiled in the near future. Even if many scholars are strongly attached to it, the complex discrepancies between the Old Testament and its many commentaries and Egyptology calls for serious study and application. As the philosopher Simone Weil[2] affirms, conclusions from a comparative re-reading of the Old Testament and ancient Egyptian history and texts could result in true revelations, since a number of passages in the Bible were adopted by other civilizations, Egypt remaining at the base.

Notes

1. Erik Hornung, *Les dieux de l'Egypt. Le un et le multiple*. Rocher, 1986, p.227.
2. *Papers of Simone Weil (1909–1943)*, edited by Marie-Eve Colin. Vol. 7, No. 1, 1984.

Index